STUDIES IN HIGHER EDUCATION

DISSERTATION SERIES

Edited by
PHILIP G. ALTBACH
Monan Professor of Higher Education
Lynch School of Education, Boston College

A ROUTLEDGEFALMER SERIES

Resource Allocation in Private Research Universities

Daniel Rodas

ROUTLEDGEFALMER
A MEMBER OF THE TAYLOR & FRANCIS GROUP
NEW YORK & LONDON/2001

Published in 2001 by
RoutledgeFalmer
A member of the Taylor & Francis Group
29 West 35th Street
New York, NY 10001

Copyright © 2001 by Daniel Rodas

All rights reserved. No part of this book may be reprinted or reproduced or utilized in any form or by any electronic, mechanical, or other means, now known or hereafter invented, including photocopying and recording, or in any information storage or retrieval system, without written permission from the publishers.

10 9 8 7 6 5 4 3 2 1

Library of Congress Cataloging-in-Publication Data is available from the Library of Congress.

ISBN 0-8153-4032-X

Printed on acid-free, 250 year-life paper
Manufactured in the United States of America

Acknowledgments

It is with great pleasure that I acknowledge the many forms of support which enabled me to complete this book. I am especially indebted to William Massy, Geoffrey Cox, Condoleezza Rice, and William Weiler for their critical suggestions and thoughtful guidance throughout the course of the project. I also received helpful suggestions and constructive feedback from Patricia Gumport, Myra Strober, Robert Marine, and Carol Colbeck.

This study could not have been completed without the generous cooperation of six universities that opened their doors to my investigations. I gratefully acknowledge their assistance and enthusiasm for this research. I am especially grateful to the dozens of individuals interviewed for this project who shared their institutional knowledge and professional insight.

From start to finish, my friends shared in my triumphs and failures. I am grateful for their support, encouragement, and belief in my ability to complete this project despite its many unexpected twists and turns.

My parents, Howard and Sally Rodas, have consistently supported my seemingly interminable educational ambitions. I thank them for their unfailing love and personal support.

Fieldwork is often expensive research, and this study was no exception. This research would not have been possible without substantial grants from the Stanford University President's Fund and the Dean's Office of the School of Education. I gratefully acknowledge this support.

Contents

Acknowledgments	v
1. Introduction and Overview	1
2. Buchanan University	31
3. Pierce University	51
4. Westmont University	75
5. Shelton University	103
6. Greenway University	127
7. Garfield University	149
8. Summary Case Analyses	165
9. Cross-Case Analysis and the Future Directions	173
Sample Interview Protocols	183
Notes	187
Bibliography	191
Index	199

1
Introduction and Overview

INTRODUCTION

The internal allocation of financial resources is a process common to every complex organization (Cyert and March, 1963; Pondy, 1970; Pfeffer and Salancik, 1974). It is a standard feature of organizational life as well as a matter of economic necessity. Through its executive managers and other stakeholders, every entity must decide how it will distribute its limited supply of financial resources. Although the trade-offs are often complex and the outcomes uncertain, resource allocation decisions are essential for achieving organizational objectives. Whether an entity is for-profit, public, or non-profit, such decisions ultimately shape that organization's failure or success.

This book addresses the allocation of financial resources in American private research universities, a subject that has received surprisingly little empirical investigation despite considerable interest among practitioners and scholars of higher education, and repeated calls for more research (Garvin, 1980; Schmidtlein, 1989–90; James, 1990; Massy, 1990; Hoenack, 1994).[1] In this introductory chapter, I examine the utility of various administrative models of resource allocation in American research universities, develop a conceptual model for investigating these core processes, and present the methodology for this research.

Because university costs have risen significantly in recent years, resource allocation has emerged as one of the most significant public policy issues facing institutions of higher education. While many factors have been cited as underlying causes of cost-growth in higher education—including the expansion of academic and research programs, higher labor costs, increased technological requirements, growing utility costs, and increased government regulation—part of the problem may lie in the inefficient internal resource allocation processes found in academic organizations (Massy, 1989). The decline in public funding for higher education, coupled with growing concerns about the cost, quality, and productivity of academic organizations, has intensified the belief that universities should allocate wisely their limited (and diminishing) financial resources (Altschul et al., 1992; Pew Higher Education Research Program, 1989, 1990, 1991, 1992). In fact, this prevailing belief may be one of the only areas in which there is general agreement among the constituent stakeholders in the academic community. But despite consensus about the need for responsible resource allocation, there is little agreement about *how* this goal should be achieved. Resource allocation remains a contentious and uncertain administrative process for reasons deeply rooted in the organizational and economic characteristics of higher education organizations.

Organizationally, as many scholars have noted (see Baldridge et al., 1977), universities are highly complex entities with decision processes variously described as a bureaucracy (Stroup, 1966), a political system (Pfeffer and Salancik, 1974), a collegium (Millett, 1962), or an organized anarchy (Cohen and March, 1974). Universities function with two distinct lines of authority, the faculty and the administration, a division of responsibility very different from the more straightforward hierarchy commonly found in business organizations (Garvin, 1980; Birnbaum, 1988). Other constituencies—including trustees, students, alumni, and public policy makers—are also stakeholders in the decision process and desire to participate in the formation of the budget (Orwig and Caruthers, 1980). Lastly, because university goals are typically general and diffuse (Orwig and Caruthers, 1980), it is often difficult to establish priorities and relate budgetary inputs to desired outputs. As this portrait may suggest, decision making—including resource allocation—is a complicated social process in academic organizations (Birnbaum,1988; James, 1990).

Economic differences also complicate the resource allocation process in higher education organizations. Although universities are fundamentally economic organizations subject to the same market constraints as for-profit firms (Garvin, 1980), they also differ economically from business firms in significant ways. In business firms, the resource allocation decision rule is a straightforward extension of basic microeconomic theory: expand profit-generating activities and contract those for which marginal revenue < marginal cost. Stated another way, resource allocation in business organizations is directed toward maximizing profit.

By contrast, higher education and other non-profit organizations are not profit-maximizers in the conventional economic sense. Instead, as economist William F. Massy has argued, universities maximize an objective function that substitutes 'subjective value' for profit and incorporates the economic constraint that deficits are to be avoided (Hopkins and Massy, 1981).[2] Subjective value, in Massy's model, incorporates the complex and multi-dimensional goals of higher education organizations. This modified economic model suggests that the senior administrative and academic staff primarily responsible for institutional resource allocation do not base their decisions strictly on the financial-economic factors that motivate most business executives to maximize profit. In theory, they also incorporate less tangible assessments of what activities are most highly valued by members of their academic community, particularly the faculty responsible for delivering core services of teaching and research in specialized units such as schools, academic departments, and organized research units.

The Massy model has important implications for the process of internal resource allocation in higher education organizations, in particular, the centralization or decentralization of budget authority within universities (Hopkins and Massy, 1981; Massy, 1990). If understanding subjective values is an important criterion for making sound resource allocation decisions, then those responsible for these decisions must understand the value inherent in various organizational activities as well as the attendant trade-offs associated with each. Herein lies a significant dilemma. If universities choose to concentrate budget authority at the central administrative level, resource allocation decisions can be tightly controlled. This arrangement enables central administrators to exercise maximum (i.e. direct) control over resource allocation decisions. Centralization of budget authority may facilitate cost control and help ensure that institutional expenditures are in line with the objectives of the executive office and governing board. A major problem with this approach is that organizational distance may prevent central administrative decision-makers from grasping the subjective value of various decentralized activities that are best known to those most closely aligned with their implementation, such as department chairs and faculty.

If, on the other hand, the central administration chooses to decentralize budget authority to major academic units (such as schools, departments, or organized research units), in an effort to capture the subjective value of their core activities, the central administration will find it more difficult to monitor expenditures and ensure that decentralized activities are consonant with central administrative objectives. From the standpoint of the central administration, decentralized units may acts in ways that are sub-optimal to the institution as a whole.

In some cases, however, the central administration may select a model that is neither tightly centralized nor loosely decentralized and that incorporates incentives or negotiated agreements to motivate unit behavior. The primary advantage of such "intermediary" resource allocation systems is that they enable the central administration to influence the behavior of decentralized academic units while still capturing the benefits of localized control and improved knowledge of subjective values. Two major models fall in this category: price-regulation systems and value-outcome systems (Hoenack, 1983; Massy, 1994). In price-regulation systems, the central administration uses arm's-length adjustments to marginal costs and revenues to influence behaviors it wants to encourage. For example, the central administration may declare a tax on physical space to encourage judicious utilization by academic units, or subsidize departmental efforts to improve undergraduate education. In value-outcomes systems, the central administration allocates general funds to decentralized units in large blocks, with general agreements about how the resources are to be used and the mechanisms for later assessing whether agreed upon goals have been achieved.

Resource allocation systems, then, can be implemented along an organizational continuum ranging from highly localized to tightly centralized decision making. Examples of resource allocation models that fall at each end of this spectrum (and points in between) can be found in private and public research universities around the United States. For example, Harvard University is the classic example of an institution with a completely decentralized resource allocation system (popularly known as "Every Tub on its Own Bottom"—the tubs being the major academic units). On the other end of the spectrum, the University of Chicago employed a highly centralized resource allocation approach until very recently. A few research institutions, such as Indiana University, the University of Southern California, and the University of Pennsylvania, use a system of resource allocation known as responsibility center budgeting (RCB)—a model that is actually a special case of the price-regulation system cited above. RCB, which will be described in more detail later in this study, uses various sanctions and incentives to influence and control the budgetary behavior of academic units on a global level—in effect creating a system that closely parallels the market-oriented allocation model commonly used in corporate world. Other institutions, such as the University of Michigan, utilize a value-outcomes resource allocation approach.

As this discussion may suggest, universities can organize their resource allocation systems in any number of ways. This research is an effort to understand and extend our knowledge of the various systems of university resource allocation. In particular, this book seeks to illuminate core processes, policies, and principles through which university executives shape and allocate the annual operating budget.

This question is addressed through case study analysis of the resource allocation process in a sample of private Research I universities. Research I universities are a particularly intriguing site in which to conduct this research because, as a group, they feature the most complex resource allocation systems, internal management structures, and decision processes. Empirical research that would point to the strengths and weaknesses of various resource allocation systems now used in American research universities is virtually non-existent. The limited literature on resource allocation in higher education organizations consists largely of conceptual pieces, informal case studies, and a small number of empirical studies focused on other issues. Very little of this work, particularly the empirical studies, has been published in the last several years.

This is also an interesting time period in which to pursue this line of research: most research universities face financial stringency, meaning that internal resource allocation processes are perhaps more important than ever before. How has this changing fiscal and market environment impacted resource allocation processes that occur inside universities? According to resource dependence theory (Pfeffer and Salancik, 1974), universities have important relationships with their environments, especially with regard to resource transactions. Hence, if environmental conditions change, one would expect the internal processes within universities to also change. Therefore, this research should shed light on the relationship between the environmental changes creating financial stringency and the internal allocation of scarce resources.

An empirical investigation of this question will fill an important conceptual and empirical gap in the scholarly literature on higher education. In particular, this research will provide insight into the economic behavior of higher education organizations as well as the perspectives of the central actors responsible for university resource allocation decisions. Equally important, because this research may point to possible ways for restructuring university resource allocation systems, the results should be of interest to executives responsible for the efficient allocation of financial resources. Finally, although this research will focus on resource allocation at the institutional level, the results should also provide insight into resource allocation processes in complex, multi-department academic units (such as a medical school or faculty of arts and sciences) within a university, as well as resource allocation in less complicated academic organizations, such as comprehensive universities or doctoral-granting institutions.

The next section reviews the relevant literature and describes the historical development of various administrative models for internal allocation of resources in research universities.

BACKGROUND ON RESOURCE ALLOCATION

Although various strategies have been developed for allocating financial resources in higher education organizations, most share in common the notion of an operating budget. Meisinger (1984, p.8) describes the operating budget as the university's 'core budget,' encompassing unrestricted income available to the institution along with restricted funds earmarked for teaching and departmental research.[3]

In most public universities[4], the operating budget is made up of income from state appropriations, tuition and fees, and a few other sources of income (such as revenue from a university endowment) which together comprise a general fund. Allocations to departments and schools are made from this general fund. Private universities also allocate resources from a centrally-administered general fund, however, major academic units such as schools are usually encouraged to develop their own sources of income from gifts, grants and contracts, tuition, and other sources. The university general fund, made up of income from undergraduate tuition revenues and income from institutional funds, is nevertheless an important source of income for most academic units. In both public and private institutions, an operating budget is prepared based on the sum total of available resources to support unit activities.

Within these general parameters, institutions have considerable choice in devising a resource allocation system consistent with their goals, culture, and traditions. As noted earlier in this chapter, a basic question is whether the allocation process should be highly centralized or loosely decentralized. In the centralized environment, decisions are made by a small, centrally managed budget group, and while consultation and negotiation with academic deans, school administrators, and trustees is frequent, formal involvement from these constituencies is limited. In the decentralized budgeting environment, resource allocation decisions are delegated to academic deans. The central administration is responsible for shaping institution-wide policy and determining what if any subventions will be awarded to the various academic units.

HISTORICAL CONTEXT

The resource allocation systems presently used in Research I universities have evolved over the last several decades as these institutions became organizationally more complex and increasingly decentralized. Following World War I, a decentralized university structure developed as faculty organized themselves into specialized academic disciplines, a situation which created a need for planning and management systems that would unify the new departmentally-based university (Jones, 1985). This trend was accelerated by the growth of federally-sponsored university research, the rise in undergraduate and graduate enrollments, and the evolution of new academic programs following World War II (Jones, 1985). It was during this same period that budgetary decisions shifted away from presidents and boards of trustees, and were delegated to administrative officers (Jencks and Riesman, 1968). In addition, academic planning and resource allocation were increasingly seen as interconnected activities.

The first attempts to integrate planning and resource allocation began with the annual budgets that most universities have prepared at least since the 1950s (Green and Monical, 1985). The budget was essentially a simple one-year plan of operation prepared for each function and budgetary unit (Berg and Skolgley, 1985). Resource allocation was largely line-item and incremental.[5] (Millett, 1973; Berg and Skolgley, 1985) and focused on the annual budget, a process that sufficed during a period when economic conditions were stable, academic programming relatively uncomplicated, and

Introduction and Overview

institutional structures fairly simple (Green and Monical, 1985). Massy has termed this era, which lasted throughout the 1950s and 1960s, the 'Golden Age' of higher education (1990, p.2), a period of rapidly rising enrollment, steady endowment growth, and an outpouring of federal research moneys. The emphasis, as Massy notes (1990), was on managing growth and maintaining quality.[6] Very little emphasis during this period was given to cost control, and budgeting remained unsophisticated (Garvin, 1980).

Signs of fiscal stress, however, were visible by the late 1960s, and by the early 1970s higher education was facing what one contemporary critic termed the 'new depression in higher education." (Cheit, 1971; see also Bowen, 1968; Carnegie Commission on Higher Education, 1972). Several reasons account for this decline: enrollments flattened, inflation appeared, and revenue streams from investments, philanthropy, and the government were no longer growing at the same rate that higher education organizations had enjoyed from the early 1950s to the mid-1960s (Weathersby and Weinstein, 1970; Cheit, 1971; Millett, 1973; Massy and Hopkins, 1979; Massy, 1990). These conditions were exacerbated by eroding public confidence in universities, as expressed in growing dissatisfaction by students, taxpayers, and legislatures over perceived inadequacies in the academy, such as curricular shortcoming, fiscal management, and the social relevance of funded research (Weathersby and Weinstein, 1970; Attiyeh, 1974; Massy and Hopkins, 1979; Jones, 1985; Massy, 1990).

The response of most universities was to retrench financially and await a more favorable economic environment (Massy, 1990). While economic conditions gradually improved, it was becoming apparent to many senior university officers that their institutions must learn to function within financial limits (Breneman, 1981; Massy, 1990), a belief reinforced by growing demand by governing boards and the political process for increased accountability of academic institutions (Massy and Hopkins, 1979). Many university officers now turned their attention to building resource allocation systems that would enable them to allocate more effectively their limited financial resources, and respond to public demands for increased accountability. A number of these efforts were grounded in the belief that higher education can benefit from the techniques of modern management science in allocating scarce resources (Anthony, 1978). Accordingly, many universities began to invest in larger numbers of professional administrators, and place more emphasis on planning and control (Jones, 1985). The next section of this paper reviews the principle allocation models that emerged during this period.

REVIEW OF RESOURCE ALLOCATION MODELS

During the early 1970s, higher education economists, policy analysts, and administrators began developing rational resource allocation models to optimize the use of available funds. A major assumption of most of these models is that budgeting and planning go hand and hand. It was quickly apparent that traditional analytic decision models used in business organizations had to be adapted to address the problem that outputs in higher education are numerous, diverse, and difficult to measure; decision processes unusually elaborate and complex; and goals less unified than those of traditional business organizations (Attiyeh, 1974; Hopkins and Massy, 1981). As the following discussion suggests, this undertaking has proved very difficult in theory as well as practice.

This section reviews the most widely adopted resource allocation models of the last twenty-five years. As Dickmeyer (1994, p.250) observes, "[d]escriptions of budgeting techniques are often vague as to whether they can or should be applied at all levels (departmental, division, school, or state)." Unfortunately, this ambiguity clouds much of the literature on resource allocation. Wherever possible, in the review that follows I have tried to make clear distinctions about the level of application appropriate to each technique, whether the model represents a relatively centralized or decentralized approach to resource allocation, and examples of institutions that currently use (or have used) a particular system. It should be noted, however, that solid case studies and secondary analysis are rare in the literature on resource allocation in higher education. The reader should also be aware that these processes are not necessarily mutually exclusive. For example, an institution may use one form of resource allocation in certain instances, and another in other circumstances. Finally, As Green and Monical (1985, p.47) have noted, "[t]here are probably as many different ways of allocating resources in institutions of higher education as there are presidents [of colleges and universities]."

1) Incremental Budgeting

a) Incremental Line-Item Budgeting

The simplest and oldest form of resource allocation, line-item incremental budgeting is still used extensively at the central administrative and unit levels. In this form of budgeting, each expenditure line item is increased (or decreased) by a fixed increment, or left unadjusted.[7] The basic philosophy is that the existing budget is properly distributed, and only requires minor incremental adjustment (Caruthers and Orwig, 1979). Thus, administrators can use the previous year's budget as the primary information for the following year's allocation, and, with the exception of a few programs designated for special review, avoid having to conduct complex, expensive, and time-consuming cost-benefit analysis or program review (Tonn, 1978). In theory, incremental budgeting provides a cut-and-dry, rational approach to resource allocation (Heydinger, 1980).

Because incremental budgeting is typically applied "across the board"—i.e., across program areas—this allocation approach does not effectively tie resource planning to specific program reductions or expansions (Dickmeyer, 1994). In addition, incremental budgeting provides little information about whether budgetary decisions support or reinforce institutional goals. It may encourage end-of-year spending to prevent loss of those funds or a diminished allocation the following year. Also, incremental line-item budgeting is static in that it generally does not provide a mechanism for considering new ways of operating (Stonich, 1977). Resource decisions are apparently not prioritized, and input from lower levels in the organization is often minimal (Dickmeyer, 1994).

2) Quantitative Modeling

a) Mathematical Decisions Models

In the early 1970s, the Ford Foundation sponsored a series of working papers published under the auspices of the Research Program in University Administration at the University of California, Berkeley. The purpose of the Program was "to undertake quantitative research which will assist university administrators and other individuals seriously concerned with the management of university systems both to understand the basic functions of these complex systems and to utilize effectively the tools of modern management in the allocation of educational resources." (Weathersby and Weinstein, 1970, p.iii)

This research generated two classes of mathematical models. One class related the inputs of the education process (e.g. student enrollments) or changes in "technology" (e.g. class size) to resources required, such as faculty costs (Weathersby and Weinstein, 1970; Schroeder, 1973). These complicated models were implemented with the aid of then emerging management information and decision support systems[8]. Because these simulation models were non-optimizing, they required the decision maker to assess the actual objectives.

The other class of models dealt more directly with the problem of optimizing the allocation of resources among competing alternatives, through application of mathematical programming tools such as linear and non-linear programmatic, dynamic-programming, and optimal control theory (Weathersby and Weinstein, 1970; Geoffrion et al., 1971; Schroeder, 1973).[9]

Although several universities adopted mathematical programming models for resource allocation during the early and mid-1970s, including Stanford, Harvard, Tulane, Michigan State, and the Universities of Toronto and California (Weathersby and Weinstein, 1970; Geoffrion et al., 1971; Hopkins and Massy, 1981), by the late 1970s the techniques had fallen into disfavor for a number of reasons. First, defining and measuring outcomes in higher education is an exceedingly difficult task (O'Neill, 1971; Wallhaus, 1980). Because the higher education production function cannot be specified explicitly, there are no universally accepted algorithms for assessing the resource requirements of a given unit (Craven, 1980). Second, the fact that many outcomes represent joint products means that resources cannot be divided among various outcomes (Wallhaus, 1980).[10] Third, because different decision makers may attach different values to different outcomes (Wallhaus, 1980), it is often difficult to express preferences or values among alternatives. Mathematical models do not sufficiently address the decision making process (Garvin, 1980). Fourth, many of the models were based upon the spurious notion that it is possible to attribute expenses across different types of academic degree programs using average costs of instruction (Smartt, 1984). In fact, such average cost models fail to capture the true marginal cost of instruction that is key to understanding the incremental impact of changes in student enrollment. Fifth, despite their technical refinement, mathematical models do not capture the flux and change that is characteristic of internal resource allocation decisions (Zemsky et al., 1978). Sixth, the cost and staff time needed to develop the models may have outweighed their actual or perceived usefulness.

b) Formula Budgeting

First introduced in the early 1950s, formula budgeting is a technique for allocating resources by means of an arithmetic or mathematical algorithm (Millard, 1979; Caruthers and Orwig, 1979). Formula budgeting has been widely applied in state university systems, where first-level resource allocation decisions among institutions are typically made at the central level (Caruthers and Orwig, 1979; Gross, 1979; Millard, 1979; Dickmeyer, 1994). Formulas vary in their composition, and range from simple enrollment-driven measures to complex systems incorporating many institutional factors and needs (Millard, 1979; Dickmeyer, 1994). Common measures include student credit units, contact hours, faculty workload, and degrees conferred (Pickens, 1982). In theory, the technique can also be applied to resource allocation decisions at the institutional level, although this seems to be a less common application, and examples in the literature are rare.[11]

Formula budgeting provides an objective basis for allocating resources that may be perceived as more equitable than other resource allocation procedures (Caruthers and Orwig, 1979). Formula budgeting may also reduce conflicts that might otherwise arise in the budget negotiation process (Caruthers and Orwig, 1979). Both of these advantages may simplify the annual budget allocation and thus reduce overall costs of administering the process. On the other hand, formula budgets are sometimes based on rather arbitrary criteria (Van Vijt et al., 1969) and, because of their simplicity, may fail to address the unique mission and complexities of a given institution or unit (Temple and Riggs, 1978). In addition, because most formulas are developed during periods of enrollment expansion and are based on average cost, they do not accurately predict resource needs

Introduction and Overview

during periods of stable, declining, or erratic enrollment (Temple and Riggs, 1978; Millard, 1979; Caruthers and Orwig, 1979).

3) Budget-Planning Systems

a) Planning, Programming, and Budgeting Systems

Planning, Programming, and Budgeting Systems (PPBS) were adopted by many government agencies during the 1960s as a means of improving resource allocation decisions (Weathersby and Weinstein, 1970; Hopkins and Massy, 1981). By the end of the decade, some policy analysts and academic researchers were recommending its application in higher education organizations, particularly public research universities (Weathersby and Weinstein, 1970). Schroeder (1973, p.896) defines PPBS as follows:

> Planning refers to the setting of organizational objectives and goals; programming refers to identifying and evaluating programs or alternatives which meet those objectives; and budgeting refers to providing the resources to support the programs. But PPBS is more than just a new method of budgeting; it includes planning and analysis functions as well. The analysis part of PPBS is usually accomplished by the cost-effectiveness approach, which considers the costs and benefits of alternative programs. Such analysis is an integral part of a PPB systems.

As this description may imply, PPBS takes a macroeconomic, centralized, and top-down approach to resource allocation issues (Caruthers and Orwig, 1979). When first introduced in the early 1970s as a potential resource allocation device, several higher education organizations including the University of California System, Ohio State University, Princeton, and the University of Utah experimented with PPBS. It quickly became apparent, however, that the problem of defining and measuring educational outputs (Schroeder, 1973; Craven, 1980; Schmitdtlein, 1989-90) makes cost-effectiveness analysis very difficult or in some cases impossible. This insurmountable difficulty is reflected in the absence of case studies documenting the successful implementation of PPBS (Caruthers and Orwig, 1979; Hopkins and Massy, 1981).

Although PPBS quickly disappeared, many institutions have adopted budget-planning systems that incorporate several key features of PPBS, particularly its emphasis on linking planning and budgeting through careful analysis of institutional programs and priorities (see Shirley and Volkwein, 1978; Arns and Poland, 1980; Long, 1980). A number of case studies (Green and Monical, 1985) document the success of various efforts to link planning and budgeting on individual campuses, public and private. In many instances, a university budget committee composed of central administrative staff, academic deans, selected faculty, and student representatives meet to assess institutional needs, review program requests, and recommend a budget. Although the actual process varies from campus to campus, the process does not demand that program outcomes and cost-effectiveness be conclusively (and exhaustively) demonstrated. Still, the process is time-consuming and demands considerable commitment from many campus constituencies.

b) Zero-Based Budgeting

Zero-Based Budgeting (ZBB) is also based on the desirability of evaluating academic programs. Unlike PPBS, ZBB does not require explicit evaluation of cost-effectiveness, but instead focuses on the microeconomic problems of transforming objectives into operating plans (Caruthers and Orwig, 1979). Under ZBB, all budgeted activities are grouped together into decision packages, and then rank-ordered according to relative priority (Schmidtlein, 1989-90). Essentially, ZBB requires that every budgeted activity be formally justified (Caruthers and Orwig, 1979). Several institutions, including Stanford, McMaster, and the University Systems of Georgia experimented with ZBB during the 1980s (Caruthers and Orwig, 1979; Hopkins and Massy, 1981). Carried out completely, ZBB requires that a large number of decisions packages be ranked and evaluated. It is a highly time-consuming process, and one that often instigates political upheaval by forcing decision makers to make controversial assessments.

Although ZBB originally meant that an institution had to justify the entire budget, in practice it has since evolved into a procedure that reviews selected decision packages (Caruthers and Orwig, 1979; Craven, 1980). A primary benefit of ZBB is that it requires the participation of managers at many levels in an organization. Thus, ZBB involves the individuals who spend the money and who are best qualified to understand the trade-offs associated with various decisions packages (Pyhrr, 1973). In the process, ZBB may facilitate organizational learning and management development (Pyhrr, 1973; Stonich, 1977). By facilitating evaluation of alternatives, ZBB may be useful during times of cost cutting or when major reallocation of resources is needed (Stonich, 1977). In theory, this arrangement should result in improved planning and management at the unit and institutional levels.

Dickmeyer (1994) notes that few academic institutions have managed to implement ZBB for more than a few years. He cites as obstacles the substantial paperwork required, as well as the practical difficulty of cutting academic programs that have been identified as low ranking. In addition, he notes that many institutions have found the technique better suited for administrative than academic areas because of the problem in systematic rank ordering academic priorities. Finally, there is often a tendency to merely justify existing expenditures needs without effective analysis of real programmatic needs (Temple and Riggs, 1978). These factors may explain why ZBB has not been widely applied in higher education.

4) Incentive Budgeting

a) Performance Budgeting

Performance budgeting has been defined as *"a budgetary structure* that focuses on activities or functions (program structure) which produce results (outcomes or impacts) and for which resources (inputs) are used and *a budgetary process* that attempts to allocate resources on the basis of anticipated or past results." (Peterson *et al.*, 1977, p.2). The technique was apparently developed to counter the problem that higher education resource allocation systems (such as formula and incremental budgeting) are usually separated from performance evaluation, and to answer calls for greater accountability (Pickens, 1982). According to Peterson *et al.* (1977), a number of state university systems used some form of performance budgeting as of 1976, including Hawaii, Washington, Tennessee, and ten other states. In performance budgeting, qualitative as well as quantitative measures of results are typically used to allocate financial resources (Peterson *et al.*, 1977; Millard, 1979).

Banta and Fisher (1984) provide a short case study of a more recent example of performance budgeting, the Tennessee Performance Funding Project. In 1979, Tennessee added a performance funding feature that applies to all public colleges and universities in the state, whereby up to five percent of an institution's annual state allocation for instruction is awarded on the basis of documented accomplishments in five performance areas that relate to academic program quality.[12]

Although determining performance criteria is sometimes cited in earlier literature as one of the greatest obstacles to implementing performance budgeting (Millard, 1979; Caruthers and Orwig, 1979; Pickens, 1982), there is growing evidence that institutions can develop valid performance criteria (and measurement instruments) using principles derived from the continuous quality improvement and assessment movements.[13] Still, many within the academy object to this belief, and consider evidence gathered through these means as unreliable or unrepresentative (Banta and Fisher, 1984).

Other issues remain to be resolved. First, because performance budgeting is generally enforced by the state higher education coordinating body, it is not clear whether it has the desired trickle down effect within institutions. Are the incentives strong enough at the department and program level to influence change? The second drawback is that performance budgeting is a highly time-consuming and potentially very costly process, one that engages faculty, administrators, and other personnel (Banta and Fisher, 1979). Finally, as Schmidtlein (1989–90) notes, performance budgeting requires consensus on appropriate performance indicators as well as an ability to accurately and equitably attach costs to reaching defined levels of performance. Both of these requirements may prove more difficult in practice than in theory. Despite the possible benefits, there is little empirical evidence that the process leads to actual programmatic improvements.

In the last few years, performance budgeting has been applied in several public university systems around the world, including the United Kingdom, Australia, and the Netherlands (El-Khawas and Massy, 1995). In the United Kingdom, separate funding councils for England, Scotland, and Wales allocate funds for the public universities. The Higher Education Funding Council for England separates funding for teaching and research. Teaching is funded through a "core and margin" funding model. The marginal funding component rewards efficiency by automatically adjusting for expected improvements in productivity, while core funding is enrollment driven (El-Khawas and Massy, 1995). Research funding is linked to assessments performed by external reviewers. By reallocating funds based on formal assessment, the British system simulates a market system with clear economic incentives. Although in theory the British funding mechanism is oriented toward achieving accountability for performance, productivity, and quality, the assessment system has been criticized for failing to influence actual improvements. A major problem in the present system is that the assessments are not formative in nature, and provide little insight into actual programmatic strengths and weaknesses.[14] However, as El-Khawas and Massy suggest, because funding in the new system is still allocated in block grants, the real responsibility for program innovation and improvement is in the hands of individual institutions.

b) Responsibility Center Budgeting

The other major incentive budget approach developed for higher education is called responsibility center budgeting[15] (hereafter abbreviated RCB). First developed at the University of Pennsylvania during the late 1970s, RCB has since been adopted by a few other academic institutions, including the University of Southern California and Indiana University. In an RCB system (Hoenack, 1978; Zemsky *et al.*, 1978; Heath, 1993; Strauss, Curry, Whalen, 1995 forthcoming), income generated through the activities of each school, and its direct expenses, are credited to that school. Indirect university expenses are also attributed to each school using an allocation procedure that measures the school's relative share of the university's central administrative costs. The central administration, in turn, apportions a certain share of the university's unrestricted general revenues to each school in the form of a calculated subsidy (also known as "subvention"). Each school then prepares a budget based upon expected total income and anticipated direct and indirect expenses. It is important to note that each school retains any excesses of income over expense.

Introduction and Overview

RCB offers several advantages. First, decentralizing resource allocation to individual schools allows budgetary planning to occur at the level where decision makers are most familiar with the needs, priorities, and activities of an academic unit (Zemsky et al., 1978). Deans and department heads are likely to be involved in and informed about the budget allocation process (Hoenack, 1978). The result may be better resource allocation decisions, improved academic planning, and broader understanding (and communication) about these issues and how they impact the academic community (Strauss, Curry, Whalen, 1995). Second, the system creates powerful incentives for individual schools to increase revenues and control costs since, by definition, both become their responsibility. (Hoenack, 1978; Strauss, Curry, Whalen, 1995). Third, because schools are charged for indirect cost recoveries, they have a more realistic understanding of how those costs are derived and are less likely to view them as discretionary income than as income that covers known (and assignable) administrative costs (Strauss, Curry, Whalen, 1995).

RCB is not, however, without drawbacks and risks. As the previous discussion may suggest, implementing RCB requires a high degree of institutional consensus about the nature of the resource allocation process and the incentives that underlie its construction. Financial management at both the central administrative and unit level, must support the elaborate revenue, expense, overhead, and cost allocation features necessary for RCB to work. Costs are allocated on the basis of average rather than marginal costs principles, and thus may not accurately reflect activity levels (Massy, 1994). But the most problematic pitfall is that RCB may create incentives for academic deans and department chairs to "game" the system. The classic example is the school or department which tries to raise attributed tuition revenues by counter-productive schemes (such as preventing students from taking courses in other schools), or by restricting use of necessary central administrative services in order to reduce costs (Strauss, Curry, Whalen, 1995). As Massy notes, once an RCB system is set up and the incentives become institutionalized features of a school's operating culture, it is difficult for the central administration to intervene with changes (Massy, 1989). Another problem is that some academic units may be too small to productively navigate the system due to instabilities in their economies (Massy, 1989). Finally, because RCB highlights cross-subsidies (Massy, 1989), the chief academic affairs officer must be prepared for the almost inevitable backlash from deans and chairs arguing over the equity of central administrative subventions.

c) Block-Incremental Budgeting

Block-incremental budgeting is resource allocation approach developed at Stanford University in the late 1980s (see Massy, 1989; Massy, 1994).[16] The basic idea is that general funds are allocated to operating units in block sums, and the academic unit head has discretion to allocate funds as he or she chooses, subject to policy constraints dictated by the university's central administration (Massy, 1989, p.46). Annual increments are awarded at the discretion of the central administration. The size of the basic block is based on the unit's size, needs, opportunities, and institutional priorities (Massy, 1989, p.46), and perhaps (implicitly) on historical precedent. Block budgeting essentially involves four planning steps (Massy, 1989, p.47): 1) The central administration develops a long-range financial forecast and tentative planning parameters for each major organizational unit; 2) The academic units (schools) prepare their own multi-year plans based on the given planning parameters and their projected requirements, including any additional requests initiated by the unit; 3) The central administration reviews, amends, and revises the unit plans and allocates funding blocks; 4) The unit prepares its own budget, within the constraints of its blocks. In order to ensure that units are operating within the conditions set forth in their original agreements with the central administration, appropriate performance measures are usually developed and monitored to ensure compliance.

The primary advantages of this approach are clear. In keeping with a "collegial" model of the academy, the faculty deans and department chairs who have the greatest stake in the outcomes also have ownership of the resource allocation process. As a result, community morale may improve (Massy, 1989). Just as importantly, block budgeting creates powerful incentives for unit heads to optimize the allocation of resources through cost-savings, productivity improvement, and efficiency gains. Even though units have considerable discretionary control over resource allocation decisions, block budgeting still affords the central administration direction over institutional priorities.

On the other hand, however, because primary discretion over expenditures is delegated to unit heads, it may be difficult for the central administration to monitor and enforce institutional priorities in the absence of direct control (Massy, 1989).

SUMMARY REMARKS

Despite all the obvious effort (and enthusiasm) that has gone into their development, resource allocation systems have a checkered track record. Perhaps, as Schmidtlein (1989–90) notes, the relationship between planning and budgeting is too complex and indirect to be captured by any *one* allocation system. Difficulties predicting future needs and conditions, and problems arising from the time, cost, and the rigidity of the planning process are also impediments. The incentive-based systems correct some of these problems, but introduce others.

A final problem—and one that will be described from an empirical standpoint in the next section—concerns the politics and uneven distribution of power in academic institutions. While seldom mentioned in the descriptive literature on planning and budgeting, it is clear that these factors play a significant role in how even the most "rational" resource allocation systems are administered.

CONCEPTUAL UNDERPINNINGS

As outlined in the previous sections, a number of models have been proposed for distributing scarce institutional resources in higher education. While each model offers a unique perspective on the resource allocation problem, they share in common a notion of rationality fundamental to economic theory. Allison (1971, p.29) notes that in economics, "to choose rationally is to select the most efficient alternative, that is, the alternative that maximizes output for a given input or minimizes input for a given output." According to Allison (1971, p.29–30), rational action is identified by four basic concepts: 1) Goals and objectives, translated into 'payoff,' 'utility,' or 'preference function.'; 2) A set of known alternatives; 3) Consequences or outcomes associated with choosing each alternative; and 4) Choice—selecting the alternative with the highest expected value.

Although the rational choice model was the dominant theoretical paradigm in management literature throughout much of the twentieth century (Scott, 1981), more recent theorists have challenged this model as inadequate. Cyert and March (1963), in their behavioral theory of the firm, argue first that rationality does not accurately portray the motivational and cognitive assumptions guiding managerial choice, and second, the theory of the firm does not capture the real complexity of these organizations. By this line of reasoning, formal frameworks for rational decision making may primarily serve symbolic and ritualistic needs for justifying choices rather than avenues for substantive change. Simon (1955), in developing his theory of "bounded rationality," argued that because of ambiguities surrounding the practical implementation of rational choice, decision makers in organizations are typically forced to select a satisfactory rather than optimal alternative.

Weick's (1976) theory of educational organizations as loosely coupled systems casts further doubt on the effectiveness of rational planning models. According to Weick (1976, p.4), because the "elements" of educational organizations are tied together loosely, planning models may be of limited value:

> There is a developing position in psychology which argues that intentions are poor guide for action, intentions follow rather than precede action, and that intentions and action are loosely coupled. Unfortunately, organizations continue to think that planning is a good thing, they spend much time on planning, and actions are assessed in terms of their fit with plans. Given a potential loose coupling between the intentions and actions of

organizational members, it should come as no surprise that administrators are baffled and angered when things never happened the way they were supposed to.

Alternative theoretical models on how organizations and managers make decisions suggests that politics and power, and not just rational decision making, may be as important or more important explanatory factors in understanding the decision process. Although relatively little empirical research has examined how universities and colleges allocate financial resources, most of this research has examined, in some way, what combination of variables influence these decisions and whether these factors fit the rational or alternative theoretical models of organizational behavior. Most of these studies (Pfeffer and Salancik, 1974; Hills and Mahoney, 1978; Pfeffer and Moore, 1980; Chaffee, 1981; Chaffee, 1983; Hackman, 1985) were conducted during the 1970s and early 1980s. While these studies parallel the development of the resource allocation models reviewed in the previous section, the studies focus less on the mechanics of the process and more on what purposes the process really serves.

In their 1974 study of organizational decision making at the University of Illinois, Pfeffer and Salancik hypothesized that resource allocation decisions are shaped by political strength as well by bureaucratic criteria. The authors found that subunit (departmental) power is significantly related to proportion of general fund allocation received. They also found that the more powerful the department, the less its budget allocation depended on traditional measures of departmental workload. Thus, Pfeffer and Salancik's study supports the view of the university as a coalition where participants struggle for scarce resources, reinforcing earlier theoretical work suggesting that budgeting is an inherently political exercise (Wildavsky, 1964).

Other research, however, suggests that the resource allocation process can be highly rational, depending upon the campus and economic conditions. Chaffee (1981, 1983), for example, tested whether the budget decision process used at Stanford University during the 1970s was rational. In contrast to previous empirical findings that the resource allocation process in research universities conforms most closely to a political or coalitional model of management decision making, Chaffee's study suggests that Stanford's budget process during this time period "shows substantial signs of procedural and substantive rationality." (1983, p.401)

Building on Pfeffer and Salancik's study, Hills and Mahoney (1978) asked whether the allocation of discretionary resources varies during periods of abundance versus scarcity. Using historical data representing periods of scarcity and abundance at the University of Minnesota, the authors found that during times of abundance, resource allocation is predominantly a function of universalistic (i.e. rational) criteria and less of power, whereas during periods of relative scarcity, the allocation process is predominantly a function of power and less of universalistic criteria. A later study by Pfeffer and Moore (1980) conducted using data from two campuses of a large, prestigious, multi-university system, lends further support to the scarcity argument advanced by Hills and Mahoney.[17] Although these studies provide compelling evidence that rational decision making is highlighted during periods of financial abundance, a recent study by Ashar and Shapiro (1990) contradicts this conclusion. In their study of resource allocation at a public research university during respective periods of resource abundance and decline, Ashar and Shapiro uncovered a "systematic relationship between objective, evaluative data and policy decisions in times of financial stress." (1990, p.137). The apparent discrepancy in these findings suggests that other explanatory variables not captured in the studies—such as institutional leadership, historical precedent, or campus culture—may determine the conditions under which resource allocation is primarily a function of power or universalistic criteria.

Hackman's 1985 study develops what is probably the most comprehensive theory to date of resource allocation in colleges and universities. Hackman postulated that a department's centrality, or how closely the purposes of a unit match the central mission of an institution, must be considered along with concepts of power and resource scarcity in understanding how institutions of higher learning allocate resources among units. Propositions are developed (rather than tested) on the basis of interviews at six varied institutions, and supplemented by questionnaires completed by administrators of a state university, a liberal arts college, and a comprehensive college. This research differs from earlier studies in several important ways. First, Hackman considered how resource allocation decisions impact academic as well as nonacademic units. Other studies have only examined academic units. Second, the methodology—extensive interviews and regression modeling—contrasts with the other studies, which were based largely on regression models, limited document analysis, and a small number of interviews. Third, Hackman's institutional sample represents greater diversity than the other cited studies, which looked at only one or two institutions.

Hackman's finding supports the view of colleges and universities as "political organizations that operate as open systems in interaction with the environment." (Hackman, 1985, p.74). Several propositions are developed: 1) Core units—i.e. those whose function is central to the mission of the organization—are relatively more successful in attracting internal resources than peripheral units, those who function is not central to the mission of an organization. 2) Institutional and environmental power interact with centrality in determining the internal resources allocated. 3) The resource allocation strategies used by the unit head interact with unit centrality and impact the internal resources it is allocated. 4) The combined effect of three uncorrelated variables—environmental power, institutional power, and resource negotiation strategies significantly explain the effect on resource allocation.

Whereas the previously noted empirical studies essentially describe how the resource allocation process is operationalized within specific institutional settings, Hackman's goes a step further in arguing that her research findings have significant implications for unit heads in developing resource acquisition strategies consistent with empirically-derived theory.

In general, the literature suggests at least one important reason why it has been so difficult to link budgets with planning. Contrary to the image of the budget process as orderly and rational, resource allocation is also a highly politically-charged activity. Even the most carefully laid out budget planning processes appear to be strongly influenced by organizational politics and power.

Significantly, none of these studies (or the theories they purport to test) describes in detail the nature of the allocation process used in the sample institutions, or how particular budgetary *systems* may impact departmental allocations. A system is labeled either rational or political, and little or no attention is given to the nuances of the allocation process itself and how it works on particular campuses. The nature of budget authority—whether the allocation process is centralized or decentralized or somewhere in between—is unexamined. This research will attempt to fill this empirical gap.

As discussed in the literature review, various approaches have been developed for allocating financial resources in higher education. Some of these resource allocation approaches—like PPBS, ZBB, and mathematical programming models—have virtually disappeared, while other systems such as incremental line-item budgeting, block-allocation budgeting, responsibility center budgeting, and performance-based systems can be found in research universities around the United States. As Massy (1994) notes, universities need not collectively adopt a single resource allocation strategy, a fact supported by the diversity of functional allocation systems in the academy. Because every system introduces trade-offs, the purpose of this research is not, therefore, to identify a single "best" model, but rather to illuminate how well the various resource allocation systems enable research universities to achieve their specific institutional objectives; the conditions under which a particular system is indicated; and directions for their improvement.

In conceptualizing this research, a key issue concerns the centralization or decentralization of budget authority. As discussed in the introduction to this proposal, universities have considerable choice in this regard, some choosing to concentrate budget authority at the central administrative level, others decentralizing budget authority to the major academic units, and others selecting an intermediate option. Concepts from the economics of agency offer a valuable lens for understanding why the locus of budget authority is a central issue in the design and implementation of any resource allocation system.

Agency, as used in the literature on economic behavior and organization, is concerned with the relationship between two figures who depend upon one another—agent and principal (Pratt and Zeckhauser, 1985; Arrow, 1985; White, 1992). Agents are decision makers who must choose an action from a number of alternatives, the outcome of which will affect both agent and principal (Arrow, 1985; Spremann, 1987). As employees, agents are subordinate to and act on behalf of principals—an organization's managers or overseers. Agency theory addresses the problems that arise due to information asymmetries between principals and agents. Specifically, because principals seldom have complete knowledge of agent behavior, an agent may consume resources or otherwise engage in activities that increase personal welfare at the principal's expense (Hoenack, 1983). Such behavior may diminish firm productivity and profitability—or in the case of nonprofit organizations, intrinsic value or stakeholder "wealth."

But principals are not completely at the whim and will of agents. Principals can devise ways to monitor agents and influence behavior through incentives. Unfortunately, however, principals cannot perfectly monitor the activities of agents and provide effective incentives (Pratt and Zeckhauser, 1985; White, 1992). In theory, to reduce or eliminate agency problems, principals should "select an optimal combination of monitoring and incentives to minimize the costs of obtaining a desired level performance from 'workers.'" (White, p.111). Although much of the economics literature on agency addresses the "optimality" problem in theoretical fashion, there are no computational algorithms for solving this problem. Consequently, in the "real" world, principals—that is, managers—must rely upon judgment, intuition, and experience in devising ways to monitor agent behavior and in developing effective incentives. In effect, principals attempt to approximate a solution to the optimality problem.

Hoenack (1983) and Massy (1994) apply concepts from agency theory to illuminate the resource allocation problem facing central administrators, and in particular, the complications that arise when the resource allocator's ("principal's") values differ from those of the recipient ("agent"). As Hoenack (1983) describes, an employer normally delegates to employees a certain portion of the organization's productive activities. Under such conditions, an employee may divert resources for personal use—the "agency" problem described above.

Many examples of agency problems arising in higher education could be cited. Three are cited below:

> The President, Provost, and governing board of a public research university declare that faculty should devote more attention to undergraduate education than scholarship and research. Individual faculty members, preferring to emphasize research, ignore the mandate.

A university central administration stipulates that all faculty and non-faculty supervisors must evaluate employee performance annually. However, some supervisors refuse to comply or perform the task perfunctorily.

An academic dean asks her department chairs to reduce the number of small upper-level undergraduate seminars and replace them with larger courses in general education. Only a handful of departments comply.

According to Hoenack (1983, pp.41–60) and Massy (1994, p.10–11), an employer may reduce resource diversion by adopting one of three global strategies, each of which offers unique incentives and possibilities for monitoring employee performance. The strategies are described below, along with examples of their relevance to resource allocation in research universities (see Massy, 1994):

1) Direct Control

In a direct control (DC) system, the most highly centralized resource allocation option, a principal dictates precisely how an agent will use resources, and closely monitors agent compliance. For example, several of the mathematical programming models developed during the 1970s enabled university central administrators to derive precise allocations for departmental expenditure categories such as teaching and instruction or student financial aid. The models left little leeway for institutions or academic units to reallocate funds as they saw fit. Although such mathematical models are no longer generally used, a few universities continue to exercise direct control through incremental line-item budgets that are centrally determined and closely monitored.

A DC system is dictated in cases where a high degree of centralized control is desired. Incentives are less apparent in a DC system because of the high degree of employer control built into the system. Massy notes that DC systems "can be effective when scope and complexity are small," but warns that "costs of information, regulation, and employee disempowerment grow geometrically as scale increases." (1994, p.10). An obvious weakness of DC models is that they distance resource allocation decisions from those most familiar with the activities they are designed to support.

2) Use Price as a Regulator

Price-regulation (PR) systems represent incentive-based models that use arm's-length adjustments to marginal revenues and costs to influence behavior. As such, PR systems represent a more decentralized and market-driven approach to the resource allocation problem. In a PR system, an institution might, for example, subsidize behaviors it wants to encourage, or tax activity it hopes to either reduce or eliminate. For example, the central administration might subsidize the purchase price of expensive equipment if two or more departments agree to share the equipment (rather than purchase it independently). On the other hand, the central unit might declare a tax on physical space in order to collect revenue and encourage departments or schools to allocate space judiciously. There is very little documented evidence that universities actually use price-regulation extensively, although Stanford, for example, has recently introduced a levy on physical space. A number of institutions also tax departmental expenditures on certain restricted accounts. RCB represents a special case of price regulation in that *all* revenues and costs are passed along to academic units. However, as Massy observes, RCB systems do not usually incorporate differential taxes or subsidies.

Massy (1994, p.10) notes that the main weakness of PR systems is that a "principal must predict how adjustments to marginal revenue and marginal cost will affect agents' behavior and then assess the resulting impact on his or her own values"—a problem demanding a sophisticated understanding of the agent's values.

3) Assign Responsibility for the Value of Outcomes

Value-outcomes (VR) systems, another type of decentralized incentive-based resource allocation model, encompass four concepts (Massy, 1994, p.22-23): 1) Principal and agent agree on what needs to be accomplished; 2) The principal provides sufficient resources to perform the agreed upon activities; 3) Authority is delegated to permit effective performance; 4) Measures are developed to assess performance and to establish a base-line for future expectations. Massy (1994, p.11) notes that "the distinguishing features of VR systems are that the principal holds the agent accountable for outcomes, and the principal does not regulate how the agent achieves the outcomes." The block-incremental budgeting model previously discussed is the best example of a value-outcomes system. In addition, other performance-based models (such as Tennessee Performance Funding Project) are based on the VR system principles. A main weakness of these models is that reasonable performance measures must be developed and routinely monitored to ensure that agreed upon objectives are being met and to offer incentives for continued improvements.

Generally, the resource allocation strategy selected by a particular university conforms most closely to one of the agency models cited above (see Figure I). For example, Chicago's previously highly centralized resource allocation model is an example of DC, Michigan's allocation process is structured around VR principles, and the University of Pennsylvania's responsibility-center budgeting system is an example of a global PR system.

The agency models described by Hoenack (1983) and adapted by Massy (1994) offer a general economic framework for categorizing resource allocation systems according to locus of budget authority, specification of incentives, and employee monitoring. Conceptually, these are salient and defining features of any resource allocation system (see Figure II). I believe

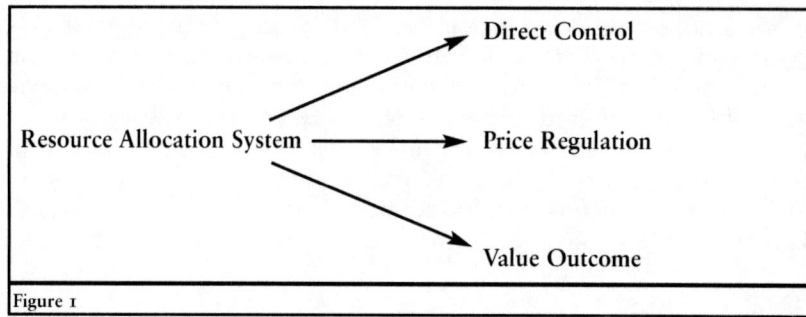

Figure 1

that the answers to the central questions driving this research are a function of how well these features work, individually and as a system. In empirical examination of resource allocation systems, I will concentrate on understanding how budget authority, incentives, and monitoring devices shape the success of the major university resource allocation systems.

While I believe that agency theory is an appropriate conceptual lens for investigating university resource allocation processes, I also recognize its potential limitations. The principal-agent problem is characteristic of every complex organization—for-profit, non-profit, or public—but the solutions proposed in agency theory may be less applicable in the academy. Property rights theory suggests why this may be so. According to Levin (1993, p.3), "property rights attempts to understand how organizations conduct busi-

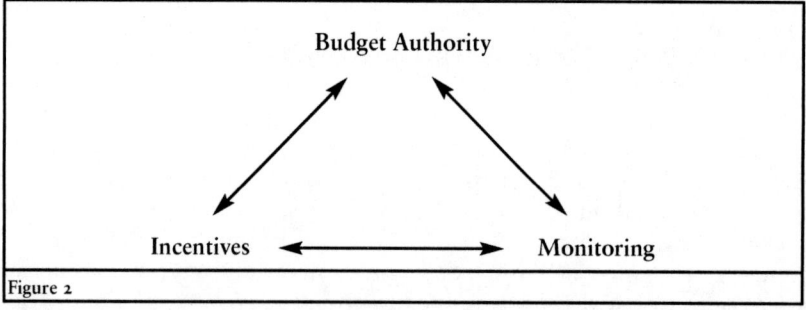

Figure 2

ness by exploring the motives of both individuals and groups in the organization to pursue their own interests, as well as the ability of the firms to alter the organizational structure and incentives to change managerial and worker behavior." Levin (1993) divides property rights into categories: *de jure* and *de facto*. *De jure* property rights are those that accrue to individuals through a legal entitlement, whereas *de facto* property rights derive from a person's ability to use resources for personal purposes without legal entitlement. In the theory of property rights, the way individuals respond to incentives is influenced by the property rights structure (Furubotn and Pejovich, 1974).

It is logical, therefore, to ask what property rights are espoused by the agents who make up the workforce in higher education, and second, to wonder how the property rights structure impacts the incentives that might be used to motivate their behavior. The primary workforce in the academy is the faculty who, by and large, teach, conduct research, and perform service—the primary "business" of the organization. Other agents—such as senior and middle- administrative managers—participate in the work of the organization, however their contributions are in support of and ancillary to the faculty. The governing board, possessing *de jure* property rights entitling them to control of the institution, delegate the day-to-day activities of the institution to faculty and non-faculty staff (Levin, 1993). As a result, faculty and non-faculty staff, acting on behalf of the governing board, are said to have certain property rights *de jure*: they use some of their resources in support of organizational objectives determined by the governing board (Levin, 1993). But as the previous examples of "resource diversion" suggest, faculty and staff sometimes appropriate property rights *de facto* and use resources for their own purposes independent of central mandates.

University faculty exercises stronger *de facto* property rights than their counterparts in other professions due the nature of the professoriate. Unlike the employer-worker relationships typical in the corporate world, faculty are not merely "employees," but members of a distinct profession with its own separate values and allegiances. The primary allegiance of university faculty to their respective disciplines (as opposed to their institutions) has been well documented (Becher, 1989). The professoriate likely screens for individuals who enjoy and even demand substantial autonomy in their everyday worklife, meaning that "supervision" is routinely carried out at arm's length. Once faculty achieve tenure, they generally enjoy even more autonomy and freedom to structure their professional lives as they see fit.

Other characteristics of the academy may compound the unusually extensive *de facto* property rights claimed by university faculty, and limit the applicability of the agency model in higher education organizations. Unlike for-profit firms, universities are identified by a diversity of goals, heterogeneity of values, multiplicity of outputs, and lack of discrete bottom-line performance measures. As noted previously, universities are loosely coupled organizations governed as much by principles of power and politics as by rational, bureaucratic procedures.

Against this perspective, the traditional means of addressing agency problems through formal authority, employee monitoring, and incentives may be less effective in research universities. Nonetheless, it is clear from the previous discussion that these agency features are firmly embedded in the three major kinds of resource allocation systems found in research universities, and therefore provide a useful paradigm for understanding university resource allocation.

METHODOLOGY

The previous section developed the conceptual underpinnings of the three resource allocation systems available to university decision makers, framed in language derived from principal-agent theory: 1) direct control ; 2) price regulation; and 3) value outcomes. As previously stated, the primary goal in conducting this research is to understand how resource allocation is operationalized in private research universities. Due to the exploratory nature of this question, as well as the paucity of existing theory and empirical research on my proposed topic, this study utilized a primarily qualitative approach eliciting data from several key campus figures responsible for developing or implementing institution-wide resource allocation policy, as well as beneficiaries of this policy—campus academic deans whose units (and faculty) are supported in part by university general funds.

This research focuses primarily on the supply side of the internal resource allocation process, represented chiefly by the activities of the university central administration. Therefore several of the individuals interviewed for this study are members of the central administrative unit primarily responsible for determining and/or implementing institution-wide resource allocation policy. These individuals include the executive academic decision makers (the President and the Provost) as well as their administrative representatives (the Director of University Budgets and the Chief Financial Officer). These positions (or equivalent titles) are found in every major research university. Other campus executives with significant responsibility for resource allocation decision (for examples, a Vice President for Planning and Budget, or an Executive Vice President for Administration), were also interviewed.

On the demand side of the equation, interviews were conducted with one or two campus academic deans, including, where possible, the dean of the faculty of arts and sciences (or equivalent).

In an effort to capture the faculty perspective on these matters, the chair of the budget or finance committee of the university's faculty senate (or equivalent body), as well as the chairs of several academic departments were interviewed. These individuals were interviewed in order to gain insight into their personal views as well as the views of the constituencies they represent. Obviously, this approach was not a substitute for in-depth interviews with individual department faculty. Nevertheless, it did provide insight into how faculty view the resource allocation process and its outcomes.

The six private research universities in this study were selected on the basis of their comparability and their diversity. In order for the data to be comparable, it was necessary to select a sample of institutions with a set of common characteristics. As outlined earlier, this research is focused on private research universities, in particular "Research I Universities" in the Carnegie Classification nomenclature. By definition:

> These Institutions offer a full range of baccalaureate programs, are committed to graduate education through the doctorate, and give highpriority to research. They award 50 or more doctoral degrees each year. In addition, they receive annually $40 million or more in federal support.[19]

Introduction and Overview

There are 29 private research universities in the United States. This study sampled six of these universities, or 21% of the total. Universities with varying resource allocation characteristics were selected. The table below shows how this sample reflects this desired diversity.

Institution	Type of System	Notes
Buchanan	Decentralized (Formula)	The system evolved incrementally and over a period of many years.
Pierce	Decentralized (Full RCB)	Classic RCB system.
Westmont	Transitioning from Centralized to Decentralized	New system attributes revenues and expenses to originating units, but avoids explicit subventions and participation of full RCB.
Shelton	Centralized (Committee)	Central committee with university representation determines base increments. Formulas used in allocation of administrative budgets.
Greenway	Decentralized (Block Allocation)	Block allocation determined by a committee of central administrators. Presidential role in budgeting unusually strong.
Garfield	Transitioning from Decentralized Block Allocation System to Decentralized System incorporating certain RCB features	New system attributes revenues and expenses to originating units, but avoids explicit subventions and participation of full RCB.

The sample accomplished the goal of diversity in that three of the institutions in the sample have a decentralized system; one has a centralized system; and two universities are transitioning from one system to another. Preliminary analysis of the institutions also suggested that elements of the three major agency models discussed by Hoenack and Massy were represented in the sample. Additional universities could have been selected to further diversify the sample, but for reasons of cost, access, and scope, this study was limited to the six selected institutions.

It is important to note that the complexity of each university's resource allocation process is not easily captured by simple terms such as "decentralized" or "centralized." These terms provide a general description of each system, but do not convey their complexity. The case studies address this gap.

DATA COLLECTION

This research was conducted using two methods. The first and primary data collection method consisted of semi-structured interviews with the campus figures cited above. The interview protocol probed for detailed information about each university's resource allocation system, how the system relates to the university's specific objectives, and the system's various strengths and weaknesses. A key goal was to understand the integration between the specific institutional goals expressed by university central administration, and the nature of the resource allocation system used on that campus.

The interviews were semi-structured in order to help focus the discussion around the key issues, but to allow room to explore other insights that emerged during the conversation. In general, each individual officer or faculty member was interviewed separately and the results of other interviews conducted on the same or different campuses were not shared with the respondents. The interviews—which were tape recorded and later transcribed—ran approximately one hour. Copious notes were taken during and after each interview. In total 72 individuals were interviewed across the six campuses.

The second data collection method consisted of document analysis of each institution's most recently published audited financial statement, descriptions of the operating budget allocation process, and related planning documents. Other published information about each institution was also reviewed, such as course catalogs and information posted on the World Wide Web. The documents provided further evidence of the procedures used on each campus for allocating university general funds and general resource allocation policy.

ANALYZING THE DATA

Data analysis was structured around the data generated from the recorded interviews, published financial statements, descriptions of the operating budget process, and other documents. After transcribing the recorded interviews and reviewing my handwritten notes, the data were assembled as individual case studies highlighting the key characteristics of each institution's resource allocation system. Each case study—organized as chapter—addresses the recent history of resource allocation in the institution; chief features of the current system, including the incentives it is designed to promote; current institutional priorities in relation to the resource allocation process; advantages and disadvantages of the system cited in the interviews and collected documents; and the current and future resource allocation challenges facing the institution.

The final chapter of this book includes a summary discussion of the case studies and a cross-case analysis.

LIMITATIONS OF THIS STUDY

This study is limited in several ways. At the outset, it should be noted that as qualitative research, this study relies heavily on interview data representing the subjective attitudes, feelings, and beliefs of key campus decision makers. Some social scientists may question the objectivity of this approach as well as the validity of the conclusions drawn from such data. I believe that qualitative methods are highly appropriate given the aims of this research and my interest in understanding a highly complex human process.

With the exception of the chair of the faculty senate's sub-committee on budget or finance and academic department chairs, I have not conducted extensive interviews with either faculty or students, two groups many would identify as primary stakeholders in the resource allocation process. While neither group generally has much direct control over institutional resource allocation policy, collectively and individually they would likely voice strong and possibly contrary opinions about the process and its outcomes[20.] They may also reject the legitimacy of the executive office to shape, define or interpret institutional objectives. I also have not interviewed university trustees in this study, and therefore cannot surmise their opinions. In sum, this study focuses on the stated opinions of executive decision makers at a particularly point in time—a perspective that may be biased or incomplete.

The sample of institutions and executive decision makers represented in this study is small and represents an elite sub-sample even within the Research University I Carnegie sub-classification. The six institutions, with possibly one exception, are considerably more selective and more financially well endowed than other private research universities. The sample is therefore in no sense a statistical sample, but it does represent a significant sample within the segment of elite private research universities. (but does not represent other kinds of universities and colleges.)

SIGNIFICANCE OF STUDY

This study is particularly timely given the magnitude of strategic and financial problems facing American research universities—a situation which many observers believe will only worsen in the years ahead. This study provides insight into these problems and their resolution.

This study advances our conceptual understanding and empirical knowledge of resource allocation systems in Research I universities. It also sheds light on the attitudes of key executive decision makers responsible for developing, administering, and implementing these policies, as well as the academic deans (and faculty) who must live by their rules. The resource allocation *process* has received very little attention in the academic literature despite the considerable interest expressed by scholars of higher education in the last decade.

The results of this analysis should generate important insights that will further our knowledge of resource allocation in research universities, and thus provide university decision makers with a conceptual lens for designing resource allocation systems that most effectively support the academic goals of their institutions.

2
Buchanan University

OVERVIEW

Buchanan University is often described as "tightly focused" and "youthful." But despite its youth, the University has achieved considerable distinction. Its undergraduate division is one of the most highly selective in the nation, and its established professional schools are equally well regarded. A number of its arts and sciences disciplines have been highly ranked in the National Research Council rankings. However, quality is uneven across the arts and sciences, and especially the sciences. Engineering disciplines are also less highly ranked.

Over the last twenty five years, Buchanan University has developed a resource allocation system built around what the University central administration refers to as "academic incentive formulas," "the management center budget system," the "decentralized management system," or, simply, "formula budgeting." The purpose of the Buchanan formula system is stated in a university planning document widely circulated in 1994:

> The management center budget system . . . provides for decentralized management at the school level . . . and general University administration and administrative support services. Formula budgets couple accountability with incentives and seeks to balance the creativity and efficiency of decentralized decision making with appropriate mechanisms to safeguard the financial health of the University as a whole and to allow for the implementation of university-wide priorities. This approach is intended to provide incentives for effective fiscal management throughout the University, to regulate the growth of administrative costs, to ensure that common administrative and academic support costs are shared equitably among the schools and to provide a stable framework for long-term planning.

The Buchanan formula system, in principle, has three distinct components according to a university document: 1) "A structure of accountability specified by the assignment of revenue and expenditure funds . . . to the management control of individual operating units;" 2) "A bottom-line contribution to (or subsidy from) the University determined by the Provost;" and 3), "An incentives mechanism regulating the disposition of both surpluses and deficits vis-à-vis budgeted 'bottom line.'"

Under the formula budgeting system, schools develop budgets based on projected revenues from sources such as tuition and fees from undergraduate, graduate, professional, executive education and continuing education programs; indirect cost recoveries; annual fund gifts; and miscellaneous income (e.g. from auxiliaries, organized activities, and service components. In turn, schools are responsible for managing expenditures, "limited as much as possible to expenditures under the dean's or director's direct control." A management document lists examples of such expenditures: instruction and research, organized activities, libraries, student services, general administration, including development, financial aid, and budgeted appropriations. The University's central budget office assists with these calculations, and ensures that each school's budget conforms to its designated formula. The budget office also "bills" each school for central or shared administrative expenses, but according to administrators, the University does not attempt to fully allocate and recover these costs. As a result, the central administration assumes some of these unallocated expenses.

With the exception of the Provost and school deans, faculty do not play a direct role in the resource allocation process. Faculty do serve as members of a committee known as PACOR—the President's Advisory Committee on Resources. PACOR was formed in the late 1980s following efforts by the academic council to involve faculty in the budget allocation process. PACOR is a policy-making board that advises the University senior administration on the budget process. In recent years, PACOR has reaffirmed the primacy of the formula system and recommended several modifications to the system which will be discussed later in this chapter. Faculty also serve on the Academic Priorities Committee, which, as the title implies, deals with academic issues related to curriculum and research. In the past, the Academic Priority Committee has occasionally addressed funding and resource funding issues, but this role has diminished over time as PACOR has assumed most of this responsibility.

Once resources are allocated, the central administration generally does not closely monitor how funds are spent, although the Provost does spend considerable time discussing general institutional and school priorities with each dean. The university budget office issues monthly financial statements with projections of year-end performance, by school, and is also involved in the year-end close. But basically, as one administrator noted, "the money within a school's budget is essentially the dean's to prioritize in consultation, obviously, with the Provost." Thus, schools and other large academic units monitor their own line-item budgets. Historically, operating units with an annual surplus have been permitted to transfer the excess into their reserves, which they are free to use as they wish. However, schools are expected to maintain sufficient reserves to cover possible operating deficits.

The genesis of Buchanan's formula system can be traced to the early 1970s, when the University central administration developed a formula arrangement for the rapidly expanding school of medicine. According to one long-time senior administrator, the Provost at the time was worried that the Medical School would present a financial problem for the University because growth in medical facilities lagged the growth in sponsored research volume sufficient to recover start-up and on-going operating costs. The Provost structured a formula agreement with the Medical School that isolated its financial affairs from the rest of the University and thus ensured that the School would not be a drain on University general funds.

During the subsequent two decades, the University's other major academic operating units structured formal agreements. The law school adopted the system in academic year 1979-90, and was followed by the newly established business school (1980-81), the school of forestry and environmental sciences (1981-82), and the school of engineering (1981-82). Finally, a decade later, the remaining academic units under the Provost, including arts and sciences, the graduate school, and the divinity school (1991-92), became formula entities.

In 1991-92, all academic units in the University were organized into three management centers: The Medical Center Management Center (which included the School of Medicine, nursing programs, and Hospital; the Central Administration Management Center (consisting of units reporting directly to the President such as development and student life); and the Provost's Management Center, which includes the University's schools and major academic units. The University central administration developed formulas for each management center, as well as formulas for certain large units within each Center.

As this evolutionary process may suggest, there was never a centrally-determined master plan for moving schools to the formula system. One Buchanan administrator feels that the system "evolved without any real understanding as to where we were going." The schools were added to the formula system, one by one, through mutual agreement of the Provost and dean. In fact, until the early 1990s when the University began to examine the status of the formulas campus-wide, conversations and agreements about formulas were confined to the dean and Provost. Each school independently negotiated a deal with the Provost at the time the formula arrangement was adopted.

Discussions with University administrators suggest several reasons why Buchanan adopted the formula system over time. As previously noted, the University Medical Center became the first formula unit. The sheer complexity of this auxiliary enterprise, as well as the not ungrounded fear of financial encroachment, undoubtedly motivated the central administration's decision to isolate the financial affairs of the unit from the rest of the University. A decade later when the University inaugurated a new business school, similar financial concerns resurfaced. A number of individuals on campus apparently feared that the new school would drain University resources. As one administrator remembered:

> And to make sure that didn't happen, they [the central administration] blocked it up, and basically said [to the prospective dean], 'You have a franchise to run a business school, but there's no money, and there isn't going to be any money . . . you're on your own . . . good luck. And if you do well, good for you.'

In addition to the central administration's desire to insulate the rest of the University from financially volatile academic units, cultural and political factors propelled the development of the formula system. A number of the individuals interviewed for this study suggested that the formula system was, in fact, thrust upon the central administration by faculty who held the view that "the central administration was incompetent, and therefore, [the faculty] should build a system in which they didn't [and] couldn't have any money." Faculty held the view that without any money, [the central administration] "couldn't do anything stupid."

Over the years, the formula system became more deeply entrenched, and deans grew accustomed to managing their resources. The deans also began to embrace the premise that resource allocation decisions are "not particularly the business of anybody else. " One administrator characterizes the culture that evolved:

> [The deans] want to be involved with the resource allocation decisions that the university is making . . . they want to be involved and they don't want central administration, maybe, making those decisions . . . They don't want the President making [those decisions]. The deans want to be the ones who make [those decisions]. . . and that's how [the institution] has been run.

Another administrator concurs, adding that a major segment of the faculty believed that the "major economic decisions that were going to affect faculty resources . . . weren't done well." Furthermore, the deans of the established schools apparently had no collective or individual desire to share the cost of running a University composed of diverse academic units.

Instead, the attitude developed, "We're going to go to this kind of system because it will make sure that I won't have to pay his bills!" Thus, the formula system offered deans a means to control University resources while at the same time achieving financial (and perhaps intellectual) independence for their respective school.

Some administrators feel that a lack of good local information led faculty and some central administrators to conclude they just didn't have "access to the information they needed to be able to judge whether decisions were being made correctly." This feeling led to "the straightforward belief that budget decisions ought to be held closely to the vest and used in ways that were determined by those most directly involved."

Finally, the formula system was in some sense the economic engine that allowed a young University to stimulate innovation and entrepreneurship at a time when the institution was seeking to improve its academic reputation with relatively limited resources. Deans were recruited with the understanding they would raise the resources necessary to attract top faculty and outstanding students. In turn, deans were given free rein to spend those resources in ways that would allow them to maximize the mission of their school. At least one of these deans was able to catapult his school into a top-ranked professional school after only a decade.

THE FORMULA SYSTEM

Discussions with central administrators, deans, and faculty reveal a range of opinions about the effectiveness of the formula system and its impact on the University. Their views illustrate how the formula system facilitates and sometimes inhibits the attainment of University priorities. They also suggest an outline of how the system might be revised to more closely achieve University priorities, as well as conform to the leadership style (and personal expectations) of the current senior administration.

Nearly everyone interviewed at Buchanan seems to agree that the formula system creates powerful incentives for deans to manage resources wisely because they are accountable for revenues and expenses directly attributable to their academic unit. Not expectedly, formula budgeting has led to what one administrator describes as "a system of strong deans, of entrepreneurial deans, and fairly independent deans." The system therefore promotes responsibility and offers opportunity for each dean. A dean of one of the professional schools illustrates this view:

> I don't have any issue over the fairness or sensibility of the system . . . I believe that people react very strongly to a federalist system or decentralized system and control . . . Under other budgeting systems, I don't think we would think as entrepreneurially as we think. I have a lot of incentive to focus on revenue building, for this school. I think that's true with every dean——they should be riding a hard course on raising revenues. I have an

absolute incentive to cover costs because we're going to have to cover our costs. I have no assumptions that somebody else is going to pay for them.

Central administrators tend to agree with this perspective and point to specific incentives. One administrator believes that the system has "provided financial incentives to all of the operating units of the university . . . and in the past four years, the formula units have beat their formulas [and] returned to reserves almost fifty-five million dollars." Another administrator notes that before one particular unit became a formula unit, there was "definitely a spend-it-lose-it mentality. You know, as you get to the end of the year, 'Why shouldn't I try to spend out my budget?'" Entrepreneurial activities, such as developing executive and continuing education programs and attracting sponsored research, are also mentioned as direct outcomes of the incentive structure created by the formula system.

On the other hand, however, not all deans regard the system equally favorably. Schools, like for-profit businesses, operate in distinctive markets, but not all schools within the same institution operate in equally favorable markets. One administrator believes that "some deans probably like [the formula system] a lot more than others. And those [schools are] Business, Law, and Medicine, and the [other] professional schools." These schools, the administrator adds, have "been in a position where what they were doing was hot and [as a consequence] they have generated enormous amounts of resources and have done generally what they wanted to do, and have accumulated significant reserves."

Another executive officer reinforces the view that the professional schools in particular have benefited from the formula system:

> Clearly, the deans of . . . most of the professional schools think the system is pretty good. They make a lot of money, and they get to keep it . . . You know, I think that arts, and some of the other more traditional or core kind of programs are less enthusiastic, because they feel like the professional schools get all the money.

The professional schools appear to have an advantage in this system because, as one administrator notes, they can "more easily slide in another ten to fifteen students" and reap the attributed tuition revenue. In addition, their mission may be more attractive to potential donors and funding agencies. On the other hand, certain units, such as Arts and Sciences, do not operate in a free market, both with respect to the tuition they can charge and the number of students they can enroll. Despite the apparent inequities, the deans apparently accept the basic premise that they are responsible for managing revenues and expenses. An executive officer summarizes this view: "I think that everyone at Buchanan has generally bought into the notion that schools and colleges need to have responsibilities for their income and expenditures." Indeed, in all likelihood, deans are screened and appointed partly on the basis of their willingness to function within the formula system. One administrator notes that in the School of Arts and Sciences, the new dean was appointed "in part because he's got great fundraising potential." When deans do complain, it is not about the system *per se*, but rather about the mechanics of the formula calculations—in particular, what costs should be counted as "direct" expense, and what costs should be shared with other academic units.

The formula system has also contributed to a kind of fiscal discipline that has allowed the university to avoid running an operating deficit. "There is the habit of people being careful here," one dean notes, adding "There isn't any thought that you would ever run a deficit budget." Furthermore, in contrast to institutions that have failed to live within their financial limits and subsequently experienced budget deficits, one of the strengths of the Buchanan formula system is that "we can't do anything of significance until we have discovered how we are going to pay for it." In fact, administrators confirm that the University has not experienced any operating budget deficits for at least the last twenty-five years. In addition, unlike certain other major research universities, Buchanan has not been forced to downsize its faculty or staff in recent years.

Despite these various strengths, the formula budgeting system used at Buchanan has serious liabilities, particularly from the perspective of the University central academic administration. The main problem is that the system is relatively inflexible in the sense that it is very difficult for the President, Provost, and Chief Financial Officer—individually or collectively—to move funds around the system. Unlike other management center systems—such as the one that will be described in the next case chapter—the Buchanan formula system does not incorporate explicit taxes or subventions that allow the University central administration to make arm's length adjustments to unit bottom lines and redistribute funds within the system to emphasize University priorities.

In theory, according to a description in a 1990 university document, the formula budget system is supposed to "provide resources for a Common Fund to stimulate academic initiatives to allow the University, upon recommendation of the Provost with the advice of the deans and faculty, to implement priorities that transcend individual school boundaries and to balance the centrifugal tendencies of decentralized management." In practice, however, the funds available to the President, Provost, and Chief Financial Officer, are relatively modest. According to a recent management document, incremental funds available to the President and Provost include:

1. The President's discretionary resources of approximately $1.25 million per year.

2. The President's Contingency Fund, included in the annual operating budget at $500,000 per year.
3. The Provost's Contingency Fund, included in the annual operating budget at $250,000 per year.
4. The Provost's Common Fund for interdisciplinary activities, included in the annual operating budget at $300,000 per year.
5. The Provost's Academic Priorities Pool for priority initiatives of the academic administration, included in the annual operating budget at $1 million for 94/95 . . .

Moreover, there is apparently no large reserve from which the President or Provost can draw. From the perspective of the senior academic administration, these modest amounts of money are entirely too small to support their ambitious institutional agenda. One senior academic sums up the budget allocation situation in the following way:

> [The system] is extremely inflexible at the moment. There are very few ways in which money can be moved around, and there are very few discretionary resources available to the President and even to some degree to the other senior officers . . . So it provides very little opportunity for support for key priorities, unless one wrests resources from other presently established pots of money.

According to one administrator, in the original conception of the revenue center, "it was clearly assumed that the Provost would be imposing taxes and moving money around the various schools . . . that the Provost would basically tax the rich and give to the poor." The administrator speculates that certain deans were recruited with the understanding that their unit would not be taxed. Taxes, where they do exist in this system, are created for special central purposes, such as "internationalization," and appear as line-items in the annual formula allocation. It is up to the leaders in the central administration to consult with the deans when resources are needed to support new initiatives and to create new special line-items which in effect become taxes. The deans are understandably reluctant to participate in negotiations that might diminish their own wealth. Deans in this system are highly territorial about resources—resources they consider *theirs*. Academic officers observe that although deans are actively engaged in discussions about university-wide priorities, few are willing to give up resources:

> You can almost see around the Deans' Council table, the protectionist turfs beginning to kick in as soon as anything is on the table that might bring about some significant redistribution of resources. You can just see it.

So if the Law School or the Business School happen to be cash cows, they want to keep all the cash. And if Arts and Sciences or [one of the newer professional schools] is having a difficult time . . . it's difficult [for the Provost] to change bottom lines in order to move money around.

Although such attitudes are frustrating to central academic officers, they are hardly surprising. As one central officer reflects:

If you're talking about the Dean of [one of the University's professional schools] who wants to protect a very important resource and a very strong reputation with a very small school and not a whole lot of alternative resources available, there's no way in which [that Dean] is going to get really warm, fuzzy feelings about helping [another academic unit's] financial aid problem . . . that's the way the motivations work.

One of the other undesirable effects of the system is that discussions of academic initiatives are often curtailed at an inappropriately early stage. In essence, as one administrator laments, the conversation is closed even before it begins:

When you run an all-out formulas system, one of the consequences is that you denominate things in dollar terms much too early in the conversation. And so that if I have a good idea, you can say, 'Yeah, but how do you pay for it?' And I'd have to say, 'I don't know. We'll have to think about that.' And the conversation is over. Because at Buchanan, if you can't figure out how to pay for it, you can't do it. And I just don't think that's a very healthy way to have those conversations.

Thus, the central administration is faced with a resource allocation system that makes it difficult though not impossible to marshal resources for major projects. According to one university administrator, under the present system, it is possible, over time, with "political will and leadership," to adjust bottom lines and redirect resources flows, from one formula unit to another. In reality, however, the President and Provost would probably rather reallocate funds without a lengthy time horizon or potentially difficult negotiations with the individual deans. Indeed, this same officer later admits "there's still a degree of independence around each management center. So that if you don't get easy consensus, it can be a fairly protracted negotiation . . . it's not easy culturally to move money across school boundaries currently, and it's not easy structurally to move money across administrative and academic boundaries."

A final consequence of the system is that it provides few incentives for deans to work together since fiscal cooperation is unrewarded in the system. Deans and department chairs are described as "very parochial." One administrator testifies that Buchanan is "much more a confederation of schools and colleges than a sort of unified entity." The situation is somewhat mitigated by the presence of the Graduate School, which oversees doctoral degree programs across the University and coordinates the academic review process. However, the Dean of the Graduate School leads through persuasion and personal influence—not by wielding carrots and sticks.

TOWARD A FUTURE SYSTEM

As the previous discussion suggests, the senior executive officers of the University are anxious to address what they perceive to be the major shortcomings of the current system. The central academic leaders in this institution find the system rather frustrating at times, partly because they are used to functioning within an allocation model that accords significantly more budget authority to the central administration. They are also accustomed to systems where discussions of priorities precede the allocation of the budget. Two quotations from senior officers illustrate these views:

> I am more comfortable starting my budget year by saying, 'What are my major academic priorities that I want to achieve?'—and then saying,

> 'To achieve those, what do I have to do in the budget to make sure those academic priorities are achieved? . . . I'd rather start there before getting into the details of the budget. And then try to make sure [we] get there.

> [At a previous institution] it certainly seemed to be more of a centralized discussion because the Provost and President were talking about allocating moneys that were theirs, which is something that we relatively infrequently do because we don't have much to talk about.

Though the three senior officers—the President, Provost, and CFO—are relatively new to the University, one of them believes that together they "have the experience in other institutions to recognize some of the major dysfunctional aspects of what we're doing here, as well as enough experience now at Buchanan to begin to understand how important certain elements of the system are to Buchanan." The CFO, in particular, was recruited to "bring together our resource allocation systems with a closer degree of attention from the center." They individually emphasize that their goal is not to dismantle the system altogether, but rather to bring the system more in line with the financial and strategic direction they have established for the University.

Before discussing possible modifications to the resource allocation system, it is useful to discuss the context in which University academic priorities (and resource allocation reform) must be addressed. Buchanan has recently undertaken a major strategic planning process, involving intensive discussions with all segments of the University community, and culminating in a published strategic plan. According to the plan, the environmental changes impacting higher education and health care "pose a range of significant challenges for private research universities in general and Buchanan in particular." Furthermore, the document acknowledges that "attracting the best students and faculty and offering the best education programs, medical care, and scholarships will not be easy." Financial constraints, including more limited endowment resources and a small alumni base, are cited as major barriers. Given these conditions, priorities must be subjected to careful and on-going scrutiny:

> Future achievement will require a careful ordering of institutional priorities and serious consideration of tradeoffs. In the economic climate that will characterize higher education for the foreseeable future, no university, least of all a university of our size and relative youth, can hope to be excellent across the full spectrum of academic disciplines. We cannot hope to answer every academic opportunity by developing new programs, nor can we respond to every need by creating a new service. We must constantly ask what is fundamental, essential, and critical. We must decide what best fits our institutional mission and what best ensures Buchanan's distinctive contribution.

The "increasing sense of the financial constraints Buchanan faces and the need to match activities and programs to available resources" means that the University must "meet these needs through reallocation, or what is sometimes called 'growth by substitution.' Growth by substitution is a growth in stature and quality derived from redirecting current resources to activities of greater priority and promise." Although the plan urges that the University aggressively build its endowment, the primary conclusion is that "growth by substitution must be our principal means of achieving quality gains a in world of constrained resources."

Together, these statements suggest that an effective University resource allocation system should enable academic leaders to reallocate funds in support of current academic priorities. The statements also suggest that in a world of financial constraints, University leaders will need to determine their chief priorities and make difficult trade-offs.

UNIVERSITY PRIORITIES

Despite facing difficult financial and environmental conditions, Buchanan has established rather ambitious priorities that reflect a desire to further improve its academic reputation. Examination of recent University documents and discussions with academic leaders point to several planning priorities, including improving undergraduate education (the University must "capitalize on and deepen [its] commitment to undergraduate education");

expanding interdisciplinary and cross-school collaboration "to maximize the effectiveness of our educational programs;" continuing to build on "the entrepreneurial spirit in program development and research funding;" expanding "cooperative arrangements "with business and civic organizations in the Region"; and providing "leadership in the transformation of academic medical care." In support of these priorities, Buchanan is completing a series of capital investments which the University believes should position it for leadership in education and research.

According to this document, five "institutional imperatives" or "strategic themes" will establish "our major priorities in the context of our distinctive character and limited resources." The themes include: 1) Enhancing Academic Quality; 2) Strengthening Citizenship; 3) Enhancing Academic 'Efficiency," 4) Increasing Academic and Administrative Effectiveness; and 5) Securing Our Financial Future. Within each priority, specific goals are described in considerable detail. The goals are too numerous to reprint in their entirety, but the summary list below represents a selection of academic goals:

- Nurture each of the schools and faculties of the university with special emphasis on securing establishing the school of the environment;
- Attract and retain an outstanding faculty;
- Continue to foster joint degree programs and interdisciplinary teaching and research;
- Provide efficient and effective administrative and academic support services;
- Secure the Graduate School as a vital component of the teaching and research mission of the University;
- Increase the diversity of our faculty and students;
- Internationalize the university;
- Provide expanding access to advanced communications technologies, including Internet and international video conferencing;
- Enhancing the quality of undergraduate life;
- Strengthen Buchanan's capability to deliver world-class scientific education and research;
- Strengthen the computing infrastructure for Teaching, Learning and Research;
- Strengthen biomedical research;
- Improve health care delivery;
- Strengthen the coordination of faculty appointments across schools;
- Modernize administrative computing systems;
- Strengthening land use and facilities planning;
- Construction of a new science center.

A number of the priorities included in this list will obviously require significant University resources, particularly the academic initiatives in the sciences and technology. The University is not only building expensive new facilities and investing in new technology, but is also planning to recruit top senior scientists from other institutions to improve the national rankings of its science disciplines.

Senior academic officers further note they are especially interested in "developing cognitive neuroscience, in strengthening the Mathematics department, the philosophy department, and putting money behind really significant faculty investments in several key disciplines." But according to one senior administrator,

> We don't have the money to do that. We've got to find it. I would like very much to be able to have more flexibility around certain projects in undergraduate life where I have put some significant proportion of the meager resources that I have, but there are things that would remain to be done that would certainly enhance the Buchanan undergraduate education. And Student Affairs doesn't have any money...

It is obvious, then, that not all of these objectives can be achieved by simply reallocating existing revenue sources. Where will the money come from? One possibility is to raise new funds for the proposed initiatives. In fact, the University's strategic planning document lists several fund-raising priorities, including funds for Unrestricted Endowment, The Science Center, Financial Aid and Fellowship Support, Faculty Enhancement, Internationalization, and Student Life. The academic leadership is ready to launch a major capital campaign in the near future, but as one University leader noted, the campaign is likely to create tensions. The formula allocation system, with its emphasis on decentralized fund raising, is a major source of this tension. One senior central administrator states:

> The major obstacle to that is going to be the fear, not ungrounded, that the people who give to such priorities might also give to any one of the schools. Since the schools are responsible for raising their own money, there will be tensions around that. But we do need university resources for university priorities. And either the system is going to have to change dramatically, or we're going to have to have some way to distill those [issues] within the present system.

The next section in this chapter discusses how the University central administration intends to diffuse this tension and modify the resource allocation system.

THE FUTURE RESOURCE ALLOCATION SYSTEM

Achieving the university priorities articulated by senior academic leaders and reinforced in several university strategic plans will demand investments in a number of key areas. The resources for these investments, as one administrator relates, "have to be . . . wrung out of a system that wasn't established with that in mind." Fixing the system will not be easy, and the senior administration acknowledges that economic and cultural change will take time.

The "mission statement" for this new system is identified in Buchanan's strategic plan:

> Effective management of a formula budget system requires a careful financial coordination, management of academic outcomes, and a delicate balance between centralized and decentralized resources. While the schools have considerable autonomy in this management system, they also have responsibility for supporting university-wide priorities. Their contributions are determined through consultations involving the administration, the Dean's Council and frequently, major advisory groups such as the Academic Priorities Committee and the President's Advisory Committee on Resources.

Efforts are currently underway to bring the resource allocation system in line with the ideals expressed in this statement. The executive leadership has invested considerable time engaging the community in critical discussion about the strategic issues (and threats) facing the University, current and future academic priorities, resource needs, and plans for achieving institutional priorities. One academic leader states that he meets "quite regularly with the chair of the academic council. And he and I have pretty frank discussions about what I think we need to do and how we do it. And the question is how to involve the right group of faculty so that they understand what it is I am trying to do . . . and get [them] to tell me what they're concerned about, what they're not concerned about. " He adds that

> the most important thing for the senior administration, working with the faculty and faculty committees, is to have a strategic plan of where it wants to go, academically and non-academically. What are you going to do about student life; what are you going to do about interactions with the community? . . . I think you have to go through each school and say, 'Where do we think we want to go?' . . . I think you need to know what you want to do strategically, and you have to update that yearly. Once you've done that, then I think your next step is to say, what are the resources to develop those primarily most important programs [and] how are we going to get them.

Such discourse is crucial for changing the way people at Buchanan think about the institution—not just their school, academic unit, or program. At the same time, it will be important for the new administration to clarify the locus of decision authority as it develops priorities and resource allocation policy. The issues, as one administrator reflects, are closely intertwined:

> I would like a system which had some sense of where we're going, that understood what kinds of resources were best spent centrally, which were best spent locally. There are certain issues that central administration can't solve and ought to stay out of. There are certain issues that deans can't fix and ought to ask somebody else. I would like for us to understand which is which, and put the money in the right pot.

The Provost's role in this transformation will perhaps be most crucial of all, because he will have to "somehow manage the transitions with the deans." Equally important, these discussions will help to build the sense of trust and community necessary for changing the academic culture in ways that support the reallocation of resources. "I think the culture here in part had gotten to the point where the trust wasn't there," one academic leader commented, adding "I think you [get there] by spending lots of time talking to the faculty." One senior administrator is encouraged by the fact that two recently appointed deans are more willing to think as "university citizens" than their predecessors, thus making the conversations a bit easier to initiate and sustain.

In addition to improving the quality of campus-wide discussions and embracing formal planning, the central administration has also recently developed a series of academic and administrative benchmarks for measuring and improving institutional performance. A recent planning document explains that the benchmarks, which are called "strategic indicators," are

> intended to provide a relatively small number of indices where we stand in the major areas of university life, including institutional finances, the faculty, the student body and key components of our academic infrastructure. The data provided is necessarily selective; each indicator presented is the point of a pyramid of data . . . The indicators are offered as benchmarks for measuring our vital signs.

Though it is yet unclear whether the indicators will eventually impact resource allocation decisions, at least one of the executive officers interviewed for this study believes that evaluating the outcomes of resource allocation should be a cornerstone of any allocation model. Benchmarks are certainly one tangible means of evaluating these outcomes.

The benchmarks are tied to five "strategic themes" mentioned elsewhere in Buchanan's planning literature. Sample indicators from four of the categories are shown on the following pages:

ACADEMIC QUALITY:

Competitiveness of Academic Programs Compared to Peer Institutions

—student applications, admission and yield rates, entrance test scores and grade point averages of matriculants; faculty salary rankings; graduate and professional program rankings.

Student Quality and Achievement

—grade point averages and honors while at Buchanan; in-school surveys of student satisfaction; placement results; acceptance rates for post-baccalaureates training.

Faculty Distinction

—peer reviewed research awards and publications; membership in national and international honorary societies; prizes for teaching and research accomplishments.

Diversity and Internationalization

—gender, race and nationality of students and faculty; number of applications and students admitted from abroad to each academic program; number of courses and extracurricular events with substantial international content or focus on multicultural perspectives.

Academic Infrastructure

—level of investment in computing infrastructure; availability of computing resources; number, configuration and quality classrooms, laboratories and other specialized facilities.

Financial Support

—Comparative tuition rankings; comparative endowment per student; development targets; university subsidy per student by program.

STRENGTHENING COMMUNITY AND CITIZENSHIP

Community at Buchanan

—proportion of undergraduate choosing the live campus; number and variety of extracurricular activities, major speakers, cultural and athletic events; campus safety statistics.

INCREASING ACADEMIC AND ADMINISTRATIVE EFFECTIVENESS

Management of Academic Resources

—Number of joint faculty appointments; number and rates of participation in joint degree programs; number and rates of participation in cooperative programs with other area universities.

Administrative Management

—Best practice benchmarks of specific administrative processes; number of paper-based and computer-based administrative systems; rates of growth in administrative costs; FTE trend by unit.

SECURING OUR FINANCIAL FUTURE

Endowments and Investments

—Value of assets under management by asset class; real rates of return by asset class.

Facilities Maintenance and Deferred Maintenance

—Aggregate routine maintenance expenditure; expenditure per foot by building class in comparison to national norms. Deferred maintenance deficiency backlog.

Capital Budgeting

—Historic and current value of fixed and movable assets; relationship between consumption of assets by type and funding for renewal by source.

It is worth noting that the indicators cover a wide range of university operations, from core educational and research activities to administrative and financial performance measures. The University has already begun collecting data and creating the summary indicators shown above. But because the strategic indicators were only recently introduced, it is impossible to predict how they will used and whether they will in fact have a beneficial impact on institutional quality. And although the University has a dedicated office of institutional research, it is unclear whether the University can sustain the resources necessary to develop and update these benchmarks. In addition, it is uncertain whether the University can develop truly appropriate comparison groups for the various benchmarks cited in the plan.

There are indications, however, that certain indicators are already being used as a basis for redirecting financial resources. The strategic plan, does, for example, discuss recently released academic program rankings conducted by the National Research Council (NRC). The plan pinpoints several programmatic clusters where the University will attempt concentrate resources, emphasizing that "investments must be selective, but equally clearly, we cannot have departments of only average national quality if Buchanan is to strengthen its position as one of the handful of most distinguished private research universities."

Academic and administrative leaders believe that these measures—improving the quality of campus discussions, engaging in formal planning, and monitoring outcomes through benchmarking—represent important first steps toward modifying the resource allocation system at Buchanan. Together these changes may set the stage and create the context for the even more politically difficult task of reallocating resources and/or introducing a more explicit across-the-board tax. As suggested in discussions with campus executives, the resource allocation process might be changed over time to support university academic priorities. Three changes in particular may be implemented.

First, central administrators believe the allocation system should enhance the authority of the President and Provost to reallocate resources without having to secure tacit or explicit approval from the deans. One campus administrator hopes that the new allocation system will "reaffirm the Provost's prerogative to move funds [including reserves] around within his management center, among the deans, based on priorities that are established by him and by the President." The administrator adds that the senior academic leaders should have "more flexibility in being able to make those kinds of decisions without having to discuss them with the deans or [other] players." Another administrator agrees: "[The Provost] should be able to change bottom lines, severely or not so severely, or with some lead time. To say, '. . . I realize you're making all this money. You're doing a wonderful job. But there are some loss leaders in the world.'" The reallocation could be used to support central priorities but also provide subsidies for schools with less robust economies.

Second, some reconsideration of the formulas is likely to occur over time. Several people interviewed voiced the belief that the formula should incorporate an explicit tax that would return more money to the central administration. The funds could then be used to support University priorities that transcend traditional school or department boundaries. In addition, such a system might incorporate the subvention or subsidy typically found in "full" management center budgeting systems. Although such subsidies are supposedly part of the formula system, the subsidies are not publicly reported in the University financial statement, or in other University documents widely circulated in the community. Formal taxes and subventions would provide funds for central priorities, and in addition, might change the psychology of the system in ways that might have an added beneficial effect. An academic leader and senior administrator contemplate the effect of such a change:

> If Buchanan were to change the system and instead start with a big pot of money, and it was up to the President and Provost to distribute, the incentive structures for the deans would be very different. [The dean] would still want to get as much as possible, but she would recognize that she would have to make the case for everything she was asking for, rather than being persuaded by some means to give up anything that she feels she already controls. It's a very different psychology. Of course, people are territorial and protective in any resource allocation system, of something that they are responsible for. But if they think the money is theirs—quote, unquote—versus ours, they're going to have a different set of incentives.

> If we more clearly allocate the costs of [all] academic and administrative support to the schools, they all need a subsidy. So instead of having a conversation about how much they're going to contribute to those support services, you have a conversation about how much they're going to contribute to those support services, you have a conversation about how much a subsidy they need from central administration. And then the senior officers can adjust the level of the subsidy. So, depending on your perspective, that can look like a pretty radical change to the system, or a pretty simple change. Culturally, it would be a big change. Mechanically, it's a pretty simple change.

A subvention pool might serve as the "big pot of money" mentioned in the above quotations. No plans are underway, however, to develop such a fund in the immediate future, though discussions with academic and administrative officers suggest that this might be a longer term objective. Everyone interviewed for this study believes that any changes to the current system will take time implement. Comments from two central administrators sum up the problem:

> Once you're on a formula system or any kind of an agreement system like that, to go in and unwind it is extremely difficult, extremely difficult. And to fully understand all the ramifications of what you are doing is just very difficult, politically and every other way. It takes a long time to negotiate all of these kinds of arrangements and then an equal amount of time probably to unwind them.

> When you want to make a major shift, a major change of any kind . . . that's a problem. There'll be a lot of gnashing teeth and screaming. That's not just a Buchanan problem. That's a problem everywhere.

3
Pierce University

OVERVIEW

Pierce University is a leading private university with an unusually large portfolio of undergraduate and graduate programs, encompassing almost every major professional field as well the traditional arts and sciences. Its professional fields are typically highly ranked in national surveys of academic quality. Quality in the arts and sciences disciplines is considerably weaker, as demonstrated in its recent standing in the National Research Council Rankings. Its undergraduate division is the least selective of the six institutions.

Pierce University is one of several universities in the United States that uses full-responsibility center budgeting (hereafter referred to as RCB). A recent (1994) university document provides a general description of this highly decentralized resource allocation system:

> RCB involves financial decision making, other decision authority, and university-wide rules and mandates. Under RCM[1], financial decision making is in large part delegated to the deans. Essentially, each Center [responsibility center] has a lump sum of annual income, and a credit (or debit) in an . . . inter-center bank; each RC decides how to spend that money. In addition, under RCM, central administration has reserved only limited substantive decision authority, and enacts only limited rules and mandates for the decisions made with each RC. Thus central administration has given up a good deal of its limited stock of instruments of leverage. A major issue of RCM is the proper allocation of decision-making between the university and local levels.

Like the formula budgeting system described in the previous case study, responsibility center budgeting attributes revenues and expenses to the academic and administrative units where they arise. Schools receive a bill for their calculated share of central administrative services, and are held accountable, or "responsible" for managing direct revenues and expenses.

Although resources in the RCB system generally belong to the units where they are generated, the Pierce central university administration also retains a certain portion of revenues through various built-in taxes. The taxes include a 1% charge on current unrestricted revenue budgets; a 10% charge on gifts as they are spent; and a 15% charge on endowment income as it is earned. Income from these taxes, along with investment income and unrestricted endowment income, goes into a central administrative pool. The central administration distributes these resources annually, at its discretion, to the major academic units—which, at Pierce, consists of 23 schools. As will be described later in this chapter, central resources are typically distributed in support of certain priorities specified by the Provost and other central academic officers.

The mechanics of the allocation process are relatively straightforward. The university budget office develops a three-year budget forecasting manual at the beginning of the budget cycle. The manual, and accompanying spreadsheet macros, are intended as a set of guidelines for deans, directors, and senior business administrators for use in developing academic and administrative center plans and budget forecasts. The manual reviews the major planning variables—-staffing and compensation, capital improvements, indirect expenses, and restricted funds—and includes detailed instructions for completing the three-year forecast. From this forecast, the business officer, working in conjunction with the dean, prepares a line-item budget.

The budget office staff views its role primarily as managing the elaborate administrative processes necessary for RCB to work and assisting units with business planning. The budget office staff does not, as a rule, assist academic units with academic planning. In the central administration, this activity is handled by the Provost and Vice Provost for Planning and Budget. The Vice Provost, who previously served as dean of a Pierce school, works with the deans and the Provost throughout the planning and budget cycles. One of his major responsibilities is to help the deans with their academic and budget planning. Previously, the budget office assumed more of this responsibility. However, according to the Vice Provost, the deans sometimes felt they had been "pressured by a budget office that didn't understand what some of the academic issues are."

The other major campus office responsible for overseeing university resource allocation is the financial systems office. This office does more than simply maintain the university's financial and accounting systems. Under the management of an assistant vice president, the office is responsible for overseeing the financial administration and performance of every academic and administrative unit in the university. Once the university budget is approved and allocated to the individual schools and service centers, the office ensures that every unit will not have overspent its carefully budgeted resources by the end of the academic year. Every month, the office tracks the financial status of every center by examining the breakdown between revenue and expense, the actual performance of the revenue budget and the variance, as well actual expenses and associated variance. If it appears that a unit may be on its way to a budget deficit, the office pinpoints the source of the problems and contacts immediately the senior business officer.

The office provides financial advice to deans who occasionally run into serious difficulty and need to close a budget deficit. When that occurs, the office helps the dean determine where to cut back. Often this means that a department is required to "dip into its cookie jars"—reserve accounts built up over the years in almost every school. At the end of the year, the financial vice president closes the books, ensuring that Pierce has once again avoided a budget deficit. The University also operates a capitalized bank, and the bottom line of every school goes into the bank. In the following year, a school is permitted to draw up to 20% of the previous year's bottom line and add it the current year's operating budget.

The success of the system is contingent on a number of factors. First, the University has an excellent on-line information system (often internally described as "state-of-the art"). The system permits sophisticated central tracking of all university financial information at the unit level. In the absence of this information-rich environment, it would be impossible to project revenue and expense with such a high degree precision, in real time, throughout the fiscal year.

Second, staff in the financial systems and budget office have developed strong relationships with the senior business officers and academic deans in each unit. When units experience financial difficulty, problems are dealt with swiftly.

Third, there are strong incentives for the central financial officers to avoid a deficit. The finance committee of the University's governing board has mandated that the institution never have an operating deficit, and with good reason: the university operates with virtually no central reserves. With two minor exceptions, the university does not budget reserves or accumulate reserves. The Provost has a $750,000 annual reserve, and the Senior Vice President for Administration has a half million dollar reserve. Both reserves, according one financial officer, are spent about five months into the fiscal year. Thus, the university operates without a "safety net" and cannot afford even a tiny deficit.

Fourth, the university relies on what one senior financial administrator calls the "good citizenship" of the deans. A dean who is good citizen manages revenues and expenses wisely and avoids creating a deficit. When a deficit does occur, the dean is willing to work with the central administration to do whatever is necessary to close the deficit. And in some cases, a dean who is a good citizen may be expected to share part of its surplus to solve a deficit created by a cost center. According to one financial executive at the University, "Most of [the deans] are really good citizens and recognize that the whole is greater than the sum of the parts. They recognize that the university has to come first, and then their school." The system has served the University very well during times of financial distress. A few years ago, the University faced a crisis when 1,000 fewer freshmen than expected enrolled at the institution. Financial aid expenses were also unusually high that year, compounding the problem. One central administrator remembers the situation and how the university weathered the crisis:

> We got through that year by going out, I think, in October and November, alerting all the deans. We had meetings with financial, senior business administrators. We walked around to everybody and explained this problem. We worked diligently, very, very closely with every single dean. Every single dean became a part of the solution to that problem. We could not have done it centrally. It had to be done very, very locally. We're all here to tell the story about the balance of that year . . .
>
> And it was, I think, one of the finest hours of revenue center management.

Perhaps the most important factor in the system's success is the leadership of the Provost. The Provost is responsible for allocating the subventions that determine whether an individual receives an rebate on its "participation," or whether it contributes a portion of its resources to the central administration, and, indirectly, to the academic business of other schools. One central administration explains that the Provost

> really has to hold [together] the system. He is the integrity of the system. Subvention can be a sieve, and indirect cost allocations can be watered down to where they aren't trusted at all . . . To the extent that he can hold firm to the general principal of indirect cost allocation and, as openly as possible, explaining and being able to defend his subvention allocations, then the system works. If he can't make these tough decisions, it's not going to work. On the performance side, we can only hold together what's been put in place at our stage of the budget process. To the extent that we're able to budget well is completely a reflection of the Provost's strengths in dealing with deans who are very needy, very vocal, very persuasive. You just have to hold them in line. You can't cut deals at mid-year. You can't make side-bar negotiations that go around the system. And we've been very fortunate in having Provosts . . . who are able to stand up in this system.

The Provost must stand firm, because, as one central administrator remarks, "[The deans] always have their own best interests in mind, whereas the Provost has to have the University's best interests in mind. And we certainly won't enhance our reputation or improve our excellence if we don't have that really strong leadership from the Provost pulling it all back together."

The President's involvement in the resource allocation process is considerably more limited than the Provost, to whom he delegates primary authority for overseeing university-wide resource allocation. The President's major role in the resource allocation process is serving on the finance committee of the University's governing board. His role on the committee, like those of the other trustees, is to provide stewardship and counsel. Recently, for example, the committee discussed the endowment pay-out policy. The President recommended a lower pay-out rate and proposed replacing the "lost" income by increasing the size of the university endowment through higher investment returns, by raising gifts, and reinvestment of pay out.

Faculty at Pierce participate in the process in at least two ways. One is by participating in the University's budget advisory committee. The chair of the faculty senate is an automatic member on the committee. Other faculty and staff serve two-year terms on the committee. According to several of those interviewed for this case study, the committee has not had much of an impact on university resource allocation policies. The committee is described as an educational opportunity for faculty and staff to learn how the allocation system works at the University and to hear about budget and financial issues. The committee does not participate in the actual allocation of resources.

At the decanal level, each dean is expected to have a faculty council or budget committee made up of faculty who advise the dean on school budgeting. The current Provost has made it clear that he would like each dean to discuss budget allocations and academic programs with the faculty, especially the school council. The effectiveness of these school-wide budget committees is said to vary from school to school, and depends largely on the willingness and ability of the dean to engage faculty in open dialogue about resource allocation matters.

Pierce has used RCB since the early 1980s. Prior to that time, Pierce actually functioned under a highly centralized resource allocation model that is quite the opposite of the system used today. The executive vice president throughout the 1970s served as the chief financial and budget officer. According to several faculty and staff interviewed for this case study, this individual almost single-handedly controlled all major resource allocation decisions at the university. One faculty leader described him as "an absolute dictator," with a vision of where he believed Pierce should go and the power to allocate resources in the directions he wanted. He focused allocations on the professional schools and invested relatively little in the liberal arts. One dean remembered that during this administration, the notion prevailed that "resources belong to the university [central administration] and they decided who got what." Another administrator described the environment as "more central than I can imagine any other private research university being managed," adding that the budget process was

> a very closed, smoked-filled room, back-door kind of management that was conducted by the Executive Vice President and a few of his favorite Deans, and the President. The President delegated all authority and responsibility to that individual. So this was not at all a democratic kind of place. Deans were given resource allocations at the whim of the very small central unit, maybe two or three favorite children, and a powerful Executive Vice President.

Under this executive vice president, "every budget was a negotiation," recalls one long-time dean. This dean remembers that his school received "an increasingly large share of resources because [his school was] particularly adept at making cases." Nevertheless, he concludes that this wasn't a particularly good way to run a university "because the people who make the best cases may not be where the institution needs to put its priorities."

In the early 1980s, under new executive leadership, Pierce developed the highly decentralized, responsibility center system it uses today. The major champions included a chief business officer who arrived from an institution which had adopted RCB several years earlier, and a new Provost and President who were willing to give the system a chance and supported it actively. The President at the time wanted to develop a system "where he and his Provost wouldn't be making twenty-three academic investment decisions in twenty-three different disciplines." One can imagine that deans and faculty were also anxious to exert more control over their financial resources.

In fiscal year 1981–1982, the senior administration developed the RCB system, working with a faculty and deans' advisory committee. The committee developing the RCB principles that have sustained the system for the last fifteen years. It was at this time that the university also developed an in-house accounting and information system to support the implementation of RCB.

THE RCB SYSTEM

RCB has now been in place 15 years at Pierce. Central and school administrators, as well as faculty, have enough experience with the system to understand its strengths and liabilities. Recently, RCB has been a subject of campus discussion. The University Budget Advisory Committee conducted an extensive review of RCB in the early 1990s, at a time when the

University was setting the stage for an intensive strategic planning process. The study was recommended by the former Vice President for Budget and Planning, and the Budget Advisory Committee under his leadership. The committee published its major findings in a 1993 document entitled "Revenue Center Management: Advantages and Problems." The stated document purpose of the document was "to summarize long-standing faculty discussions of budgeting and financial decision-making at Pierce with the Revenue Center Management (RCM) system." At the outset, the document lays out the problems associated with RCB:

> From the start, Pierce faculty have seen many problems with RCM. RCM is accused of encouraging a business mentality, thus allowing financial priorities to drive academic decisions and subvert academic values, so that we forget we are a university. Moreover, RCM is charged with shattering a university-wide vision, thus promoting intellectual balkanization and sabotaging inter-disciplinary cooperation; so that we forget we are a university. For these reasons, many faculty would like to replace RCM totally.

Nevertheless, the report ultimately concludes that

> A complete change from RCM would be disruptive . . . and, paradoxically, would focus too much attention on accounting issues rather than academic ones. Moreover, no budget system is perfect. And, whatever the system, the sum of the limited resources will always be less than the total list of needs and aspirations.

The document explores the basic features of RCB and its implementation at Pierce, as well as its advantages and problems. Many of the same points were also raised during the course of interviews conducted for this case study. The summary below highlights the major points that emerged in the many interviews conducted for this case study, as well as the Budget Committee's document. (Quotations are taken from the Budget Committee document unless otherwise noted.)

1. RCM is a decentralized system of management in which schools are held accountable for decisions and resources.

As a decentralized system of management, RCB provides strong incentives for deans to "be businesslike, concerned with enhancing income and minimizing costs." Furthermore, the system creates obvious incentives for deans to maximize income and minimize expenses. In addition, units have powerful incentives to create surplus income to support new or existing programs. One dean summarizes his view of the incentives created under this system:

> If you want human beings to have an incentive to generate resources, you have to provide it for them . . . if the central university wants me to go out and raise money, they have to tell me that I'm going to get to keep it—so that we can hire more faculty, or have greater student aid, a better library, or more computers, or whatever we think the priorities are that will enhance the quality of the institution we're running . . . So if the central university wants me to go out there and raise money . . . they've got to say to me, 'You get to keep it if you raise it, to enhance the quality of your institution.' They've got to make a bargain.

The Budget Report notes, however, that because deans keep all surplus income, these resources are not available to cross-subsidize programs outside the school, including programs that may be important institutional priorities. The Report also points out that because deans are expected to be "businesslike," "collegial processes and academic values" may be "downgraded." In addition, university-wide issues in this system can only be addressed by "indirect leverage of the deans."

2. RCB encourages entrepreneurship.

The Budget Committee Report notes that RCB "creates incentives for deans to maximize income and minimize expenses, at least to meet the budget, and beyond that to create a surplus that can support other programs." As a result, deans tend to be creative in developing new programs. One faculty leader states that:

> the advantage, or course, is that some of our deans are extremely innovative. They can go out and develop programs, find potential people outside [the university] who are interested in their programs. They . . . know exactly what their budget is, so they have this stability, they can plan ahead of time and do a lot of things. So . . . the entrepreneurial part is the top advantage.

Deans are selected on the basis of their ability to thrive in an entrepreneurial environment. One central executive notes that:

> we attract people who are risk-takers, entrepreneurs. I think there's always a distribution within the deans, but I think for the most part we've hired good deans who have the abilities to make the decisions they should be making.

One administrator describes the role as somewhat different from the dean's role at institutions that use a more centralized resource allocation system:

it takes a very different set of skills to be successful. It's not a traditional academic role for deans . . . it's a lot of fund-raising, it's a lot of management, both administrative and academic. And it's both being a lot more entrepreneurial and savvy about the market you're in and different kinds of revenue opportunities.

Deans here are expected to behave more like a college or university president in the RCB environment. And that includes significant bottom-line accountability and responsibility for procuring and managing resources.

On the other hand, the entrepreneurial culture at Pierce sets up incentives that sometimes compromise academic standards. A widely cited example is that schools sometimes offer courses on the basis on their perceived popularity in order to draw imputed tuition revenue. Interdisciplinary activities, both teaching and research, are complicated to arrange, and discouraged in the system because units would rather not share attributed indirect cost recoveries or tuition income. It has not always been easy to create faculty joint appointments. The result is an entrepreneurial culture that is sometimes unproductively competitive.

3. RCB holds central services accountable.

Because all costs in this system are explicit, deans know exactly how much everything costs, including the share of central administrative services for which they are annually billed. Thus, according to one dean, the deans keep a careful watch on administrative costs and the quality of services they receive:

> I think that we are all more vigilant; we are all more eager to talk to the people who run these administrative units and say, 'This is what I'm getting.' I always start meetings by saying, 'This is what I pay.' . . . And [then] I say, 'This is what I'm getting.' Or, 'I want . . . 'And I think it works very well.

As a result, central administrative units are said to be accountable to the revenue centers that pay for central services through indirect cost pools.

Still, as noted in the Budget Committee Report, some of the formulas used to allocate indirect costs are "challenged as unfair." And while central administrative units may be "accountable" to the responsibility center, the Report points out that the responsibility centers have "only limited influence over the amount spent on those services."

4. RCB is an open and objective system, with visible subsidies.

The RCB system is remarkably open at Pierce. Deans are aware of the items that together make up the indirect cost pools for which they are billed, and how much they cost. Perhaps most important, levels of participation and subvention are explicit and published annually in the University's annual audited financial statement. Thus, as one administrator observes, "The Provost's decisions are open to everyone, in terms of the academic investments or contributions required of the different schools." As one central administrator describes:

> The deans do know who's getting what, and there's a lot of pressure that comes, both from the people who are being treated well and the people who are not begin treated well, to change the resource allocations or to maintain the current resource allocations. So it is difficult in that way. We have worked hard to in a sense open it up even more, and in the last three years have brought the Deans very closely into the process of providing resources for what we call the costs centers—the administrative centers that don't have revenues associated with them, so they, if you will, live off taxing the revenue-producing groups. We now have Deans sitting down with all of the budget presentations in areas like student affairs, plant operations and so on . . . Their budget presentations have Deans sitting in on them and asking questions.

The budget committee notes that financial openness "can foster jealousy" among units. In addition, whereas data on financial performance is widely available, systematic data and benchmarks on academic quality and achievement are currently absent from the system.

5. The units created by RCB are variegated.

Under RCB, small as well as large units operate under the same rules. Both have the same opportunity to manage their own resources and develop appropriate goals and priorities.

On the other hand, however, a number of the schools are exceedingly small. Four schools—Fine Arts, Architecture, Music, Theater—each have between fifteen and twenty-five tenure-line faculty—the equivalent of academic departments in most universities. In fact, these smaller schools were once part of a larger division, a School of Performing Arts that encompassed cinema, fine arts, music, and architecture. The School was broken up into its constituent units because some central administrators felt that breaking up the school would stimulate entrepreneurial activity by allowing units to be closer to their markets. It is not clear that whether breaking up the school has had the desired effect. Despite their size, each unit is organized as a school, with a dean, with separate administrative staffs, and a direct reporting relationship to the Provost. As one administrator observes,

> there's an opportunity cost of having so many people report to the Provost . . . it's just too cumbersome. If you take the schools, add all the vice-

provosts and all the other people that report to him . . . he's probably got thirty people that report to him. It's crazy. It's just nuts.

The large number of deans also makes it more difficult for the Provost to achieve consensus around academic planning issues.

The Budget Committee Report also notes that small responsibility centers results in "unnecessary bureaucratic duplication" and an inability to take advantage of "economies of scale possible in operations like admissions, fund-raising, and financial management." In addition, the Report notes that the academic choices of small schools are "unshielded against immediate financial realities," and implies that in large units authority is overly-centralized.

In general, the faculty, deans, and central administrative personnel interviewed for this case study believe that RCB works reasonably well. One central administrator summarizes a perspective heard repeatedly during the course of interviews conducted for this case chapter:

> I think [RCB] works. And I think it's just been the kind of spirit of [this institution] . . . and that's just the way we operate. And we've been able to operate that way, and make this university run without a deficit. So the model seems to work by holding the deans accountable to their bottom line and giving them the power to do that. From the financial standpoint, it's worked.

On the other hand, however, the system has been less successful from a strictly academic standpoint. This same administrator sounded a familiar criticism:

> some of that translated into success at the academic level, and that has been much more uneven. You would think that would enable deans to create schools that are highly ranked . . . we have [seen] some of that, but it's much more uneven. We haven't seen as much of the academic benefits as I would like to see.

The remainder of this case chapter discusses the current academic priorities articulated by senior leaders at Pierce, and some of the ways in which the resource allocation system is changing to support the achievement of these priorities.

PRIORITIES

University priorities were discussed in conversations with central academic administrators and are explained in a formal strategic plan approved by the University's Board of Trustees in 1994. The plan discusses four institutional priorities:

1) Improving undergraduate education

A number of specific goals are suggested, including improving the liberal arts core curriculum required of all Pierce undergraduates, regardless of major. The report also recommends stronger faculty involvement in undergraduate education, especially senior faculty. Another major goal is to establish stronger linkages between the liberal arts and the professional fields for which the university is better known. The report discusses the importance of facilitating collaboration in teaching between revenue centers. Lastly, the report recommends improvements in student services and facilities, and the academic advising program.

2) Interdisciplinary research and education

The report notes that the "most interesting and important problems facing society today tend to be highly interdisciplinary." While acknowledging the university's current strengths in several interdisciplinary areas, the plan recommends that the University

> encourage research that is creative, interdisciplinary, and has high societal relevance; develop programs to stimulate faculty interest in selected broad interdisciplinary problems; eliminate existing disincentives and provide positive incentives for excellent interdisciplinary research, with emphasis on areas that are truly innovative.

The report also recommends that the university develop a "management structure" that will allow the institution to develop "promising interdisciplinary and interdivisional programs." Such programs should also include provisions for program review and "program discontinuation."

3) Initiatives to build on the resources of the local region

The document notes that the local region is "an invaluable resource for teaching and research on a wide range of topics, including the urban condition itself, immigration, multiculturalism, health care, post-industrial economic conditions." The plan recommends that the University use the local region as a "laboratory for teaching, research, service, and internships" by developing curriculum and research related to urban problems of national concern and by building programs that are closely linked to emerging and established industries. The report also urges that the university coordinate the several health-related schools in the university in ways to create "new and innovative approaches to health care for a complex urban region."

4) Internationalization

The plan describes the University's desire to foster international involvement aboard thorough connections with other universities, communities, alumni, and corporations. The university hopes to create "internal structures and policies that support educational and research linkages abroad and that coordinate major international activities across schools."

The plan notes that the stated strategic priorities for the university "do not focus on a single school or department, but rather on programs that generally involve multiple schools and departments." Given this vision of the future, the document notes that the "allocation of resources and the organizational structure" must support these objectives. The plan states that the university must focus on resource allocation and utilization. With regard to resource allocation, the plan includes five recommendations. The University should:

1. Utilize objective data and national surveys, along with other factors, to determine the relative strength of programs at Pierce vis a vis their national competitors.

2. Sustain areas of . . . excellence . . . throughout the university. Focus doctoral programs more sharply, so that Pierce develops great strength in fewer fields at the doctoral level. . .

3. Sustain areas of teaching and research most important to the perception of a leading researching university: key liberal arts programs in the college and elsewhere that are the most critical to our stature as a center of liberal learning; and key programs in those professional schools commonly acknowledged as being most important to the external perception of universities . . . Key programs will be defined by the individual schools based on their knowledge of the disciplines.

4. In building new levels of excellence, focus first on areas of current excellence and visibility where the strategic initiative identify sustainable competitive advantages.

5. As resources become available, build up other areas where the strategic initiatives identify sustainable competitive advantages.

The plan also urges that the university "utilize resources as efficiently as possible in order to maximize resources available to improve academic programs." Specifically, the plan recommends that the University:

1. Reorganize administrative and support activities as necessary to minimize redundancy and maximize effectiveness.

2. Improve utilization of physical plant, and most especially of classrooms and teaching laboratories.

3. Combine or like . . . smaller, quality programs in order to create larger programs that achieve demonstrable excellence and visibility.

TOWARD A NEW SYSTEM

The priorities described in the previous section of this chapter will demand that Pierce focus its academic investments in several areas that transcend disciplinary, school, and department boundaries. Historically, academic initiatives have been concentrated in the academic units that make up the university's responsibility centers, with limited cross- school initiatives and minimal direction from the university central administration. The university's decentralized culture and resource allocation system have resulted in the development of strong, independent schools. The university central administration is seeking ways to preserve the strengths of RCB while at the same time modifying the system to more closely achieve university-wide priorities.

Many of the changes were recommended in the University Budget Committee in its 1993 Report, and subsequently reinforced and expanded by the Task Force on Revenue Center Management, which issued its own report a year later.

The most important change is that the central administration is now taking the position that distributions from the subvention fund should support the attainment of university priorities. One university central administrator summarizes the new perspective on subvention:

> [Subvention] represents our investment in these [academic] units, and we expect some payback on that investment—just as a business, where you're making strategic investments. So we took the four largest subvention-eaters, users, and cut out 25% of their subvention this year, and said, 'You've got to come back now with some proposals why we should invest in you, to get some, all, or even more of that money back . . . we're trying to see subvention as investment in units that are going to pay off for the university, not an entitlement.

Another central administrator states the process will take time because the central administration cannot simply withdraw funds overnight. Still, the central administration is working hard to dispel the notion that certain schools—especially Law, Engineering, and Music—are entitled to permanent subvention. Quotations from the supply and demand sides of the resource allocation process illustrate this view:

Central administrator:

> So there's a weaning process that's going on, and in fact those schools have all had to provide me with very detailed business plans which show how they're going to work their way out of the subvention over the next two to three years. Each of them has come up with inventive programs that they might not have otherwise come up with.

Central administrator:

> I get a lot of outraged phone calls from [two of the deans] . . . you know, ones that took a lot of subvention . . . saying, 'You can't do this! How can we survive?' And I say 'Well, you come back and tell us why we should make an investment in your unit, not just because we've done it in the past, but why we should continue to do that.' . . . So, I think that's how you have to view subvention. It's not an entitlement, but an investment. It has milestones and benchmarks and payoffs down the road. And it fits in with where the university wants to go.

Academic dean:

> I think [this Provost] has more a view that people who are getting subvention should be doing it temporarily while they're trying to get their house in order rather than as a permanent kind of thinking; whereas the old Provost felt that there were three units in particular who, for a variety of reasons, deserved sort of a permanent subvention . . . basically he said, 'You'll get a couple million dollars a year . . . plan on it.' And this Provost is more like 'You can take that money temporarily if you have a plan to get on your own feet.' But it's more of a 'Let's get this closer to everybody being zero.' At the same time, he also has this view that it's within his right to tax the different units this one percent tax for the Provost's Excellence Fund.

Even "poor" units are not protected citizens in this culture and cannot expect to receive an automatic subvention. One administrator states:

> I would say it really depends on how central [the unit] is to the university's mission, whether or not they are a priority and therefore receive subvention. If they are, I think there must still be a push toward excellence so that they can justify the investment from the university. If they're not a priority, then they really have to focus on what they can do best, or how they can serve the university more broadly.

In addition to altering the traditional "rules" of subvention and participation, the University central administration is attempting to raise additional funds for reallocation. The University recently introduced a 1% tax on each school's revenues which become part of the University's Fund for Excellence. Its purpose is to fund enterprises the individual deans would not likely support, but which the university's strategic plan cites as institutional priorities. The fund will allow the Provost to help move the university in a direction he feels it should be going. The dean of each school is free to submit a proposal to the Provost requesting a grant from the Fund. Resources from the Fund are distributed based on concordance of the proposal with goals and priorities articulated in the University's strategic plan.

In addition to the Excellence Fund, the Provost has also carved out a second, $1 million dollar fund called the University Fund for Investment in Excellence. The Provost has invited deans to submit multi-school proposals for each initiative and writes that "the goal is to promote cooperation, not competition." The three initiatives which the Fund targets included a proposal for developing a laboratory for the study of basic and applied social sciences in the local region; an initiative in health care that would use "as broad a spectrum of our faculty resources as possible" and perhaps result in some "interesting and perhaps unique experiments in the organization, provision and evaluation of health care in an urban area." A third possibility is to use a portion of the fund initiatives in ethnic and American studies.

Over time, the University central administration would like to raise the "at-risk" revenue tax up to 10%, which, together with revenue from central fund-raising, participation-subvention, and other centrally-imposed taxes, would generate $45 - $50 million dollars for the Provost to allocate based on university academic priorities. Right now, the annual fund available for allocation by the central administration is about $ 14 million.

The purpose of this fund is described by a central administrator:

> Our role is to stimulate innovative new programs with that fourteen million dollars . . . So, in the last two years, I've been having a meeting in September or October with each of the Deans, where we sit down and we talk about the strategic plan for their school . . . [and] how it coincides with the university's strategic plan. We talk about programs they could be setting up. We try to understand their options and opportunities, and it's more or less out of that particular meeting that I should be make the allocation of the subvention.

Such discussions are in keeping with the recommendations of the Task Force, which urges that

> university decisions on investment or levels of investment should make use of the following criteria: the Provost's judgment of a unit's academic excel-

Pierce University

lence in light of the University's strategic plan, an assessment of the unit's priority for support in light of the categories of subvention, and an assessment of the feasibility and the benefits of possible support.

In keeping with the direction outlined in the University strategic plan, the central administration is trying to use the fund for programs with a strong cross- or inter-disciplinary orientation. The Task Force document favors "making the categories of university investment manifest," and divides them into several categories: 1) investment in academic initiatives: teaching and curriculum; 2) maintenance of excellence programs: teaching and curriculum: 3) investment in academic initiatives: research; 4) maintenance of excellent programs: research; 5) investment in academic support centers (i.e. units that "directly support the research and instructional mission of the University, but do not engage in teaching or research"; and 6) Loans to ensure unit viability. One senior executive states the problem, and his proposed solution, in the following way:

> Our revenue center management systems, which really focuses on, if you will, sort of the vertical structure of the schools, although it's wonderful system for building entrepreneurial activity with the school, is a real hindrance to sort of horizontal activities that cut across [schools], and this tax has been my way of trying to break down some of those barriers, but of course the people who built the barriers don't like the ideas.
>
> I'm trying to pull themes out that I can combine in some useful way that increases the visibility of the whole institution. We are working very hard to increase excellence everywhere, and for a long time there has been an unwillingness in this institution to really set priorities and to work on those priorities.

As might be imagined, the deans are not highly enthusiastic about the tax, even a one percent tax on revenues. Two quotations from central administrators and an academic dean illustrate this view:

Central administrator:

> The deans don't like it for the most part. We operate on the margin here. We're not a very rich university. And we've never had a deficit. We're very proud of that. But there isn't a lot of money in the system. So I can think, 'Gee, one percentage of somebody's budget isn't very much.' But to some of the smaller, less wealthy schools, one percent is on the margins and a lot. Given their druthers, they'd rather have that one percent and spend it themselves than contribute it.

Academic dean:

> In terms of the Provost tax, whenever you tax people, the general view is that 'I could spend it better than the Provost; and therefore, even if it's then reallocated in part to my unit, it might not be my highest priority.' The Provost's response naturally is that there are public goods, and by definition, these are goods that it is in nobody's individual interest enough to pay for it; and therefore, they're not going to be done. It's just a well-known case of market failure in economics. So you're not going to get too many deans to step up there and say, 'Boy, I love this one percent tax.' On the other hand, that's why it's needed.

Despite the strong resistance of the deans, the Provost and President remain firmly committed to moving part of the subvention fund into a strategic investment pool. They are aware the idea is unpopular, and realize they are going to accomplish this goal only by "kicking and dragging some of the people with them." Although the senior administration recognizes that some disciplines are simply more expensive to run that others, over time the concept of subvention will gradually be changed, and even units with high fixed costs will need to demonstrate that they represent an important university priority.

Certain deans understand the new rules and are becoming more savvy about what it takes to acquire resources from the central administration. One dean explained that he regards the President and Provost as prospective donors to his school. He believes that

> They require the same kind of treatment, the same kind of selling [as outside donors]. 'This is what your subvention, your gift . . . will do for my school. This is what it will do for you. This is why you will feel good about it.'

This dean tries to demonstrate to the Provost and President the "payoff" for their investments by communicating the achievements of faculty, students, the strengths of research and instructional programs, and contributions to the local community. Other deans, however, particularly those who have benefited the most under the "old" rules, are less enthusiastic:

> And I think the deans who are used to getting large amounts of subvention and have been getting it for a long period of time obviously say, 'Well, this is a change in the rules. I'm allocating my budget. I've hired faculty in the past based on this idea that I'm going to get this kind of money for a long time.' And when you change their rules of the game, people get pretty upset. On the other hand, the people who are participating or are at

zero probably are pretty happy that these welfare states are now going to be eliminated.

The Provost and President realize that they cannot change all the "rules" at once. As one administrator notes, "I can imagine the deans would get really upset if every budget cycle they had some new tax. Even if it were a small tax, the very fact that something else has a surcharge attached to it would probably make them really angry." The taxes are likely to increase over time. One senior executive states that the "real reallocation is probably two or three years down the line [when] I can really start working on my venture capital model as well as I would like to."

As part of its strategy to more selectively allocate central funds, the central administration is working with schools to devise methods for evaluating the performance of academic units. The university's task force on RCB urged that comparative benchmarks be used for determining a unit's eligibility for subvention. The document notes that "in choosing which units will be supported, which maintained, and which phased out in light of the university strategic plan, the Provost will need to make an evaluation of unit performance and assess the unit's eligibility for subvention."

The report notes that while measures of fiscal performance have been explicit in the RCB system for some time, academic measures of performance have been lacking. The report urges the development of "internal assessments of performance" and external measures of reputation. The report mentions internal measures of students (quality of students, as measured by standardized test scores, undergraduate records, size and quality of applicant pool); output measures such as acceptance into graduate programs, academic honors, and job placement; faculty quality, as measured by scholarly distinction, teaching evaluations, and grant and contract procurement; contribution to strategic plan; and institutional climate. External measures include the national ranking of graduate programs.

The report recommends that "each unit, working with the Provost, or appropriate vice-president, be measured against a set of internal performance benchmarks that can be used to determine the University's 'investment' strategy relative to that unit." Central administrators agree that this is an important objective but recognize the difficulty in developing appropriate performance measures, especially in the academic realm:

> Every school, recognizing that each area is different from every other area, is trying to create some metrics that will reflect on how well they are doing their job . . . We're really going to start to using those as judges or better indicators of how each school is actually doing compared to its peer group. Because, of course, you ask any school how they're doing and the Dean says, 'Just great! We're wiping out the competition. I can't tell you how good we are,' and the response is 'Says who? What make you think you're that good?'

> And that, of course, is a very tricky thing, because it's difficult, exceedingly difficult, to get comparative data between institutions of higher education . . . There are just not easily obtained metrics. We're all very petrified that one of those metrics will turn out to be a really useful metric, and we won't look good in it. So we do the best we can to prevent there being a lot of data out there relating to our own institutions. We are up for Reaccreditation through [our regional accreditor]. We have proposed and they have essentially accepted that we would like to demonstrate that as complicated as this can come up with metrics that can be used both to demonstrate that we are accreditable, that is that we meet the minimal standards, and can be used to measure improvement. So basically our reaccreditation will be essentially totally based on data, and with the working assumption that both we and [the accreditor] have that nobody knows what the right data are at this point . . . It's a great challenge for us all.

The new tax, central investment fund, and the development of performance metrics, are three of the ways in which the central administration is working to bring unit behavior in line with central university priorities. While economic incentives are important, they are not a substitute for strong central leadership. The Provost, Vice-Provost, and President are attempting to engage the community, and especially the deans, in on-going conversation about the strategic direction of the University and the need to emphasize central and not just school priorities. The following passages illustrate one central leader's recent efforts to communicate these values to the deans, create new structures for cross-school collaboration, and involve deans in planning and budgeting:

> I have been trying to emphasize to the deans that they are university officers, and that they bear responsibility for the health of the institution as well as for the health of their own school, and that they will be judged according to their success both in handling their own school and in contributing to the health of the university . . .
>
> So I think part of making all of this happen is to change the atmosphere—change the attitude. And certainly as I bring in new deans . . . one of the things I emphasize to them is the importance of working with their colleagues in ways that have not happened. So I think part of it is creating new structures, and I haven't figured out what those new structures are; part of it is creating a change in the mindset on the part of the administrators, and the deans just have to be viewed as managers for the institution. Bit by bit, we'll figure out how to do it, and hopefully a few of the things we do will turn out to be successful, and the people will say, 'Hey, I'd like to get in on that.'
>
> That's part of way I brought them into the budgeting in a much more direct way that they were before; that is, I want them to instead of complaining about how much plant operations spends, I want them to take

responsibility for making sure the university's physical plant is good ten years from now and that we haven't left our successors with some collapsed shell. It is my hope that by this process I can get more of them to take a longer view of how they can work together in order to make things happen.

I had three deans in here just two weeks ago to talk about putting together a joint [academic] program. We have [an academic program that spans three schools]. [The deans] found that they were having dinner on successive evenings, trying to raise money from the same group of people, and it was crazy, they should be working together. So we're going to put together [a program] that brings together the strengths of these three schools, which will make one of the better . . . programs in the country. So they're beginning to see that if they're not quite so competitive, and not quite so worried about their borders and the separation between the schools that they can make things happen that will be good for everybody.

The current Provost is trying to lead through a mixture of persuasion, wise counsel, and authority. One administrator states: "[The Provost] has to be strong enough, as we have recently seen, to wrest a couple of million dollars aside and say, 'This is for steering the ship. This is not for running any part of our on-board operation. We've got to make a direction change.' One faculty leader describes the Provost's role:

See, the deans control the budget . . . The Provost has very little budget. The deans form a group . . . you have twenty-some people, a very powerful group . . . they actually literally veto whatever the recommendation . . . but the new Provost has reversed the trend . . . [he] really works very closely with the faculty.

Under the previous administration, [faculty] usually 'got their way.' But right now . . . policy is agreed upon strongly by both the faculty and the Provost's office. So, slowly, the power moves back to the Provost's office.

While the Provost is apparently trying to gain more control over the schools (and their budgets) through a combination of persuasion and authority, he must avoid an overly heavy-handed approach. It's a fine balancing act because as one faculty leader notes,

once [the Provost] gets more control, then the deans will feel less. Because, then . . . the dean will say . . . you know, the accountability on the dean's part becomes less . . . because the dean can say, 'You know, I try so hard, but you take everything away from me . . . so, you know, I'm not accountable for what happens because you're the one who makes the decisions, right?'

The Provost is also developing performance criteria for each dean which, according to the Task Force Report, should take into account the dean's success in promoting "university performance," the "school's contribution to enhancing sister disciplines," and "the school's active support of interdisciplinary teaching and research." Each dean has to describe to the Provost how his plan advances the University's strategic plan. The Provost uses these criteria for determining the size of the annual bonus awarded to each dean.

SCHOOLS

The new emphasis on strategic investments in resource allocation is also beginning to trickle down into the schools. The University's Arts and Sciences school, for example, last year formed a committee that resulted in an objective analysis of where the school should concentrate its resources. The school's central administration evaluated departments and programs on the basis of eight criteria, including teaching at the under graduate level, research quality, centrality to the college and the college's strategic plan, student placements, grant, publications—and something called predictive investment return—defined as the number of faculty who would nee to be hired to move the department ahead in the national rankings. The school has also looked at how departments have used faculty appointments in the past, with particular emphasis on whether the department hired top notch faculty and whether the new hires advanced the department's strategic plans. The University central administration, as the following quotation suggests, endorse these efforts:

> Our [arts and sciences school] . . . has sort of always tried to improve all its departments. Well, it's got too many departments and not enough money. You can't improve them all. So they're now focusing on a half dozen departments and they're trying to improve those so that they develop some real excellence.

Over time, therefore, the strategy of individual schools may parallel the efforts now underway in the central administration.

CONCLUSION

Pierce will continue to use responsibility center budgeting, though over time the central administration will likely claim a larger share of revenues which once "belonged" to the academic units where they were generated. The revenues will still be distributed to the academic units, but with an eye toward achieving university-wide priorities, including those which transcend school and department boundaries. Senior officers are optimistic about their ability to reform the system in ways that will achieve a better balance between school and university-wide priorities. Despite the constraints it imposes on the central administration, RCB will remain the backbone of Pierce's resource allocation process. One senior central administrator reflects:

> I often envy my colleagues who just have this big black box of money and they say to deans, 'Here's your share. Go away and do the best you can with your share.' Many, many times that seems to me to be a really nice idea. But I think our system really stimulates . . . The deans know they're accountable for absolutely everything, they know that they can generate more money, they know that if they save money they get to keep it, and they know nobody can take it away from them. I think it's a wonderful system for bringing out the best in a dean.

4
Westmont University

OVERVIEW

Westmont University, known for unsurpassed quality in education and research, offers broad liberal undergraduate education, and graduate education in the arts and sciences and in several professional disciplines, including law, business, and medicine. Its celebrated faculty is among the most highly distinguished in the United States. The University's academic standing is confirmed by its exceptionally high standing in the recent National Research Council rankings.

Westmont University's resource allocation process is presently in a state of transition. Long regarded as having one of the most highly centralized resource allocation systems, Westmont recently adopted a substantially more decentralized resource allocation model under which deans are more responsible—and accountable—for managing financial resources. At the time this case study was under development, Westmont was implementing and refining the new decentralized resource allocation system. A major purpose of this case is to understand the factors that led the University to adopt a more decentralized resource allocation model, and to study the impact of this transition on the University's internal organization and financial economics.

Prior to 1994, resource allocation was a highly centralized process at the University. The central administration gave each dean an annual allocation in the form of a line-item budget which deans were allowed to spend within certain fairly specific guidelines. The allocation did not represent all resources available to a department—just unrestricted moneys from the university central administration. Schools were discouraged from moving resources from one expense category to another. Deans would negotiate directly with the central administration for incremental increases for such items as graduate fellowships or faculty appointments. In terms of managing revenues, deans outside the professional schools seldom engaged in external fund-raising and had little incentive to manage enrollments or introduce new degree-granting programs. The tuition revenues never trickled down to the departments, at least not in a manner transparent to the deans or department chairs, and there was no clear relationship between a school's revenues and its annual allocation. Moreover, very little information about university finance was shared—not with the deans, and not with other members of the university community. "We managed everything from the center, behind a curtain," one central administrator recalled, adding that "requests came up to the center . . . and from behind the curtain, people either said yes or no."

Consequently, deans did not worry much about matters of university finance, partly because, in the eyes of one university central administrator, it appeared that their requests "were being adjudicated purely on matters of academic merit and that finance was just . . . an accounting matter that occurred some place . . . It was a good noble myth." According to several administrators interviewed for this case, the "myth" had prevailed since the University's founding a century earlier.

The transition to the new budget allocation model was motivated both by financial distress as well as the central leadership's belief that while the current allocation system in many ways "promoted a certain type of behavior that was positive for the institution, academically," the system was nevertheless, "financially wasteful" because it provided few incentives for deans to raise funds. A senior academic leader notes that

> deans, for example, in the prior world . . . in most of the university . . . would get no benefit of a gift given to that part of the university. So they therefore had no incentive to go out and try to raise any money, since if someone gave a five million dollar gift to support the humanities to create three chairs, the chairs would exist but the money supporting the chairs would disappear into the center. And so for the most part, deans had very little incentive to pay any attention to fund-raising . . .

Similarly, on the expense side, deans had very little incentive to conserve resources:

> Since deans didn't manage to a bottom line, they had really no incentive to be creative about saving money and about allocating money sensibly. They were basically given a series of discrete line items in the abstract and told [for example], 'You have this much to spend on financial aid' . . . But if they saved money on administration, they couldn't use it for financial aid. It just disappeared, again. So they had no incentive to do anything other than to spend all the money available.

In the world of the deans, revenue and expense were unconnected. The dean of one of the University's professional schools remembers an episode several years ago when more students matriculated than expected at his school. Even though the school was receiving more tuition from these students than it was distributing in financial aid, the dean was "scolded" by the central administration for overspending his financial aid budget—"even though," he remembers, "there was a net benefit to the University no matter how you measured it!"

Despite its apparent drawbacks, the centralized model nevertheless benefited the University in several important ways. One administrator summarized a view echoed throughout the interviews conducted for this case study: "[The centralized model] focused the faculty and the deans on what they really should be doing, which is excellent scholarship [and] good teaching." In addition, the centralized model facilitated the development of the cross- and inter-disciplinary programs for which the University is renown. As one administrator notes, "Maybe one reason that Westmont's so good at being interdisciplinary is that people have no idea what resources go to other parts of the university."

Changing economic circumstances led the University to examine the utility of the resource allocation system and the incentive structure that it reinforced. As recently as the late 1980s, the University financial position was generally regarded as healthy. In fact, in fiscal year 1989, net income was $11 million; the following year net income increased to $19 million, and in fiscal 1991, net income reached $24 million. But in fiscal 1992, net income dropped to $9 million. The following year, the University experienced a net operating deficit of $10 million. In fiscal year 1994, the deficit was $14.8 million, and in fiscal year 1995 the deficit was $17.8 million.

Conversations with university administrators and examination of university documents point to five main reasons for the deficit. First, tuition growth had not offset shortfalls in other revenues or in the cost of new facilities. From 1984–85 to 1992–3, the University enjoyed a rapid growth in (net) tuition revenues, due partly to an increasing enrollment, and partly to significant annual increases in the tuition rate. According to a university document, from 1991–92 to 1994–95,

> the growth in tuition revenue has been sufficient to cover the increase in student aid, faculty compensation (including the faculty retirement incentives program) and new instructional costs . . . but [the growth] has not generated additional dollars to compensate for shortfalls in other revenues, to fund investment in facilities, or to cover inflation in support and administrative areas.

Second, the University has had to make considerable (and expensive) investments in physical plant in recent years, including new facilities, physical infrastructure, maintenance and safety programs. An academic officer noted that although the University performed

> necessary maintenance [in the decade 1985–94], we did not invest the extra funds that would have enabled us to modernize many of our buildings. It was, in part, this 'under investment' in our physical facilities that enabled us to experience significant operating surpluses in the last decade . . . Although this was a financially sound policy, it increased the need for us now to 'catch up' in renewing our physical facilities . . .

Third, University fringe benefits have grown rapidly and in excess of inflation according to University documents. Growth in revenues between 1984–85 to 1992–93 enabled the University to increase faculty compensation and to provide enhanced medical and other benefits for faculty and staff—benefits the central administration claims were necessary to "maintain the University's market position for staff."

Finally, revenues from government and private grants, gifts and endowment payouts have not kept pace with inflation. The University also recently reduced its endowment payout formula from 6% of market value to 5%. Other income had also fallen. For example, the University lost $9 million of income from certain investment royalties and invested cash balances.

The University had also experienced losses in its health sciences division, which includes the biological sciences, medical school, and medical center. These included losses of key clinical faculty in several important revenue-generating programs, including transplantation surgery. Reduced Medicare payment rates for many specialty physician services have also had an impact. The division has also felt the effects of diminished reimbursement for health services due to conversions in private insurance from fee-for-service to discounted managed care. In addition, the health sciences division had incurred significant interest, depreciation, and operations and maintenance costs for a new learning and research center. Lastly, the health sciences division is recruiting a new dean/vice president and is planning a number of investments in key research and clinical programs which will entail high start-up costs.

In addition to these factors, the central administration points to a more general problem which the University has perennially faced: Westmont competes with institutions which have stronger basic financial structures, including larger endowments and greater ability to raise money because they have a richer, larger base of alumni. This partly explains why deficits are not unfamiliar to the University. An administrator notes that the

Westmont University

University had a "huge deficit" in 1986–87, adding that "These deficits keep popping up because . . . we've got a tough basic set of economics."

The University central administration, represented chiefly by the chief financial officer, President, Provost, and Budget Director, studied the situation and realized that in the base-case situation, deficits would continue to grow, and eventually deplete cash reserves. According to the Provost, "By requiring us first to spend down our reserves, and then to invade our endowment, these deficits, if left unchecked, eventually would erode not only our financial strength, but our values as well. We determined to take strong and decisive action, and we have."

The decisive action referred to by the Provost included several steps. The first step was to understand and analyze the problem through financial analysis and discussions with the University community. The Provost and CFO spent a great deal of time talking to trustees, deans, administrators, faculty committees, and staff about the financial problems facing the university, both to inform them of the nature of the problem and to solicit advice. The Provost states that he met with the faculties of more than 30 departments and schools around the University.

The University undertook corrective action in fiscal year 1994–95 to close the deficit by decreasing expenses and by increasing revenues. On the expense side, the University undertook a major effort to cut University administrative costs by $10 million dollars in real terms over four years. Second, the University postponed a number of proposed capital and building projects, "on the premise that in these circumstances, [the University] can afford to undertake only those projects that are of both immediate and compelling necessity." Third, the University has constrained the growth in student aid, ensuring that it does not exceed the growth in tuition. Fifth, the University has postponed a number of faculty appointments. Academic units therefore will appoint only about half as many new faculty in 1995–96 and 1996–97 as they would normally. Finally, overall expenditures for staff and administrative expenses will be held constant from 1994–95 to 1996–97.

On the revenue side, the University has resolved to expand its development activities, while also increasing the enrollment of unfunded graduate students.

In implementing these changes, the University has created special incentives and economic structures for schools to act in accordance with the centrally established guidelines. In a public document widely circulated on campus, the Provost testified:

> I should emphasize that these guidelines are not meant to be applied mechanically across the University. To the contrary, we recognize that different parts of the University have different needs and concerns. Thus, to put these guidelines into effect, we have significantly altered the budget process to give individual units greater authority to control their finances

than they generally have enjoyed in the past. In the past, most deans and directors did not have a comprehensive budget that showed total revenues and expenses. Rather, they were presented with particular line-item allocations, such as 'dollars for financial aid' or 'dollars for faculty compensation,' and were directed to manage those specific line items. Most units had little incentive to raise funds, increase enrollment, tighten financial aid or cut administrative costs, for they ordinarily did not get to retain the benefits of such actions.

The next section of this chapter discusses the University's decentralized resource allocation model which sought to correct these problems.

THE DECENTRALIZED RESOURCE ALLOCATION MODEL

Reforming the Budget Process

During the budget process for 1995–96, the University central administration for the first time created budgets for each dean or director which showed explicitly direct revenues and expenses. Schools and administrative areas were divided into 35 units. These included the College (the University's undergraduate division), the Division of Social Sciences, the Division of Humanities, the Division of Physical Sciences, the professional schools (Business, Law, etc.), and various administrative entities, such as Information Technology or the Development Office.

Direct revenues, such as tuition, federal grants and contrasts, indirect cost recovery, restricted endowment payout, and gifts were attributed to each department. Direct expenses were also attributed to each department, including faculty salaries and expenses, student aid, and expenditures on federal grants. The University chose not allocate overhead or central revenue from unrestricted endowment. According to one member of the central administration, the choice was deliberate: "We made the strategic decision to basically only count things that were direct, on the argument that any methodology would open up a can of worms that was kind of essentially unsolvable."

After preparing a revenue and expense statement for each unit, the chief financial officer shared each statement with the respective dean, highlighting the bottom-line difference which the central administration calls "net position." According to the central administration, the net positions were "all over place"—some positive, some negative—an outcome consistent with the microeconomic theory of cross-subsidies in non-profit endowed institutions (Hopkins and Massy, 1981). After the margins were computed, the budget office spent considerable time trying to understand the economies of the various units.

According to a central financial executive, the collective net positions represented the underlying economy of the University:

So [one of the professional schools], which has very few faculty and which teaches a ton of students who pay a lot of tuition and receive very little financial aid, had a large positive net position. [Another division], which has very few heavily aided students, a lot of federal grants that don't really cover all the costs of research, and a lot of faculty, had a big negative number.

The net positions were used as a starting point for increasing each department's contribution to closing the University deficit. To illustrate how this would work, a financial administrator uses the hypothetical example of a department whose net position in 1994–95 is minus 10 million dollars. In 1995–96, the department would be expected to have a net position of say, minus 8 million dollars. And by 1996–97, the department would be expected to improve its position to minus 6 million dollars. If a department fails to achieve its target in one year, the difference would be added to the following year's target; if a department over-achieves its goals, the surplus could be applied to the following year's target. The policy is not limited to departments identified as having an economic deficit; departments in a net positive position are expected to become "more positive." So, the thrust of these efforts, in the words of one senior academic officer, has been to move the deans toward "more ambitious bottom-line numbers." Although the University administration doesn't publicly refer to it as such, the new policy could be described as a lump-sum tax system.

At the same time, the University central administration has given deans much greater responsibility for managing their resources. In a public forum, the Provost noted that

> [W]e have empowered deans and directors to allocate resources in the best interests of the unit, and we have enabled them to reap the benefits of their own revenue-generating and cost-cutting activities. Thus, the guidelines described above are presumptive rather than prescriptive. We have used them to establish a bottom-line target for each unit, but then freed each unit to decide for itself how best to achieve that target in light of its own needs and circumstances. I am pleased to report that, for the past several months, our deans and directors have been hard at work putting in place plans to achieve their 1995-96 and 1996-97 targets.

Thus, the deans have greater financial autonomy over their academic unit, along with more accountability for managing resources. One central administrator states simply that "We had to figure out a way to improve the net position for each unit, letting the deans do as much as they possibly could, giving them as much freedom . . . the Provost just said, 'Well, of course, that's the only way you could do it.' " Another senior administrator adds that the University has attempted to create better incentives for deans to begin thinking of their academic units as economics units and to give them incentives to both generate revenue and effect savings, so that they could keep the benefit of those revenues and savings or at least most of the benefit of them.

Essentially what we've been working with over this last three years is a period of really completely wrenching around an economy and trying to change the ways in which deans think about their units and the ways in which they manage them. And the primary focus has been on avoiding disputes over 'How come they got this, and we got that?' And trying to push all into a mind set into which they're all changing, and leaving to a somewhat behind-the-scenes readjustment on my part that is designed to sort of soften a bit here, relative to a different part of the place. So there haven't been large resource allocation differences across different parts of the university so much as putting enormous pressure on the entire university to be more efficient and generate more revenue and to improve its bottom line, whether it was positive or negative, and then the allocations were much more gentle.

Imposing targets and allowing units to retain surpluses were the primary economic incentives for deans and directors to manage resources wisely. For its part, the Provost and budget office tried to create ambitious, but attainable targets:

> We put pretty aggressive targets in place for people in terms of increasing whatever outside revenues they would have. I think we had a three percent increase, or maybe four percent increase, applied to federal grants . . . basically based a little bit over inflation . . . And then the other thing was on tuition. We realized that tuition was an area that we had a lot of control over. And we put pressure on people to increase the size of their programs for unaided people . . . that's Masters students, unaided PhD's, and undergraduates, and asked them to reduce the size of the average first-year award, in the first year, by ten percent.

As will be discussed later in this case chapter, deans in the new system enjoy much more freedom than the had in the past to manage revenues and expenses. One administrator notes that deans now have

> the ability to shift money across lines and to make decisions about whether they would rather have more money for financial aid and less money for administration, or less money for faculty and more money for administration. So for the first time, they're kind of free to begin thinking in that way.

This fungibility represents a major shift in the budgetary process. Rather than attempting to resolve the budget deficit by reallocating resources across units and downsizing staff, faculty, and programs, the central administration has focused on restructuring budgets and incentives:

> We've gone from a system in which there were essentially no budgets for the divisions or the college, in which they had no direct sense of what their revenues were or what there expenses were, what their net was, and no incentives to manage to any net because it didn't exist to them . . . to one in which they do have those structures in place. And that has taken a tremendous amount of energy and time and work to recreate the structure.

Under the current ("new") system, the University Budget Committee, chaired by the Provost, meets to make judgments about budgetary priorities and guidelines for the University. The Committee's membership includes the Chief Financial Officer, the Budget Director, three Associate Provosts (two of whom are academics), one of whom is a full-time administrator but clearly with an academic bent, the Vice President for Research, the Associate Vice President for Human Resources, and the University Controller.[1] The Committee looks at general issues related to resource allocation across different parts of the university. Based upon their general assessment and recommendations, the University budget office builds a comprehensive model of the University's thirty-five key units. The model consolidates all sources of income and expense. The office then tests several scenarios based upon growth rates in various expense and revenue categories and then decide what's affordable. At this stage, budget personnel meet with the university budget committee to discuss and "tweak" the budget. (The new system has also been a transition for the central administration, which has had the task of creating "rules" for the assignment of direct revenues and expense under a very rapid timetable.)

Under the old system, the major academic units submitted thick budget proposals to the central administration. Now, the budget office sends a brief letter to each unit along with a page that has guideline growth rates for revenues and expenses, and a target. There is a space with boxes that asks units to fill in their proposal. Only a few pieces of back-up information are requested by the budget office. Units are required to submit enrollment projections and expected average financial aid awards. With this information, the budget office can assess whether tuition income will be reasonable. Units are also expected to provide information on faculty. Units must explain variances in excess of 3% on a line-by-line basis.

Deans are expected write an annual report to the Provost discussing areas where they want to make investments and the current status of their programs, but, as one budget officer states "they don't have to go through a whole bunch of rigmarole with the budget."

Budget meetings have also changed as a result of the transition to a more decentralized model. "Our meetings have changed dramatically from being adversarial, the deans working off one set of numbers, us having another set." Now, "We all agree on numbers when we walk into a budget meeting and have a discussion. We all absolutely agree on the twelve points that we would raise have a discussion on." Nevertheless, as one administrator points out, deans still argue about the numbers, but now they argue over their targets, and how the "right" target was determined.

In addition, deans seem to be meeting on a more regular basis with the Provost to discuss academic priorities and related financial concerns. Partly this may reflect the change in leadership, but to some extent it likely reflects the new budget allocation process. When a dean is considering a major new investment that would require significant reallocation of existing resources, a targeted fund-raising effort, or bridge funding from the Provost, the dean is more likely to initiate discussions with the Provost. Since budget targets are prepared for two years, a central administrator states that "we don't have any expectation that going into a meeting in February, you'd have a unit missing their budget by a million dollars because they wanted to invest in a particular program area."

In the past, deans could go directly to the Provost and request incremental resources. The deans are still free to make those pleas, but the Provost is now much more likely to encourage a dean to reallocate resources or raise the additional funds. An administrator uses the following hypothetical discussion between a dean and a Provost. The dean has requested an additional one million dollars to support teaching assistants. Under the current system, the Provost's reaction is likely to be:

> Well great, spend a million dollars more on teaching assistants. Go find something else, somewhere else, to make up the difference. And if you want to give up faculty appointments, great I'll do that. If you want to give up a new building, I'll do that. But this is constant: you have everything within your control. I don't have any other resources in the center. You find them . . . you make the trade-offs . . . We don't think that we're in the best position to make those decisions. You make them within your operating unit.

In other cases, the Provost might be willing to willing to invest in a new program, but only if deans are willing to share the risk through revealed preference:

> What I've tended to do in a world in which deans now have resources is to say to them, 'Convince me that this is a good interdisciplinary program. If you'll put up a certain amount of money, if each of the three of you will put up a certain amount of money, then I'll match it, or I'll double it. But

if you're not willing to put it up, then I'm going to assume it's not that important. And if you're willing to let it go by the boards, then so will I.'

In some sense, this notion of trade-offs is not very different from the past. Financial trade-offs were always part of the resource allocation process at Westmont. The difference today is that the trade-offs are now being made by the schools, not by the center. The central administration now feels that most of the deans, "having lived with this or come into it when they became deans actually have a pretty positive view of it . . . they understand the incentives. They've managed to use it to their advantage. And I think at this point, the downsides have been pretty small."

The central administration has made it clear to deans, department chairs, and faculty, that the trade-offs are now in their court. Still, some are more comfortable than others navigating the new system. A central academic officer remembers meeting with the faculty in the Music Department:

> After laying out for them what we were doing and why we were doing it, one of the faculty members raised her hand and said, 'Can we have a new piano?' And I said, 'You didn't get the point. Don't come to me and ask for a new piano. The answer's going to be, 'I've given out all my money. It's all been distributed. If you want a new piano, make a decision whether you're better off having one fewer fully funded graduate student next year and using the money for a piano than you are without the piano. And you are now free to make that decision. And make a recommendation to that effect to your dean. And the dean, presumably, as long as you meet your bottom line for the department, would be willing to let you make that trade-off.'

The Provost and other members of the central administration have a critical role in communicating the new system to University constituencies. It is clear, however, that deans must also bear some of this responsibility, as the comments of one dean suggest:

> I have a good set of chairs now, and in general I feel that I work with them well. And there's been kind of a changing of the guard among the chairs. See, under the old system where the resources were centrally controlled, for example, if a faculty got an outside offer, the way it was put to me was that the chair of the department and the dean would go up and pick the Provost's pocket, on behalf of that faculty member. Now that I have to manage this out of a fixed set of salary dollars, it's no longer a matter of advocacy; it's a matter of making tough decisions, and that's the way the Provost wants it.
>
> The old guard of department chairs didn't understand that. They thought that it was all a matter of bluster and advocacy and threatening

to leave, or threatening to resign. I have a younger set of chairs now who I think understand now that it is a world of tough tradeoff of resources, and what I need is their best advice on where they think we can get the most out of our resources.

The deans are also finding it necessary to collect and share more financial information with their faculty. In the past, very little financial information circulated within the schools. In the current more market-driven environment, such information is more important, as one dean attests:

> Many faculty members just assume that they can hire a full-time research assistant if they want . . . which wasn't consistent with our past practice. And in order to be able to say no to faculty, you have to be able to tell faculty when they say, 'Well, gee, isn't that what we've always down?' . . . you say, 'No that isn't. And here's the list of every faculty member and how much each spent on research assistants last year.' No only wasn't it the case that people used information like that before; they never even had it. They had no knowledge of how much money was being spent on this, that, or the other thing . . . The starting point of any resource allocation system in an organization that is as large as [this professional school] . . . is having information.

Entrepreneurship and Revenue Generation

A central academic administrator, reflecting on the current state of affairs at the University, stressed the importance of cultivating new sources of revenue generation:

> My view is very simple: we have to generate the resources. We have only two alternatives, basically, in my opinion. One is to preserve the core of what we do exceptionally well and find ways to generate the revenue to support that. And that may mean things like this kind of program. And we should do it well. But it may not serve the core mission of the university, other than financially. But it should done well, with good students, with good faculty. And if we're going to do those things, we should welcome it.
>
> If we can't succeed at that, then I think our alternative is essentially to rethink the entire university and to recognize that we cannot survive as a first-rate institution doing only those things that we've done in the past. And therefore we have to basically redefine ourselves entirely and take our endowment and become the world's best Law School. Get rid of everything else. Or the world's best Law School, Business School, and Public Policy School, and just say, 'We cannot afford to have Arts and Sciences.'

Now, that's obviously not a particularly attractive message. But I think the reality is that those are the two avenues we have available to us. We have to figure out a way to become financially not only stable but vital as we move forward. And that primarily means generating revenues that were not ever generated. And if we cannot do that, then we have to downsize big-time.

The University has tried to avoid downsizing and other drastic cost-saving measures by identifying new sources of revenue. It has done so primarily by creating new incentives for academic units to generate resources, especially tuition revenue. The University plans to expand the size of the undergraduate college and feels that a targeted recruitment strategy will result in additional incremental tuition. Westmont is currently recruiting a Dean of Enrollment Management who will implement the College's new undergraduate enrollment objectives. One administrator describes this transition, and its impact on the academic units:

> A lot of what we've done is to push on the units. We've explained to the university that we've got serious financial challenges; they're real; we're not making them up. We've persuaded the deans, if not everybody else, that the only way the university can address this is if the academic units do better because they are the core of the economy of the university. And not only what we do, but they also, whether we like it or not, are the core of the finances of the institution. I mean, development can do something, but fundamentally tuition is what most universities run on. And then what we've done is basically try to push upon them the responsibility for figuring out how to solve those problems in each of their own units. And it's been very hard, and different units have used different mechanisms.

A recent planning document notes that certain departments are developing terminal master's degree programs for "specific groups of students who need advanced work in particular areas for professional advancement but who are not interested in research or in careers in higher education for which the Ph.D. is required." The document notes that because

> students pursuing a master's degree in general receive little financial aid, this would seem to be a promising area for the University to expand with the reasonable expectation of increasing revenues, while, at the same time, providing programs of the highest quality to students who would benefit from what we have to offer.

The document further notes that in the future, "master's students will constitute an increasingly important segment of the student body." Schools which have not traditionally encouraged terminal master's students have either introduced or are planning to introduce such programs in the near future. One such program is a Master's degree program in the social sciences, which, according to a school administrator, tends to attracts students from "small colleges or second-class state universities" who think they might want to do a Ph.D. and who need to sample courses before choosing a discipline or need to build a track record before applying to a prestigious graduate program. The program is said to be academically worthwhile: "It's a well managed, well structured program. I think we provide them with good educational and career value . . . and it's a program that makes sense." The program has grown from an enrollment of about 50 in 1993, to a program of about 120, and may rise to 140 in a future year. The Humanities division is also planning to introduce a similar program.

The Social Sciences division is also thinking about introducing a master's program in computational psychology that would be of great interest to businesses. A dean in the division is careful to add "It is also—and this is crucial—an area where our faculty would like to teach. Whatever the financial pressures, we're not about to invent programs that distract faculty from their intellectual interests." He hopes to find a curricular blend that will satisfy "the demand of the academic marketplaces and satisfy our intellectual interests at the same time." The dean cites the example of a proposed M.A. program in quantitative survey methods. This program was particularly attractive because, according to a dean,

> It fit well with the intellectual interests of our faculty who are already here, but also because I looked at where the faculty are under-utilized or over-utilized. And there are some department that have much heavier teaching loads than others. Sociology happens to be one that under-utilized. So this would be a way to increase the number of students they have to teach.

The University academic administration recognizes that some schools, such as the Business or Law Schools have greater "capacity to admit substantial numbers of additional paying students, without any difficulty in terms of the availability of those students." They worry a lot about the quality of those students, whether they want to teach that many students, and who they are, but it's financially easy for them to address those issues [by admitting more students]." Other Divisions, such as Physical Sciences, apparently have fewer options, but the central administration is not very sympathetic, as the following quotation suggests:

> For the Physical Sciences Division, which hasn't been able to figure out any way of imagining Masters programs and which believes that in the competitive world in which it exists, it cannot admit additional PhD students and expect them to pay anything. And indeed it can only admit PhD students to the extent they have grants, the faculty have grants, to

support those students. Their view is, 'We have no real revenue generation capacity, unlike the Business School. So how do you expect us to respond to these pressures?' So different units are clearly at different places in terms of their ability to respond . . . and we've tried to set our targets in some degree with an awareness of a lot of things, and one of them is their capacity to respond. But we've essentially been pretty ruthless about saying, 'Be creative. Don't tell us you can't do it. Do it.'

The University's Physical Sciences Division is now developing a new masters program in financial mathematics which one faculty believes will be "quite successful . . . both academically and in terms of the market." This terminal master program will be offered by the Mathematics Department in association with the Departments of Economics and Statistics. The program would be offered at a downtown location for professionals in finance.

Other entrepreneurial programs include a new program sponsored by the School of Social Services which provides advanced training to social workers for the Department of Children and Family Services. The Humanities division has also recently launched a new M.A. program in Japan. The University is also considering a premedical program for college graduates who wish to complete requirements in the sciences for admission to medical school.

Some departments have also admitted more unfunded Ph.D. students, though one dean points out that "it's pretty clear that faculty don't think it's a good idea to have a lot of unfunded PhD students." Given the choice, deans have responded by developing unfunded master's programs.

Although it is still to early to evaluate the effects of these new programs, the university central administration is cautiously optimistic, but recognizes the potential liabilities of admitting large numbers of unfunded students:

> The graduate divisions had to generate more paying PhD students or Masters students in order to meet the targets that we set for them . . . far more difficult targets than whatever the bottom line was before. That has generated a good deal of concern. What does it do to the quality of the graduate programs to be adding weaker, presumably weaker, students who are paying you something to be here, relative to having fewer students who are paying you something to be here? It clearly adds dollars, but what does it do to the average quality of the students, to the classes, and so on? I think that has been the issue that has generated the most anxiety on the part of deans, and rightly so.
>
> And what we've tried to do is to use the pressure of their desire not to live in that world to force them to be creative about other ways of achieving their goals than simply admitting a horde of unfunded PhD students. And that's led to a good deal of interest in creating Masters

programs, which at least are terminal. The students come, knowing they are here for a year or two, hopefully for a coherent, sensible academic program, and where they don't stay twelve years but they are in and out in two years.

And that's actually been, I think, cautiously promising. So, that's an area where I think they've worried a lot about the effects. And fairly so. Then the alternative way, of course, they could meet the goals is by having fewer funded [Ph.D.] students. I mean, it doesn't matter . . . We don't care if they have fewer funded students or more paying students. It cancels out. They have not wanted to do that. Even in the world in which their students can't get jobs. So it's put a lot of pressure on the units to think a bit more . . . and, I think, ultimately in a constructive way, about what they're trying to accomplish with these PhD programs, and how much of their resources they're prepared to invest in them. I mean, one of the things they're beginning to understand now is they can pay their faculty more money if they have fewer paid graduate assistants, and maybe that's a better use of their money.

As one might imagine, many faculty are worried that the new emphasis on revenue generation may have negative consequences for the academic character of the institution. There is concern, for example, over the impact of budgetary changes on the interdisciplinary character of the University. One administrator states:

> The worry here is that putting into place some of these budgetary changes will make units more parochial and less cooperative in terms of letting faculty teach across the institution without transfer payment. And so there's a worry about the permeability of the institution, and it's a reasonable concern.

Most of the concerns, however, are embedded in the tensions between the core academic values of the institution and the demands of the marketplace. In a recent university publication, a prominent member of the social sciences faculty noted concern among some faculty, "partly associated with change of any kind and partly associated with the fear that [budgetary] decentralization will change the priorities or distort how the University should conduct itself. Would we turn into entrepreneurs, selling the time and talents of our faculty to the highest bidder?" One of the deans raised a similar issue, candidly admitting that, "There are large cultural issues, as you could imagine, involved in all these things. I mean, a lot of people say, 'This university is not supposed to be involved in training a bunch of people who are working for Lehman Brothers.'"

With regard to the master's program in financial mathematics, one dean comments that the proposal has generally been favorably received, but it raises the question, 'Is this what we want these departments to be doing?' The frank answer is there's money in it. If there wasn't money in it, we wouldn't be doing it. This is an indication of the concerns about the entrepreneurial role the University has to take. There is general affirmation of the changes, but concerns will remain that the President, Provost, and deans be vigilant concerning those things that make us a unique scholarly enterprise.

Less controversial are efforts by the Divisions to pursue fund-raising and development opportunities beyond generating additional tuition revenue. Professional schools at the University have traditionally engaged in fund-raising, but until recently the Divisions (Humanities, Social Sciences, and Physical Sciences) did not. In the past, as one Division dean notes, there wasn't much incentive "because the center absorbed all of [the revenue]. And now if I can raise a chair, and I haven't yet, but if I can raise the endowment for a chair, I will get to add that on to the faculty headcount in the division."

Now, the Humanities Division has its own development operation, with a staff of two. Although the Social Sciences Division has not yet developed an independent development operation, the Dean has assigned development duties to an assistant dean, "which will mainly take the form of trying to keep the attention of the central development staff and make sure that they keep an eye on our needs." A dean in this Division is uncertain whether development is worth the investment. "I don't know what the payoff will be at this point." Still, he is beginning to make development trips and mentions that he recently visited the West Coast last month to meet with potential donors. For the time being, however, he believes that the immediate gains are to be found in student tuition dollars.

SUMMARY VIEWS OF THE NEW SYSTEM

As the previous sections may suggest, the movement from a centralized economy to a more market-driven decentralized resource allocation system represents a major cultural shift in the way administrators, faculty, and deans approach financial matters. A major concern noted throughout the interviews and discussed in various university documents is the fear that the University will "compromise" its core intellectual values and gradually become nothing more than a business. The faculty has expressed particular concern over the new system and the values of the University. According to one central administrator:

> Well, basically, I think it is an attitude on the part of many faculty that the administration of the university cares only about the budget, about finance, and that we don't understand the values of the university . . . which are scholarly excellence and intellectual community, and an

interdisciplinary approach to problems . . . and that we are doing things for their monetary value, and that we're creating a structure that is going to make it very difficult for people to pursue scholarly excellence and, in particular, there's a great deal of worry that people would not be able to pursue interdisciplinary work because we have now created budgets on a divisional basis, so there could be jealously of work teaching across divisions.

The Provost and the President are constantly on the lookout for any sign of adverse impact and making adjustments when they occur and, indeed, very few signs occur. But I think the biggest problem is that we sort of exploded this noble myth that this was just purely an academic enterprise that had no [financial] activity going on.

The Provost has reiterated the sentiment that he will not let the University fall astray, in a recent public document where he attempted to explain some of the changes now occurring at the University:

This is hard work, for we are attempting to rethink and, indeed, to reinvent the ways we fulfill our responsibilities across a broad range of tasks, from budgets to admissions to appointments, in a stunningly short period of time. In this context, some individuals have expressed concern that, as we make these adjustments, we may undermine the very values that make us special. This is a serious concern. Thus, as we move forward in this process, we must constantly attend to the unintended consequences of what we do. Some changes will not work as intended; some may even have perverse effects. As the President has emphasized, when that happens, we must go back to the drawing board, and we will.

One of the key reasons the transition seems to be working, according to central administrators, is effective communication and a willingness to be flexible in the face of uncertainty. The current administration has spent considerable time discussing University finances in the campus community. One administration notes that there is "a much more detailed sharing of information than tended to be the style before," adding that "this is an administration that is much more open about sharing financial information than the previous administration." Though this has contributed to a "collective sense of knowledge," it has also "focused the attention of the institution on financial issues." Information about financial issues is critical, as far as the central administration is concerned. One central administrator states:

And for the most part what I have done is to try to create an environment in which they are doing that with much greater information than they had before, with much more of an awareness of the financial implications of those decisions, and trying to get them to understand that there are real constraints and that they have a limited amount of positions and dollars to give out.

And for the most part, the deans are rising to the challenge of the new economic order, even though their jobs are more difficult. The following quotations illustrate viewpoints of the supply and demand sides in the resource allocation process:

Central administrator:

> We've tried to monitor them. We talk about them a lot. We worry about them. I ask them to always bring to my attention any time they find negative things happening as a result of this. But I think if you talk to the deans, their view at this point would be that this is a more sensible world. It's a much harder one for them; their jobs are much more difficult. But they're able to see the power it gives them. And if this was not happening in a world of constricting resources, I think they'd love it. The point they don't love, really, is that it is a world of tighter resources, not the fact that we're giving them more power to make decisions and more incentives to make decisions. So basically, I think, the deans at this point would be quite positive about this. They understand it. They see why it makes sense to them. And they've lived with it long enough that they can see where they've been able to do things they would not have been able to do before that have benefited their unit.

School dean:

> If you look our endowment compared to the other comparable research institutions, we're sort of dreadfully low. And I think [the Provost] is determined to turn that around. I think he's right about that. The problem is that what the faculty hear is constant talk about dollars and fund-raising. And they draw the conclusion that he doesn't have strong intellectual standards. That's not true. I know for a fact that that's not true . . .
> What I've told faculty is, 'If you gave me a choice between a President who is trying to tell me what to do with my departments, or a President who is out trying to raise new funds so that I could help departments pursue research and educational projects, it wouldn't take me any time at all to decide which I'd rather have.' And put in that way, I think most of them would agree. That does mean, then, that the dean is kind of the mediator between the attempt to get the financial house in order and to find new resources, and then the faculty and the departments who think that this is a very special place in its intellectual atmosphere and they don't want to see it change. I don't know, maybe I'm a Pollyanna, but I don't think they're doing anything that risks really changing the intellectual

atmosphere around here. In part, because I think there's a tremendous inertia in the faculty. Faculty come because they want this kind of place, with a heavy tilt toward graduate study. And unless we just change that out of all recognition, I don't think that the character of the place will change.

Not all deans, however, have been equally enthusiastic about the new system. According to one central administrator, some deans feel that they

> didn't really sign on to be financial mangers, quite frankly. That wasn't the job. They changed the job description in the middle of the play, all right? And [though] everyone has basically stepped up to the plate to do that, some have done that more enthusiastically than others. And some really resent the fact that they are supposed to be recruiting the best faculty and making programmatic decisions, not managing budgets. On the other hand, at least some if not all, have noticed that this gives them considerably more flexibility and that it has a lot of . . . well, call it 'entrepreneurial energy' in the sense that you can create new programs like Master's programs that add new revenue and you get to actually spend it on something you want, which never occurred before.

There has been at least one casualty since the new system was inaugurated. Administrators refer to one dean in particular, who

> hated [the new system] with a passion and resisted it, and regarded it as terribly corrosive and destructive. . . Because it was making the units take into account finances rather than excellence in some abstract sense . . . And what I tried to explain to the deans is that this was dirtying their hands and their department chairs' hands and even their faculty's hands by making them think about trade-offs, but that it was my view that they could make those trade-offs more wisely than I could, sitting at the center.

According to central administrators, the dean referred to in the above quotation continued to believe that the "targets were not in the best interest of the division, and his job was to watch out for the best interests of the division." As one administrator put it, the dean found the whole notion of targets to be "profoundly incompatible with the values of the institution, which are excellence at any cost. And somebody else is supposed to worry about the money." In the past, this dean "always made pleas; he had always won. And he just didn't buy in with the program. He didn't do any of the planning. Two minutes before the budget cycle was supposed to start, he'd begin; he hadn't done anything." This individual is no longer a dean at Westmont.

The "new" dean, therefore, must balance a commitment to academic values with the financial realities of running a school. While most of the deans have apparently embraced this new role, it is still source of discomfort. One dean felt compelled to close his interview by affirming his values:

> One of things that I want to emphasize . . . is that I am actually a dean who runs a school, who believes in higher education, who is a serious scholar, who is quite willing to be an entrepreneur . . . but ultimately, at the end of the day, I have to have a strong sense of the academic mission of the place. And I have to be committed to it. And I have to make decisions in a way that vindicate that.

INSTITUTIONAL PRIORITIES

The institutional priorities of the University Westmont stem from a long and scholarly tradition that is well captured in the following quotation, taken from a recent University planning document:

> Since its inception, Westmont University has been characterized by single-minded focus on excellence, depth, and originality in scholarly research and education. At all levels, the commitment of members of the university to these qualities has created a scholarly community remarkable for its unit of vision and sense of purpose. We possess a research atmosphere of striking openness within and across fields, and we undertake education at all levels with intensity and seriousness. The success achieved by the University has been due to its core of outstanding faculty and students, both undergraduate and graduate. We believe that this focus, on excellence, depth, and originality, together with the distinction of our faculty and students, must remain at the heart of the University and that all discussions of its future need to be understood in the context of the absolute important of sustaining this triad of characteristics that define who we are.

Discussions with senior academic officers and examination of university documents suggest that Westmont University, in broad terms, is seeking to retain and expand its core values during a period of fiscal retrenchment. These core values are described in one recent university as "scholarly excellence," "intellectual community," and "interdisciplinary approach."

The University core values have made it difficult to develop a targeted investment strategy, even during a period of fiscal retrenchment. As one administrator states, "The guiding principle at Westmont is excellence . . . excellence across divisions, excellence across the departments. That's not a very targeted strategy, and we're almost wealthy enough to pull it off." What this means is that the University will continue to concentrate on strengths, as one university officer notes:

> Fundamentally, it's a lot easier to build on excellence than it is to build on weakness. And this is a time when I think we need to preserve and build upon those places where we really are great, rather than to let them deteriorate and try to build up other things that are mediocre. . .

He adds that:

> Unfortunately, we don't have departments in the university at the moment that are both relatively weak and relatively expensive. We have some that are relatively weak, but they tend pretty much to pay their own way, and if they disappeared completely tomorrow, you wouldn't have that big of savings. And we have some units that are real drags financially, but they are really quite excellent and played an important role in the history of the University . . . So unfortunately, we won't really feel we have any low-hanging fruit here. We got rid of [one of the professional schools]. We got rid of [a department] some years ago. There's not a whole lot now, when you look across the institution, where you can see both weakness and significant financial gains from eliminating programs.

Even though the central administration has no apparent plans to eliminate academic programs, many individuals interviewed for this case study are nevertheless worried that the University's financial problems and decentralized resource allocation model may, over time, adversely affect the academic character of the institution. The university central administration has tried to reassure the community that it remains committed to retaining, and, indeed, strengthening its intellectual core. A recent university document summarizes this perspective:

> As we now look toward the future of the University and the renewal and enhancement of our strengths, what remains paramount are our commitment to recruiting and support outstanding faculty and to admitting excellent Colleges students who can thrive in our intellectually demanding atmosphere, as well as excellent graduate students. In addition, we want to support intellectual initiatives of our faculty, to begin new programs that promise increased intellectual vitality, and to expand in directions ready for significant long-term intellectual development.

Within these general aims, University officers mention several specific priorities in 1996 briefing materials on the state of the University:

1. Moving out the demand curve for the College to increase enrollment while enhancing quality.

2. Building on the success of the [Capital Campaign] to raise fundraising to a new level.

3. Continuing to strengthen the quality of our world-class faculty.

4. Achieving budgetary equilibrium in the near term.

5. Maintaining a competitive rate of capital formation in the long term.

Three of these—priorities 2, 4, and 5—might be considered strictly financial priorities, while priority 3 refers to the academic enterprise. Priority 2 has both financial and academic implications. It should come as no surprise that the chief priorities preoccupying the University are financial in nature. Discussions with University executives suggest that the University first needs to restore financial equilibrium before it can engage in long-term academic planning. It should come as no surprise, then, that the University is not currently making large-scale investments in new areas:

> What I've tended to do thus far is to be relatively cautious at a time of stringency. At a time in which we are forcing people to tighten their belts, I have intentionally avoided large-scale investments in things that are seen as beneficial to only particular aspects of the university. On the other hand, we have supported international studies and gender studies from central funds. I've done that primarily by matching.

Conversations with other University administrators suggest that most of the investments in these areas have been relatively small.

Recently, the University has begun to address certain educational priorities through three University task forces. The task forces were organized around Undergraduate Education, Graduate Education, and the Quality of Student Experience. All three concern student life and education, which in some sense are also related to the objective of increasing enrollment because improvements in student life would make the University a more attractive place for students.

The Task Force on Undergraduate Education examined "such fundamental issues as financial aid, the size of the College, the proper role of graduate students and other non-faculty instructors in undergraduate teaching, the appropriate relation of the departments to the College, and the curriculum of the future." The Task Force on Graduate Education considered such issues as "graduate financial aid, the appropriate size of departments and programs, the goals of graduate education, the appropriate role of graduate students in teaching, the length of time it takes students to complete their studies, and the responsibilities of faculty for teaching, scholarship and colleagueship." The third Task Force on Quality of Student Experience has focused on "how we can best provide students with a superb educational experience." Areas under review include the curriculum, teaching, facilities, advise and counseling, and creating "an intellectual and social environment in which students can flourish." The task forces were charged with "examining our current situations . . . and with gaining perspectives on future development and renewal of our faculty and educational programs in light of our distinctive financial realities."

At the time this case study was researched, only the first two task forces had completed their work. The task forces issued extensive statements in Spring, 1996, which were reprinted and circulated to the University community as a combined report. The task forces recommended that faculty increase their involvement in undergraduate instruction and participate more actively in "making educational decisions, and participating in the legislative processes of the College Council." Furthermore, the report urged that departments evaluate their teaching and advising programs, and course offering for concentrators and non-concentrators. The goal of these efforts is "the creation of an ongoing process of Departmental involvement and self-accounting with regard to developing and maintaining superior undergraduate programs as well as administrative review and assistance for this process."

The task forces also examined the benefits and drawbacks of master's programs, and concluded that "despite the costs and complications," the programs are apparently a "reasonable way in which the University can garner additional revenue" to students who "would benefit from what we have to offer."

The task forces addressed the issues related to the faculty, and in particular, the allocation of resources for faculty recruitment across the University. In making these decisions, the task force urged that the University take into account two general principles. First, decisions about faculty size should be based on two considerations: "the preservation and enhancement of the University's intellectual strengths, and the University's capacity properly to fulfill its educational responsibilities." Any downsizing, according to the document, should take these factors into account, particularly as the university

Finally, the task forces urged that the University preserve one of the most distinctive features of the University—its emphasis on interdisciplinary research and teaching.

The report only indirectly discusses current University priorities. The report is less a compendium of recommendations and more an intellectual discourse about long-standing academic and educational issues facing the University. The report is a relatively long narrative, written in dense, academic language. It does not include a summary list of recommendations, and the recommendations it does provide are tentative at best. A senior academic officer states that the Task Forces were supposed to make recommendations about the growth of the College, faculty size, use of graduate student to teach, and the use of instructors to teach in the

College if its enrollment is expanded—all issues with significant implications for resource allocation and the academic character of the institution. This officer was disappointed that "the faculty was completely unable, totally unable to do it. They were very turf-conscious." The result is a report which discusses many issues but offers little course of direction.

Despite the lack of direction provided in the reports, the central administration is moving ahead with plans to increase enrollment of the College.

EVALUATION

The University monitors financial performance by assessing how well each unit has managed its resources in the previous year. The budget office does not attempt to continuously monitor unit financial performance and does not project the bottom-line financial performance of each unit on a monthly basis. "We just depend on the units to give us projections and to keep us informed," notes one financial administrator. A few units are monitored more closely, however, possibly because they lack the in-house financial skills required in a decentralized resource allocation system. At the end of the budget cycle, each unit is, of course, evaluated on the basis of how well it has performed relative to its targets and net position.

In the academic area, performance measures are not systematically collected, though the university central administration and deans often mention using the quality rankings of the National Research Council as a reasonable benchmark of excellence. One administrator states that "We know that [the ratings are] correlated pretty well to what we thought were good departments and what weren't." But beyond using these ratings, the University does very little to quantify academic performance. One central academic officer laments that

> We have a virtually non-existent institutional research capacity at this university. And so one of the frustrations is there's a very real sense in which we often at the center feel we are flying blind, that we could monitor the finances, but we've learned how to do that, and we are continuing to learn how to do that. But in terms of being able to measure the effects of this on academic matters, we have to rely much more on anecdotal evidence.

In general, however, the University central administration is comfortable with this arrangement, as the following comment suggests:

> [I] trust them to write them to worry about the academics. I mean, basically, what I've done is to say to the deans, 'We can monitor the finances. I want you to do it right on the finances. And I trust you to it right on the academics.'

FUTURE SYSTEM

As stated at the beginning of this case study, Westmont's system is currently in a state of transition. Although it has effectively decentralized the resource allocation system, much work remains to be done. Over time, there will be minor adjustments in the "rules" used to establish unit targets, as one administrator statese:

> I think it will be necessary to begin questioning the starting points a bit more, and asking whether those historical baselines were the right baselines, and to begin making more difficult choices about how resource allocation goes to different divisions or schools . . .

Implicit in this statement is the possibility that the central administration might begin to use these funds more strategically, reallocating resources and moving bottom lines through the rules of subvention and participation commonly found in responsibility center systems. A central administrator notes:

> And where this all leads to three, four, or five years from now . . . I imagine that there will be more allocation decisions being made from the center about how much goes to the humanities versus social sciences. But we've been pretty much preoccupied with turning the whole thing around during this time period.

Another administrator believes that the central administration has "put a bit too much pressure" on the academic units in the last two years. Although such pressure was probably necessary to address the University structural deficit problem, the same administrator does not think they can "continue that degree of pressure on the institution" in the long-term and sustain academic quality.

Relief may come partly through invigorated fund-raising efforts, as well as administrative cost savings. As part of the University's effort to close the budget deficit, Westmont recently engaged a management consulting firm to assist the University's Administrative Cost Reduction Steering Committee in the redesign of the University's major administrative processes. The objective was to identify at least $8 million in administrative costs savings, and to identify ways to improve the quality of services to students, faculty, staff, her university constituencies.

The Steering Committee and outside consultant recommended a number of changes in administrative organization related to structure, process, practices, and required technology support. The specific processes included finance, procurement, student services, faculties management, development and alumni relations, grants and contracts, human resources, auxiliaries enterprises, and academic administration. The University expects to cut administrative costs by $10 million over four years. The consultant believes it can save $11.6 to $15.1 million in annual savings if the University is willing to make on-time investments of $7 to $14 million.

Time will tell whether the combination of administrative cost reduction, revenue enhancement, and resource allocation reform will improve the University's financial standing—and perhaps alter Westmont's academic character.

5
Shelton University

OVERVIEW

One of the oldest and most prestigious research universities in the United States, Shelton's reputation stems from its exceptionally strong undergraduate education and distinguished graduate departments. It is the oldest university in this study, the wealthiest, and arguably the most selective undergraduate program. It's academic departments, with few exceptions, are ranked among the strongest in the country. Professional studies are available only in a handful of areas.

Shelton University has traditionally had a highly centralized resource allocation process. With only a few graduate and professional schools, and a relatively modest total student enrollment, Shelton is a comparatively small institution. As such, the distance separating the organizational center from the academic and administrative operating units is not as pronounced as that found in larger, more complex institutions with more numerous graduate and professional schools and organized research units. It is perhaps not surprising, then, that resource allocation is highly centralized at Shelton and has been ever since formal budgets were first used at the University. But although centralization has prevailed over the decades, the current system, in place since the early 1970s, is a significant departure from the system used in previous generations. Before examining the present resource allocation system used at Shelton, it is useful to understand the historical context from which it emerged.

Prior to the 1970s, resource decision-making rested primarily with three individuals: the President, the Dean of the Faculty, and the Financial Vice President (Shelton did not have a Provost at the time). Though the three officers consulted widely in the preparation of the budget, it was not, as one university document noted, an era of participation. A brief summary of the process illustrates this point. The budget process began in the summer when the Controller and Financial Vice President estimated how much new income would be available. The Dean of Faculty, meanwhile, studied various data to determine the size of the salary pool to be recommended for faculty the following year. His recommendations were presented to the Finance Committee for approval at its November meeting. Departments were notified of the outcome shortly after the November meeting.

The remainder of the budget was gradually prepared between November and May on the following standard timetable. The Dean of Faculty reviewed requests submitted by departments for new faculty positions, and informed departments of his decision shortly after the announcement of new salary pools. Requests for non tenure-line faculty were considered on a less formal basis throughout the year. Salary pools for nonacademic staff were determined in January on the recommendation of the Director of Personnel and the Financial Vice President. The remainder of funds for each academic department—mostly funds for clerical and administrative support—-were determined through interviews conducted in March and April between the Financial Vice President and the department chairs.

Budgets for the Library, Computer Center, and all administrative departments were also determined by the Financial Vice President, through a series of meetings occurring in April and May. Decisions on tuition, room, and board were made during the course of the year "as adjustments seemed necessary" and were apparently not closely connected to increases in financial aid, which was managed through a separate process.

Throughout the year, the Controller tallied the collective commitments, and at the beginning of May, the cumulative decisions became the basis for an extremely detailed document entitled, "The Shelton University Budget," which was subsequently presented to and approved by the Board of Trustees.

Decisions were thus carried out by a small number of individuals in the central administration. Faculty were minimally involved in the process, and budget work was distributed throughout the year. The system apparently served the University very well for many years. According to one document, the system was

> well suited to the economic circumstances of the period, to the nature of the changes occurring within the University, to the generally accepted views regarding University governance, and to the particular administrative pattern which had evolved at Shelton in the years after World War II.

The disadvantages of this system were becoming obvious by the end of the 1960s and are summarized in University documents from the period. One document notes the following six disadvantages:

1. "Spreading of decisions through the whole year meant that the various sorts of requests could not be treated as competing claims against an overall limit of available resources."

2. The rather sharp division of responsibility between the Dean of the Faculty and the Financial Vice President, the former making academic decisions and the latter making non-academic decisions, "discouraged a single review by a single group of all claims on University resources."

3. Because decisions were made throughout the year, and major budgetary proposals were not considered in concert, administrators may be subject to the "mood" and "nature" of the administrators. Early or late requests might receive favored or unfavored consideration.

4. Finally, because the budget process ended in April "if the overall budget picture revealed by the April total is unacceptable, the opportunities to make adjustments are severely limited."

5. It was not "constructed along programmatic lines."

6. "The budget system described above did not encourage any general sense of participation in decisions on resource allocation."

At the same time that these disadvantages were becoming clear, the economic climate for higher education was changing. According to a university document, "the period of relative affluence in university finance came to an end . . . we concluded that a new budgeting system had to be developed which could cope with what promised to be a growing gap between needed expenditures and available funds." The same document notes a wave of interest, both at Shelton and at other universities and colleges, in more participative decision processes. Furthermore, campus officials realized that more systematic planning and analysis would be required because of the strong likelihood the University would become coeducational.

In 1968, with support from the Ford Foundation, the University embarked on a demonstration project to develop a more systematic budget process that would address the short-comings of the existing resource allocation process. The outcome of this project is the resource allocation system that Shelton still uses today, and which is described in the next section of this chapter.

THE PRIORITIES COMMITTEE

Since the early 1970s. Shelton University has determined its annual operating budget through the deliberations of a central committee known as the

Priorities Committee. The Priorities Committee consists of sixteen members, including three administrative officers (the Provost, the Vice President for Finance and Administration, and the Dean of the Faculty); six faculty members; four undergraduate students; two graduate students; and one other representative. The Provost, who at Shelton is responsible for all academic as well as non-academic resource allocation decisions, chairs the Committee. Two staff members from the budget-finance office serve as administrative resources to the Committee, and a member of the Provost's Office staff serves as executive secretary to the Committee. Beginning in early October and continuing through mid-December, the Priorities Committee meets twice weekly for two hours. Normally, the Committee meets fifteen to twenty-five times in a typical year. During the course of these meetings, the Committee makes the major resource allocation decisions for the next year's operating budget.

The Committee is assisted by staff from the budget-finance office, who prepare base budgets, summary tables, and other analysis, thus ensuring that the Committee's recommendations are consistent with available funds. The budget-finance office prepares a consolidated statement which incorporates all sources of funding. Thus, for example, when the Priorities Committee considers the amount which the salary pool can be increased, the budget office has already taken into account the fractions of resources available from general funds versus restricted funds. The process begins with a comparison between last year's projections and actual performance. The central administration will try to determine how closely revenues and expenditures match earlier projections, and determine whether the projections will be on target. This process thus enables the central administration to determine the general shape of the resources available for next year's budget. At this stage, the President meets with the Provost, Vice President for Finance, Dean of the Faculty, and trustees of the University to discuss institutional issues before the Priorities Committee meets.

The Committee considers the funding requests from campus officers representing various academic units, as well as administrative departments such as physical planning or the library. For example, the Dean of Faculty may request faculty salary increases, the Dean of the Graduate School will solicit funds to support graduate students or to develop a new academic program, and the Director of the Library may present a request for additional staff. One member of the Committee sees this as a strength of the process: "each of the unit heads comes forward in an unfavored way and says, 'This is what's important to me and my people.'" Normally, requests are first submitted to the Committee in writing, and, following an initial review of all requests, the Committee develops a balanced budget based on projected income. In addition, the Committee also interacts with other campus committees and holds an annual opening meeting for the entire campus community. The Committee meets twice with the Finance

Shelton University

Committee of the Board of Trustees, once in the November to discuss issues of concerns with the Board, and once in December to present tentative recommendations. The output of the Committee is a report issued in the Winter and made available to the entire Shelton community, entitled "Report of the Priorities Committee to the President: Recommendations Concern the Operating Budget for FY __."

At the outset, it should be noted that the Priorities Committee primarily deals with the annual incremental increase to the University budget, not the base budget. Nevertheless, one university financial officer notes that the Committee does look at the base, and sometimes addresses the hypothetical questions, "What would happen if we had to cut the budget two percent to five percent?" In lean years, and especially in years where a budget deficit is projected, the Committee looks more closely at the base. And in years where cutbacks are indicated, the Committee does in fact go through each major unit and expect those requesting an increase to justify their base. A faculty member who served on the Committee in academic year 1995–96 feels that the Committee has become "more hard-line than in the past" and has taken the position, "Let's force these groups to really look at what they're doing, and how much money they need to do it." Still, as one administrator acknowledges, "we don't do zero-based budgeting." In fact, as another administrator states, zero-base budgeting is beyond the scope and capabilities of the Committee:

> It is impossible for a transient group to look at the base on the level of sophistication. They're all sophisticated enough, but the time and effort and experience and knowledge you need to have to understand the base takes years to accumulate. You can't accumulate that in a minute or in a semester or two semesters or two years. So, it would be quite fatuous, in a way, to look at the base. Not because it is unimportant - it's very important, but you just cannot, if you're going to use a structure like this, you just cannot ask them to look at the base.
>
> [The participants] don't know enough and can't know enough, because that committee, here at least, changes somewhat every year, and nobody serves on it too long. I think three years may be the longest time. So that's why these initial decisions in the fall that the President makes with the policy group regarding his views and the strategic plan are so central to this process. That plan . . . really sets long term directions in an envelope in which we operate and we do look at the base.
>
> We look at the base of the school of engineering and the [another professional school] or whatever other school we're considering or the Romance Language department or something like that. But I think in general, our experience is, as in most universities, that these bases change rather slowly over time.

The Committee is apparently not equipped with the institutional knowledge or the continuity to dramatically impact the base. In the eyes of one central administrator, this is a weakness of the Committee:

> It's harder to take a dramatic step, whether it's down or up, to say, "Why the hell do we teach Economics?" or "Why do we have an athletics program?" or "Why do we have graduate programs in essentially every department?" These are fundamental questions.

Though the main focus of the Committee is on developing a balanced budget for the next year, the Committee does make projections for a four-year horizon. The central administrative staff develop the projections beyond the upcoming fiscal years based on the Committee's recommendations. A major purpose of the exercise, according to a university officer, is to "see if there's anything involved in those recommendations that will produce problems later on." If problems are indicated, administrative staff will ask the Committee to perhaps reconsider some of its recommendations, or possibly begin a planning process to address the financial consequences of the recommendations.

On the other hand, however, the central administration believes that the Priorities Committee has sometimes had a subtle but important impact shaping resource allocation policy in the long term. An administrator cites the following example:

> Two or three years ago, when the beginnings of the Washington cutbacks were obvious, and some of our other sources for supporting graduate students had already dried up or were in real danger of drying up, the Committee basically said, 'We should begin to cut back.' Now, that didn't lead to a recommendation per se, like, 'Next year we want a hundred fewer graduate students; but it did push the Provost, the Dean of the Graduate School and others to begin to explore [the matter] and so we've come down a hundred and something graduate students over about four years, and we're probably going to come down more. The people who raised that question four years ago probably don't realize how much of an effect it had as it played itself out over several years.
>
> But another example on the other side was in the early '80s when the initial Reagan budget cuts basically froze undergraduate financial aid programs, at that point federal support for scholarships, either the campus-based programs or the Pell Grant accounted for something like 35% of our scholarship budget . . . When that first started to happen, the Priorities Committee said basically our commitment to need-based, open need-blind admissions policy is so strong that we have to make up the difference. The first year that was two hundred thousand dollars. Basically that's been confirmed year after year after year, and the result is that we now spend

something like 90% of our scholarship budget comes from university money . . .

[The Committee] set a direction; they articulated a policy and set it up resulting in millions of dollars being shifted around. I think that's what we would have done - if any one of us in the administration had gone about putting the budget together in 1980 we'd have done the same thing . . . The Committee process helped strengthen that resolve.

Formally, the Committee makes recommendations to the President and Board of Trustees, but in practice, its recommendations are ordinarily endorsed. An administrator notes that the Committee's recommendations have "been accepted in every detail by the President and Trustees every year it's been in existence." One administrator speculates that this successful "track record" reflects the substantial analysis and discussion that precedes the Committee's final recommendations, as well as the fact that the Committee is chaired by the Provost, who works closely with the President throughout the process. In this way, the President can and does exert considerable influence over the process, as one central administrator reflects:

[The President] certainly heavily influences some of the major parameters of the Priorities Committee. He is a strong advocate, this year, saying, 'I want on your table of requests a request for lower fees. I'm making that request on behalf of myself and the Board of Trustees. We won't tell you have to do it, and we're not going to give you a number, but we're going to tell you, we'd like you to consider that.' So he influenced them that way. This year, when we're making reductions, he certainly concurred with the areas we said we're not going to touch. We're not touching the number of faculty slots, we're not touching the student aid programs, we're not touching major maintenance budget, we're not touching the salary pools this year; he concurred in all those.

[The CFO and Provost] will take that information with them to the priorities committee. Now, it may or may not come back just exactly as I've seen it, but at least I will have some significant input. They know what my own views are on this area, and so if they come back reflecting my views, fine; if they don't they either have a good reason, which is normally the case, or we continue to negotiate, because the way it works here is the Priorities Committee makes a recommendation to the President, and he make a recommendation to the trustees.

His strong desire is to be able to accept the recommendations of the Priorities Committee. That is, it's an important committee, people spend a lot of time and effort on campus, from various campus groups to look at it and look at the choices we have to make, so he very much respects the process, and it would take a really major difference of opinion for me to say that I don't accept their recommendations. But that's never been the case, and the reason that's not the case is because people go into the process knowing what his general initial feelings are, and either they get good reasons why he's wrong, which is often the case - you know, they'll point out that there's something he hasn't fully appreciated, which is often the case—or, he'll convince them that this is really a good idea.

As this passage suggests, the central administration still exerts great influence over the final direction and shape of the operating budget, even though the final report represents the Committee's recommendations. Because the Provost chairs the Committee, he has special influence over the process, as one administrator attests:

> It helps that the Provost chairs the Committee. It means that if he really does disagree with something that the majority of the Committee wants to do, he has the ability to in effect lock the door and say, 'We're not leaving here until either you convince me or I convince you,' and that's very valuable. The administration is going to end up being comfortable with what gets produced. In order to get that, though, we have to be prepared to really include the faculty and students, so the things that are really important to them, we've got to find some way to be responsive, either by simply accepting what they've brought forward or by developing some sort of compromise or persuading them why it isn't the central thing. And so it is in that way a collaborative effort; it's not an equal partnership—the administration—because we work at it full time, because we continue from year to year while committee members serve two or three years and then rotate off, we control a lot of the knowledge that the committee has. But I think the success over the years has been that we also listen to them.
>
> There's a greater level of community support than would be the case without this process, and that's most important with respect to faculty, and while most faculty will poo-poo the Priorities Committee process to a certain extent, saying, 'Oh, well, it's just the administration telling the faculty what to do,' I think deep down enough of them have either been on it or know people who were on it that they realize there's some real substance to the process and that knowing that good people have been on it, they're a lot less inclined to believe that we're just playing games.

The Committee also forces the administration to "be more careful." One central administrator notes that the Committee process:

> really does improve our own processes. It forces us to write things down, it forces us to answer tough questions that we might not in a polite way ask ourselves or each other . . . Those are very significant advantages that outweigh any of the disadvantages for me.

Other faculty members are less persuaded that the Committee has a significant impact on University resource allocation matters. One faculty member who served on the Committee in the 1970s feels that the role of the Committee is often overstated, and believes that the primary role of the Committee is largely symbolic:

> It was useful in some ways and not useful in others. In the sense that it actually influenced the budget in any meaningful way, I don't believe it. It didn't. The members of the Committee didn't have the information to make any meaningful [recommendations]... if they had the information, they didn't have the capabilities for processing it - again, that includes me. So I don't believe that the Committee ever had a substantial impact on the budget. The reason it was useful was entirely political, because what it meant was that if an unpopular decision had to be taken, it could diffuse responsibility. So if tuition was going up, you could say, 'Well, Jimmy Jones who was a senior was on the Committee.' Or if faculty raises weren't high enough they said, 'Well, Professor Smith was on the Committee,' or 'A member of the library staff.' But, would you really want a Committee with a member of the library staff, [an undergraduate] junior, a history of art professor, an economics professor, and a psychologist to be drawing up the budget of this multi-million dollar enterprise?

The same faculty member also points out that the Priorities Committee does not control capital expenditures. Major new initiatives are funded through the capital budget, which the President to a large extent is said to control with assistance from his senior advisors—on the academic side, the Provost and Dean of Faculty, on the finance side, the Vice-President for Finance and Administration. This faculty member cynically notes:

> So basically some other group determines whether we're going to build a microbiology building, which could cost $28 million, and then Priorities decides whether there should be three more janitors or two more janitors.

The other main weakness, from the central administrative perspective, is that the Committee demands a degree of consensus decision making they would rather avoid. Once central administrator feels that

> The system places special burdens on the University: Every year I think, 'Oh, my God, how am I going to talk the committee into this, this, or this?' Every year, I end up swallowing and saying, 'That's not quite the way I would have done it. I had the perfect plan here, and they monkeyed with it.' That's in the back of my mind every time.

Administrative expenses for such items as basic computing needs, staff salaries, and materials and supplies, are allocated to academic departments by means of a formula that has existed since the mid-1970s. The system evolved, according to one administrator, because

> we felt that it was totally a squeaky wheel system and it was not particularly equitable, and we wanted to get out of that. The Vice President and the Deans wanted to get out of approving half secretarial slots in general.

The allocation formula has been based on two variables: the amount of sponsored research volume and the number of faculty FTE's in the department. The formula attributes $11,161 for each faculty FTE under 20, and $6,006 for each FTE over 20. The result is then summed with 10.8% of the sponsored research volume. For the most part, the formula has worked well, according to one central administrator:

> When everything is out there on the table and saying, 'This is it, and this is how we're going to give you the money,' and they understand that and they understand that there's some logical process by which this formula was derived - it wasn't just plucked out of the air, has worked for the past three years and so therefore it should work for the next ten years; then at least they can also themselves see how much they're going to get next year; they don't have to wait until the Dean or whomever says, 'This is how much money you're going to get.'

The formula has recently been under review because it does not accurately reflect the educational needs of departments such as Engineering and the natural sciences, which require expense laboratories. One central administrator explains, "Increasingly, we've made exceptions from the formula which is one of the reasons we've decided to look at it." The formula does not currently take into account the capital costs of running a laboratory in allocating administrative funds. In addition, departments that run programs which involve faculty from different departments have few "real" FTEs on paper. As a result, every year the central administration makes significant off-formula adjustments with perhaps a dozen (out of forty) departments. According to the central administrator responsible for evaluating the formula and its effects on University resource allocation, the new models should limit the number of time-consuming" off-formula" adjustments. Still, administrators believe there will always be requests for additional resources. One states:

> I assume even after the new formula is put in place [sometime in FY 97], I would imagine that it will come closer to meeting the department's needs, but people will always be asking for something, I'm sure. But we have no experience with whether that will be better with the new formula.

Shelton University

Another administrator agrees, adding that:

> I think the [new] formula [will] work . . . but there will still be departments which will come and say, 'We don't have enough money.' And there won't be any departments which come and say they have too much money.

Once administrative funds are allocated to a department in a lump-sum allocation, departments have great latitude in determining how to use it, as one administrator explains:

> We give them a dollar number and say, 'That's yours. You figure out what you want to do with it.' So, for example, in the '80's people were trying to automate word processing, and later with the more general purpose of desktop computing. We basically said to most of the departments, 'If you want to do that, that's great. We urge you to do that. But you've got to cut staff to do it. You've got to reallocate some from your existing budget.' And that's what happened.

Though the Priorities Committee and the administrative formula are the key formal features of the resource allocation system, resource allocation also operates in many informal ways at Shelton. Small requests do not necessarily go through the Priorities Committee, for example. When one department chair needed more computers for his students to handle increased enrollments, he wrote to the Dean of the Faculty, made a case for the increase in computers, and received the following response: "Well, I can give you money for four computers this year; if you need more you will have to go through the Priorities Committee." Another department chair also seems at ease soliciting the senior administration for additional resources, as needed:

> Well, once in a while I get a memo from somewhere that says, 'Here's your administrative budget for next year. If you want more money, make the case now,' but I really don't pay very much attention to that, because that's really dealing with things like, 'Do I want a bigger telephone budget? 'or stuff like that? I'm just not going to put a lot of energy into thinking about that. But, if we do need new computers, and I want to make a case, I'll just write a memo. It doesn't have to be part of any particular cycle, I'll just write the memo, and again, they'll either say yes or no, or let's split the difference or something.

Department chairs seem at ease in dealing with school and central administrators when additionally resources are required. One chair notes that when additional resources are required for his department, he has no difficult obtaining access to the right people:

> The first person I'd be most likely to talk to would be the Dean of the Faculty, then sometimes the Provost, sometimes the Vice-President for Financial Affairs. One very nice thing about this place is that department chairs have very easy access to high level administrators. When a chair calls the President or the Provost or the Dean of Faculty or the Dean of the College, the call gets returned and it gets returned quickly. I think that's wonderful. They're a very responsive group of people; everyone knows everyone by their first name and it makes things work very smoothly.

Because the central administration and the school administration work together so fluidly, the cultural of informality can be a bit frustrating to central administrators, who generally prefer that chairs and faculty first deal with school administrators:

> Sometimes the departments that are part of the school remember to consult with us, and sometimes they don't remember. Shelton is highly centralized, it's still a small enough institution that the central administration can reach out to virtually any department and any department chair relatively easily, and our faculty have existed in a culture where they feel direct access to the Provost and President's office is their right and privilege, and they exercise it sometimes. We've tried to educate the central administration to send them back to us—to first ask the question, 'Have you consulted with the Dean? And if not, please do so.' It gets a little confusing, but as I say, it's a small enough institution and we work it out. Shelton does not operate by very many rules. It's pretty much ad hoc.

As is typical at highly endowed universities, many departments also possess their own restricted fund accounts which they are free to use, though some departments have more resources than others. One department chair notes that

> History, philosophy and art and archaeology are all extraordinarily well endowed in various ways, but there are restrictions in each case on how the money can be used, but they all have serious endowments. Comparative literature, German, Romance Languages, they have nothing or very little in terms of endowments. We're kind of a middle-class department; we have enough to do things that we wouldn't be able to do otherwise, but we don't have enough to support entire positions, we can't offer reduced teaching loads because of using our endowment to hire lecturers and so on and so forth, so what we use our endowment for is, in part, really to pick up the slack that the administration can't or won't give us

to do what we feel needs to be done. For example, hiring this graduate student to keep our computers running. It's not, in some ways, an ideal use of restricted funds, since it seems to be that sort of a thing that the central administration should be handling, leaving us to use our endowment for actually interesting things . . .

A central administrators notes "Some departments are quite wealthy in those ways and they're able to support extra faculty members, able to support all kinds of special programs for their departments." She adds that those kinds of departments are found in every division of the University.

Unlike some institutions that actively encourage schools and departments to engage in their own revenue-generating activities, the central administration has apparently not encouraged departments to do their own fundraising. One department chair states that "We had to fight for what's sometimes called a hunting licenses. You have to fight in order to get the right to go out and find donors." Fund-raising is permissible if cleared with the central administration. This may be changing. One chair notes that

> The administration has recently signaled that it is trying to make it easier for departments to engage in fund-raising; that they are trying to make it easier for departments to engage in fundraising; that they're going to encourage departments to raise their own funds and that they're not eager to make difficulties for departments to raise funds . . . there does seem to be willingness on the part of the administration to make this easier.

It is likely, however, that the central administration will still retain control over the fund-raising enterprise at the University.

MONITORING AND EVALUATION

The central administration actively monitors financial performance of academic departments. In August and September, the central administration does a thorough review of the budget for the current year—the budget which the Priorities Committee recommended the previous January. According to a university financial officer, "We go through in August and September, line by line, department by department, and say, 'Is there anything that we should change?' . . . And we go through and we change a lot of those."

Similarly, at the end of the academic year, the central administration conducts a financial review:

> We'll get every department and we'll say, 'All right, here's where you ended up . . . All right, what happened and why.' If you came in right on budget, your explanation is very simple. If you came in over, we want to know. If you came in under we want to know. And then we say, 'Okay,

here's your budget for the current year. Tell us whether that's adequate or not.' And then we go through those and make whatever changes we feel are necessary . . . That becomes the base for the priorities committee in looking at the next year's budget. That's what we do in advance. We have the best estimate we can make of the current year's numbers.

During the course of the academic year, the central administration monitors departmental expenditures, although in general it does not attempt to monitor individual line-items. The budget-finance office has developed a program review process which enables central officers to project expenditure information using historical extrapolation to determine whether a department is likely to experience a surplus or deficit. If a problem is indicated, the office will contact the department and try to ascertain whether corrective action is needed. The budget-finance office tends to focus on unrestricted balances rather than gifts and endowments, except in cases where a particular department had a history of problems because "You can always make them pay off out of their future endowment earnings, so given the fact that we have a small staff, it's not as high-priority as some of the other areas we monitor." This officer further notes:

> There are sanctions to the degree to which the department has restricted funds and they've overspent their general funds, we will pretty routinely go in and take enough restricted funds to cover their overdrafts. Departments understand that, and they understand that we give them wide latitude because we operate under that assumption. If the department routinely goes into overdraft and does not cover them, we would certainly have a discussion involving the Provost and make some decision as to whether we put them under tighter control or not. Most of the departments are relatively responsible.

The office also attempts to monitor expenditures in the non-academic, administrative areas:

> At the end of each year, we try to do an assessment and get an explanation from any department that was over about exactly what caused it, and then we have to make an assessment as to whether that was legitimate, and if we think it was, we might make a budget adjustment, and if we think it wasn't, then we'll probably ask for a plan on how they're going to get back to their budget. But we would not penalize in the sense of, 'You were over by $50,000 last year, you get cut $50,000 this year to make it up.' After the fact, we try to resolve the problem.

Financial controls are not rigid however, partly because the University has not invested heavily in the systems area. "Our budget tools—they're OK; they're not state of the art," one administrator frankly admits, adding

"We would never tell someone to come to Shelton to learn about how the budget information systems work. They work only because there are some very good people in the positions." As a result, monitoring is somewhat relaxed:

> So, could a department wander off course and end up with a pretty good size overrun that we didn't know about? Yes, actually, they could. We catch up at certain times, but the horse could be out of the barn by then. We just don't have the staff to do that. That's a judgment call, though, to assign staff. I believe we're OK. [We have] very good people they smell when something is starting to go wrong.

From a department standpoint, controls also seem relaxed, as comments from one school administrator suggest:

> We prepare an annual report, but curiously enough it contains no information on how we distribute our resources . . . Nobody ever asked! . . . Our annual report addresses all the statistics on the student enrollments, and admissions statistics, and research income, and highlights. . . and all research grants, an appendix of research grants, and some text on major grants and major happenings, and major changes, but it does not contain one single data point on how we distribute our resources.
>
> It's not formal . . . the block grant that we get is determined by discussion and presentation of needs by the Dean to the Provost . . . But, curiously enough, there is no reporting on how we spend the money. The data are there for anyone to analyze; we work through a central accounting system, and I don't know exactly to what degree the Treasurer's office or Controller's office examines our accounts to determine how we spend the money. You'd have to ask them that. If they examine it closely, I certainly don't get any feedback about it. It's very loose.
>
> It's a curious mix, isn't it, because Shelton tends to be very centralized in distribution of resources, but when it comes to measurement, there's very little . . . that I'm aware of, at least. Other than some gross measures of the numbers of students . . . if it's tracked, it's tracked by the central administration; it's not through our preparing any reports. We are not asked to prepare reports. Why that is? I guess they trust us. I don't know.

The same administrator speculates that the University may pay less attention to analysis than more financially challenged institutions, adding that "Shelton is a fairly well-to-do institution, and perhaps that leads to the level of, one might say even casualness, about financial controls."

On the academic side of the institution, quality is also monitored. Like other institutions, the University pays particular attention to the ratings of the National Research Council:

The NRC report that came out earlier in the fall ranked graduate programs. I don't think there were any surprises there for us. Whether something is four or six or two or one, you can't always . . . there weren't any things that we thought were in the top five that showed up on that list as fifteen.

In addition, the University monitors the quality of faculty, of undergraduates and graduate students, and of academic departments and programs. There are also academic reviews conducted periodically by a team of outside reviewers called an advisory council. According to one chair,

> From a departmental point of view, you get your peers saying what you're doing well and what you're not doing well. So they write recommendations. They also can push the university to reorder their priorities by saying, 'It is an outstanding department, and, you know, they need more space, or they need more resources.' I suspect most advisory councils, do this. But on the other hand, depending upon the credibility of the people and the reasoning they use, the administration can or cannot listen to them. We've been very fortunate. So we've had good advisory councils, and we've gotten good support from the university as a consequence of the reviews.

One chair states that the reviews sometimes lead to additional allocations:

> I haven't gotten any [faculty] FTE's from them, but we've gotten a lot other things, yeah. So they take them seriously if they're well constituted. And then they use the ad-hoc outside review every five years, where they will get a select group of people to come in and review the department or any program.

In general, however, processes for monitoring and evaluating the academic performance of departments and programs are relatively informal. One faculty member states:

> On a day-to-day basis, they [the central administration] are getting information from us, they meet with us once a year. At least once a year. They meet with the chair, they meet with the faculty and provost and talk about our staffing, tenure, our needs, our undergraduate program. The dean of the college is always watching each department's program, based on course evaluations. They hear complaints from students or favorable impressions by the students—they pass them on to us. So, Shelton's small; so it can work very effectively. And so there's not a lot of memos going back and forth, but people are monitoring how you're doing.

Shelton University

A central administrator apparently agrees with this assessment: "So all of that adds up to a picture, and I think we can tell you very, very precisely where our problems are and where our strengths are. "

INSTITUTIONAL PRIORITIES

University priorities are developed through a number of formal and informal processes. One of the most important processes has already been described—the annual work of the University Priorities Committee. The narrative report of the Priorities Committee describes the fiscal circumstances of the University, current University priorities, and the outlook for the future. The reports for the two most recent fiscal years, 1996 and 1997, are very similar in content, organization, and style. Both are relatively short documents—30 double-spaced pages with brief appendices. The report begins with a brief review of the structure and procedures of the Committee. The second section of the report details the factors influencing the budget recommendation. In the 1995–96 Priorities Committee Report, the Committee notes that several factors could "hamper efforts to achieve balance between income and expenses":

1. A decline in annual long-term rates of return in capital markets that could result in lower rates of growth in spending from endowment earnings;
2. Continued pressure and our own desire to reduce the rate of increase in tuition and fees;
3. Government support for sponsored research and student aid is expected to grow considerably more slowly in the 1990s than it did, on average, in the 1980s, and more slowly than the cost of our existing programs in these areas.

The document notes that "challenges on the revenue side are matched by both current and anticipated problems on the expense side of college and university budgets," and mentions such factors as the elimination of mandatory retirement for tenured-faculty, cost of providing competitive salaries for both faculty and staff, the rising cost of instruction and research, and finally the cost of maintaining a fully need-blind admissions policy for undergraduate students.

The third major section of the report discusses requests and recommendations for the next fiscal year and is divided into the following subsections: Tuition and Fees (undergraduate and graduate); Graduate student support; Undergraduate Financial Aid; Faculty and Staff Salaries; Employee Benefits; Faculty Staffing; Computing and Information Technology; Research Support; Facilities; Administration and Academic Supporting Services. A short paragraph discussion of each the above areas includes the Committee's financial recommendation. The Committee notes that the recommended budget for 1995–96 achieves the following results:

- A balanced budget;
- Continued moderation in the rate of increase in tuition and fees;
- A salary program designed to sustain the gains made in recent years that have helped Shelton continue to attract and retain excellent faculty and staff;
- An increase in the budget for undergraduate scholarships which provides the funding required for the anticipated needs of Shelton students;
- The funding of a new Summer Scholars Institute;
- A modest increase in faculty positions and the number of graduate teaching assistants.

The 1995–96 Committee Report concludes with a section entitled, "Outlook for the Future," which briefly addresses the long-term resource needs of the University and includes four years of budgetary projections—for the year immediately ahead, and three additional years. The 1996 report also includes the following discussion of long term university priorities:

> Although this Committee's number one priority for the future is to continue the pattern of lower growth rates for tuition and fees, we are concerned that there do not appear to be sufficient funds available in the future to address any of the unmet needs that the Committee heard this year. These included, among other things, more adequate support for instructional costs, particularly in science and engineering, and the need to improve salary levels for certain segments of the faculty and staff where the relationship to market is not ideal. Further, it is clear that other new exciting possibilities, such as the new summer scholars institute presented and recommended for FY 96, will emerge in the future and that subsequent priorities committee may well wish to fund them. This means that all segments of the University's operating budget should continue to be reviewed closely, looking for opportunities to reallocate existing funds to support emerging activities. As last year's committee concluded, 'Indeed, it may be that thinking about what we can do best and what we should do next will help put in perspective those areas which are less essential. Trying to approach the future in such a way will be a challenge not only for future Priorities Committees but for the entire University community.' We believe this remains true now and for the foreseeable future.

The Priorities Committee is not the only forum in which academic priorities are openly discussed at Shelton. The University also has a standing committee on academic planning, and various faculty and University committees engage in planning. The University has also engaged in formal strategic planning in which "we have tried to identify steps that Shelton might take to strengthen its programs of teaching and research, and to develop a set of broad strategic themes that can help guide and focus our ongoing planning activities."

In 1992–1993, the University carried out a strategic planning exercise which culminated in a written report entitled "Shelton University— Continuing to Look Ahead." The Report notes that the plan has been guided by several themes, one of which is "allocating resource to areas of highest priority so they will have the greatest possible impact on the *quality* of our faculty, students, and programs of teaching and research." In fact, the 1996 fiscal year priorities report describes the relation of this mandate to the University's campaign initiatives."

> The discussion of the campaign-related issues and the general outlook for the University's revenues helped the Priorities Committee in weighing the short- and long-term budget requests that came before it in the ensuing weeks. This discussion of major long-term needs and revenue sources set the stage for what proved to be an ambitious set of requests.

WHY THE SYSTEM WORKS

The resource allocation system at Shelton is characterized by several features: a central planning and resource allocation committee composed of members of the university central administration, faculty, and students; informal procedures for allocating resources that operate almost as a shadow to the more formal Priorities Committee structure; limited formal monitoring of financial and academic outcomes; and extensive informal communication among faculty, department chairs, and central administrators. These structures seem well suited to the University's culture and relatively focused academic portfolio, characteristics which is described in a recent strategic planning document:

> Shelton is distinctive in its relatively small size; in its commitment to a single faculty; in its strong dual emphasis on excellence in teaching and in scholarship and research; in its focus on the arts and science, along with its schools of engineering, architecture, and public and international affairs; in its special commitment to undergraduate education; in the value it places on independent work; in its extraordinary investment in student aid, to support a truly need-blind admission policy at the undergraduate level and to insure the quality of its programs at the graduate level; and in the importance it attaches to the residential experience of a increasingly diverse campus community.

As this description suggests, Shelton has a relatively small portfolio of academic programs as well as clear and focused institutional priorities. These characteristics—along with less tangible cultural factors—may explain why Shelton's unique resource allocation system is successful. The following quotations from Shelton administrators and faculty provide additional insight into the reasons underlying the success of the resource allocation process:

Central administrator:

> . . . We take pride in the sense of community that we have here, and the administration—the upper levels of administration are filled by people who have strong academic backgrounds and also the faculty and administrators at the department level feel like they can talk to people, that they can pick up the phone and get whoever makes the decision on the phone, or just send an e-mail . . . they are able to express their views . . . they at least have some sort of control of their destiny, which is quite hard in a much larger institution where it takes several phone calls to get to the right person, and even then you're usually sort of headed off at the pass before that happens.

Department Chair:

> Certainly the current . . . Dean and the Provost are most responsive. That doesn't mean they always say yes, but you get yes's or no's, and that's why people like it. And again, getting back to the scale of the thing, probably the reason the system works is because people learn to know each other and I think the Dean and the Provost know who they can trust when a Chair comes and says, 'This is very important, I need the money' and the person isn't yelling wolf all the time. Our dean really has an intimate knowledge of what's going on in each department, and what chairs can be trusted and which can't, and she can use that to her advantage. It's hard to imagine how that could work out at a place that was sort of monster size.

Central Administrator:

> I think there's an enormous advantage for this kind of process for Shelton in our size, and the fact that we are basically a liberal arts university. It means that when we sit down around a table, students and faculty in particular, when we start talking about our university, we're talking about the same university. We're talking about what is the university trying to accomplish. We start out with similar assumptions about what the university ought to be trying to accomplish.

If you tried to do that at Harvard University, and you put the Dean of or a faculty member from the Business School, the Law School, Arts and Sciences, the Divinity School together in a room, and say, 'What are we trying to accomplish?' you'd get at least four and maybe eight or sixteen different answers. Establishing priorities when you don't share the same assumptions or the same objectives is impossible. Then it just becomes, who's going to outvote whom? Or who's going to feel sorry for whom? It's not going to be legitimate disagreements and coming together about the best ways to achieve objectives. It's going to be battles over whose objectives are more important.

So we're not exactly like anyone. We're more homogenous than anybody . . . I think it's the homogeneity that's almost more important than the scale. [Homogeneity] in terms of our fundamental academic issues. Educational issues. The fact that we're fundamentally an Arts and Sciences institution. That's what I mean by homogeneity. . . We don't have a Business School, Medical School, and so on. We've got Engineering. . . You can judge for yourself, but my sense is it's much more like a division of a university of Arts and Sciences than a separate school. There's a lot of overlap in student traffic. There's a lot of overlap in terms of faculty collaboration between engineers and people in sciences or even in the social sciences. So it's not a separate engineering school doing professional engineering training; it's a set of disciplines within a liberal arts institution and we produce very competent technical people and engineers, but they also produce competent economists and classicists. Shelton has consistently chosen to focus itself on Arts and Sciences, and do those really well.

Central administrator:

I've seen budgeting committees or priorities committees that have failed at other places; part of it may be that Shelton is of the right size and it's homogeneous enough to make this work in a way that Harvard, for example, wouldn't be. We don't have the professional schools, [and we are] basically an Arts and Sciences university.

Also . . . there isn't a separate process by which the Provost or any group of us sit down and say, 'This is what the budget ought to be,' and then we let this committee go on and produce its recommendations and we see if they're even close together. We basically do our budgeting in that room, with the students and faculty. And so they say, 'We think something's important,' we go in and argue with the committee about that, and we generally win most of those arguments. Hopefully, it's because our arguments are good ones, and persuasive.

On the other hand, could the process work somewhere else? According to one senior administrator, the answer is yes.

But I don't see any reason why [a similar budget process] couldn't work at a place that is larger. I've seen it work. We had it working very well the years I was president of [a large, public research university]. . . . I then became Provost and used it with the President the whole time I was Provost and the whole time I was President. So it was, give or take some nuances here, similar. The differences were, at a place like that, with tens of thousands of students and so on, you were making decisions at a much more macro level. That is, you were allocating not to Natural Science versus something else, you were allocating to the colleges, that is to the Arts and Sciences college, or the Engineering school or the Medical school. The level at which you were discussing things was dealing with larger items . . .

For instance, I've just received the tentative report of the Priorities Committee, and it deals with something that turned out to be a small allocation to the Dean of the Colleges office to strengthen the administration of our freshman seminar program. . . At [a large public university], you would never get down to a decision like this; there are just too many such decisions. So when you really have a large complex university like that, you really have to think of it almost as a confederation of a few different universities . . . but the principles are the same. The principles are really very much the same. The main decisions you make, the huge macro decisions you make, like what is the salary program, and what is the tuition going to be - those big decisions have to be made no matter how big or small you are. So I see no reason why it couldn't work at a big place.

CONCLUSION

Shelton has no plans to dramatically alter the resource allocation system that has apparently served the University so well for over two decades. One important change, however, is that the Priorities Committee appears to be considering a longer-range planning horizon in setting future priorities. The 1995-1996 Priorities Committee Report notes that "budgeting decisions should be made in the context of the long-term needs and resources of the University rather than by focusing on a single budget year." While acknowledging the difficulties of making long-term budgetary projections, the Report reinforces their importance:

> It was the sense of the Committee that they wished to include, therefore, in this report—in addition to the specific recommendations for tuition, salaries, and other allocations which appear below-several recommendations for targeted study of issues which, in their view, will remain very significant to the University's future priority-setting and which call for a more thorough, more broadly, or simply more current analysis than was available for this Committee's consideration.
>
> One theme that surfaced several times in the Committee's deliberations this year was the need to balance short-term financial decision-making

Shelton University

(which, most agree, is successfully address by the Priorities Committee process) with longer-range financial planning and priority-setting.

The Report goes on to note that the University's processes for longer-range financial planning and priority-setting "seems less fully articulated," adding that "the need for such long-range planning is well indicated." Consequently,

> The consensus of this Committee is that one contribution they can make toward longer-range planning is to identify particular areas or topics which seem, on the basis of what the Committee has learned in the course of its meeting thus far, to merit further study. This further work can assist University decisions-makers in the future to establish priorities and set both goals and limits.

In its consideration of the "long-term financial health of the University," the Committee examined cost-cutting as well as revenue-generating possibilities. Noting that the University has not traditionally had "open discussion on some sources of revenue," the Committee felt it might be helpful to review the experience and practice of peer institutions in this area. With regard to savings, the Committee urged against "across the board" cuts, noting that

> it is unlikely that across the board efforts will prove the most effective or desirable means of instituting reductions. Rather, the immediate measures taken this year to address the deficit have the benefit of providing the time and opportunity for more focused and selective decisions in the future, concerning both those aspects of the University that are as lean as possible and areas in which some further reduction could be achieved without seriously jeopardizing the University's central missions. In addition, future re-assessments of the University's budget will need to adopt a broad, institution-wide perspective, seeking the most effective ways to accomplish operations and deliver services which reach across the institution, spanning traditional divisions of accountability.

The Committee concludes by noting the opportunities which financial constraints may stimulate:

> The prospect of constrained financial circumstances may actually present the University with the opportunity for a wider view of its mission and of its structures . . . By recommending that a number of questions raised in this fall's deliberations be studied at a depth that is simply not possible for the Committee over the course of one semester, we hope to foster continuity in the consideration of issues with long-term financial implications and thus to strengthen a consultative process which has served the

University community very well, as we move into a period in which long-term strategic planning may need to take its place as a full partner with more immediate, shorter-term priority-setting.

In addition to reviewing budget projections four years into the future, the Committee also urges that the University develop a more strategic approach to long-term planning:

> The Committee believes that a number of options should be pursued in coping with these projections. First, there must be a dedicated effort to ensure that each unit achieves the base cut targets which have already been announced. While in such efforts there always needs to some leeway to deal with factors absolutely beyond the control the University, keeping the variances to an absolute minimum will help diminish the deficits as now projected. Second, some of the longer-term strategies for both expense reduction and income generation which were alluded to in the beginning of the report must be discussed and studied. Finally, we can hope for greater success from the Campaign, particularly in targeting funds to support the growing burden of the financial aid programs on operating funds. To these ends, the Committee has agreed to meet several more times during the spring to address the first two of these areas in more detail.

At the conclusion of the case, it was not yet clear how the Priorities Committee would integrate the long-range planning efforts described in these quotations with the annual operating budget process. It seems likely that time constraints would likely be an issue, as the main task of the Committee is the formation of the annual operating budget, an objective for which the Committee has but a few months to complete. Long-range planning would presumably also demand a more sophisticated understanding of University priorities and financial planning.

6
Greenway University

INTRODUCTION

Greenway University offers undergraduate and graduate degrees in the arts and sciences, as well as professional degrees in law, medicine, dentistry and business. Though its professional schools are highly ranked, its graduate programs in the arts and sciences are generally solid, but with a few exceptions, not among the nation's leading academic departments. Its undergraduate program has becoming increasingly more selective in the last ten years.

Greenway University uses a decentralized resource allocation process in which funds are allocated in blocks to the major academic units. Although the University central administration does not generally monitor individual line items of schools, academic departments, and organized research units, resource allocation policy is for the most part centrally determined and administered. Since the mid-1980s, the allocation process has been characterized by two other features: the leadership of an active and involved president, and a program review process in which every major academic and administrative unit is examined and evaluated on a regular cycle.

To understand the reasons why Greenway adopted its present system of resource allocation and program review, it is helpful to understand the past. From about 1976, until about 1985, the University's financial condition was precarious at best. The University routinely operated in a deficit, and the president at the time was apparently unable to instill a sense of fiscal discipline or engage in appropriate institutional planning. According to one administrator:

> I don't think there was good internal discipline, principally on the academic side, about how people were going to live within their budgets. We had a couple of renegade Deans who basically just said, 'Well, I don't care what your planning process says, this is how much I need to spend in the

name of greater glory for my school.' The President and the Provost at that point in time didn't shut them down.

There was no meaningful sanction—and no one was willing to say, 'Fine, Dean So-and-So, if you're going to do that, then you're gone.'

The situation became so acute that the governing board was finally forced to intervene and terminate at least one dean. The board was critical of the president's lax fiscal management and could not understand why the University continued to run a deficit year after year and or why buildings were not being maintained on a current basis. In recalling the situation, an administrator felt that "the University had lost its way. I think that people felt like it wasn't achieving excellence in any particular way; I think that the leadership was tired and the finances had started to get out of control."

When economist Jack Goodman become President in 1986, his first task was to close the budget deficit and improve the University's financial condition. In the system that evolved under Goodman's leadership, University revenues—including tuition, indirect recoveries, and endowment earnings—are pooled and then allocated to the ten schools by the central administration. Thus, the University does not delegate responsibility for revenues and expenditures to individual academic units. The one exception is the Business school, which has a revenue-sharing contract whereby 70% of the school's revenue goes to the school, and the remaining 30% to the center.

The allocation process for the other nine schools is relatively structured. A central budget team, consisting of the President, the Provost, the Vice President for Research, the Vice President for Business, the Budget Director, and the Associate Provost, is the permanent standing committee responsible for making all University-wide resource allocation decisions. The Provost is designated the official chair of the committee.

Prior to the beginning of the budget process, the central academic administration compiles and reviews an annual faculty hiring plan. The faculty hiring plan summarizes recent faculty hiring activity by school, as well as projected faculty hires. The hiring plan allows central administrators to identify openings by various ranks, and the budgetary implications of these projections. Similar central controls do not exist on the staff side, as one central administrator states:

> So over the last decade, the faculty members haven't grown a lot—we've managed it through that process—but where we have not had any significant overall management discipline is on the staff side. Our staff numbers keep going up, particularly at the School level; centrally they haven't grown significantly but they have at the School level.

At the outset of the budget process, the central budget team meets to review, on a macro-level, the estimated total resources available for allocation. The university budget office examines various economic gross measures, and evaluates the university's comparative position on tuition and faculty salary. In the process of making its allocations, the central budget committee reviews the relative economic standings of each school by looking at the gross margins based on direct revenues and expenses, before the allocation of central subsidies, including credit for attributed tuition. According to a senior university administrator, Greenway has conducted a cost allocation study for about 25 years:

> We basically take all of the revenues and all of the expenses and we allocate them back to the Schools and to the Research Centers, and we basically then come up with a fully loaded revenue and expense allocation. It assumes that the primary reason for the university is to support these ten schools plus the research centers, so if you take all of the support costs, the President's office and [all other shared central administrative expenses] and allocate them back—and then you allocate the revenues back to how they're earned by those centers—how would they look? We don't do it at the department level; we do it at the School level. We use that each year to help guide—it's not a rigorous guide but we keep an eye on it. . . . We have some that are significant contributors, and then we have some that are benefactors. We try to move the benefactors more closely to being on an equilibrium, but in some cases we're not making much progress.

Every year, the central administration looks at the distribution of gross margins. "We look at that on an annual basis, and so we're always asking, 'Are we happy with the relative balance?'" reflects one administrator. At times, the central administration has worked with various individual schools, to change the degrees of subsidization and contribution suggested by the gross margins. One central administrator cites the following examples:

> [One of the professional schools] has had a negative gross margin, so we've been working on them. [Another professional school] is one we've urged to be more aggressive. There are some professional graduate programs that they've mounted because the market [in this area] is very healthy and we have a good reputation and so they've grown those programs. The other side that has really helped the school is that under the new Dean, who is in his second or third year, he's much more research-oriented. [The school] basically did no research, very little research, and he has brought them into the research enterprise, and that's going to help quite significantly because of the indirect cost recoveries associated. But then there are other areas where we've been frustrated. [Another school] has been a negative contributor for years, and no matter what we do, it doesn't seem to get any better. It's always the same.

In some cases, the budget committee will not grant special budget requests to certain schools "because we already subsidize this particular school for quite a significant amount." Thus, in making resource allocation decisions, the central administration and budget committee does take into account the economies of the various units, including their ability to raise resources through tuition or other sources, in making resource allocation decisions.

Nevertheless, the central administration does seem to accept the fact that different units have different operating economies, and not all can operate at a surplus. As one administrator states,

> I think we accept that . . . their production functions are radically different. You're in the business school, they're doing largely master's education, the classes are relatively uniform; you're not doing a lot of specialized doctoral education—that's one form of a production function. Another would be in the sciences where you don't have big undergraduate enrollment, and therefore it always costs more . . . or music, [and] performing arts; our music school is very much music performance as opposed music theory, and so it is a very expensive form of education to offer, but we expect that. That's what we are—a very exquisite music performance school. It's inherent in that, and we accept that. Similarly, our theater department is not going to be a money producer, and we accept that.

This administrator adds that "whereas other [universities] have the expectation that every unit ought to be sort of in line with business in the profit making sense, I really think that's misguided." Instead, they recognize that "some are money producers and some are money consumers. That's accepted."

In addition to studying the gross margins of the various schools, the central administration performs other kinds of comparative analysis:

> We do a lot of other ratio analysis. We look at research productivity of faculty across the schools, at least the ones that are players. I mean, it doesn't make much sense to look at journalism because they do very little research. But for the College, the Medical School, Engineering, and Education . . . we keep an eye on those ratios. Then we do an instructional workload analysis, using what we call course registrations, and again, we do that for the undergraduate schools too, and that basically demonstrates what kind of instructional workload each of the school faculty are handling, and we've been doing that over time.

The administration also prepares an annual "fact book," which is shared with the academic deans. It contains various statistics, tabulated by school, including faculty counts, various ranks, tenure/non-tenure, by ethnic group, men/women, the salary data again by school. It also includes information on student enrollments, including graduate, undergraduate, admissions data, statistics on students, SAT's, and graduation rates, and tables on the finances. The book also contains some comparative financial information as well as a roll-up for the entire university.

Deans, through their administrative officers, submit requests for funding to the central budget committee. For the most part, the system is incremental. The exception to the rule are those cases where a unit gets into financial difficulty. "Then we go back and we go right down to the zero and review the whole financial structure," reports a central administrator, which was necessary in the case of professional school that ran into trouble a few years ago.

Following a preliminary review, the detailed funding plans are submitted. During this process, the Dean, Provost, the President and their analytical support staff meet to discuss funding plans. According to one central administrator:

> I've heard it's a tense interchange. Various kinds of challenges are made towards these budgets. 'You really don't need this many people over here,' or 'You really don't need to be spending more money. [The President] was a very aggressive budget maker, very interested in details.

The central budget committee then meets and decides which proposals it will fund, and final allocations are made. Historically, schools have received an increment that was essentially based on the macro-economic price level, plus any special requests that are funded. The budget team makes preliminary estimates about the amount of money left over for "special allocations." Special allocations are the incremental requests for resources which units are permitted to submit. Special budget requests, as they are known, are considered by the central budget committee.

Special budget requests are requests for one-time or recurring funds that are not part of a school's current regular budget. A special budget request might, for example, support a new faculty line, a capital expenditure for equipment, or a new facility. The criteria for awarding a special budget request are somewhat murky, as the following comments from central administrators and deans suggests:

Central administrator:

> [Special budget requests] vary widely by their very nature, so there's not really a general statement, other than obviously you want to prove the educational mission as much as you can with the given amount of money. The emergencies come first. If there's a roof leaking or a statue deterio-

rating, those are higher priority. Then perishable opportunities—things that if you don't act this year, they're gone.

Central administrator:

Apparently, the requests are rank-ordered eventually in the Central Administration, and they're addressed in some sort of a way. Once each Dean makes such requests, it disappears, and later on in the spring the Deans are informed which of their requests, if any, are going to be funded. My presumption is they're funded only to such a level that the President and the Provost feel there are new funds available, or that they can drop three bassoonists from the School of Music and squeeze a little extra money out and get a new economist.

Dean:

The process has been to tell you which ones were granted, and no comment on any others . . . we send [the requests] over there, and some months later we get something back, these things are funded. No mention of anything else.

Comments from central administrators suggest that the special budget requests are not used as strategically they could be by the central administration:

Under Goodman, we had grown into the habit of not being very discriminating on those special budget requests. In some cases, we had a strategic objective that we were trying to address. It sort of depended on the school, and the Dean in that school and its leadership; in some cases we had some pretty definitive plans that required multiple-year investment, so we'd guide the annual allocations on that strategic objective, and at the end of three or four years we achieved it—we mapped out a target and we'd accomplished it. For example, in the College of Arts and Sciences, he'd identified some initiatives where we basically made the contributions over a period of time and achieved that particular objective. That process that we've done over the last decade has some major hazards, because it does not do anything with respect to the question of how well your base resources allocated—it assumes that everything is optimally allocated, and that isn't necessarily so.

The remainder of the budget—the bulk of the following year's budget—is allocated fairly incrementally—which one central business manager calls "a flaw in the system." Another administrator adds:

> We have tended to be more incremental, so I think that says perhaps we're not as happy with the way resources have been distributed. I think we have concentrated more at the margin, and now we're asking ourselves, should we do some more fundamental analysis of looking at the base budgets, whereas we've tended to make the differential allocations right at the margin.

In the last ten years, there have been two or three attempts to force units to look a little more closely at their base budget through cost containment initiatives:

> A couple of years ago, we asked all units to come up with a two percent reduction plan, for just the non-personnel side of the operations, we asked them to put a two percent plan together—how they would live with two percent less, and then we in fact took some significant dollars out of the base budget—I think it was about $2.7 million in round numbers—just out of the non-personnel budget. Essentially, the central administration asked the schools to remove a small percentage from their base budgets.

In many respects, the resource allocation process is not very open. In fact, one central administrator freely admits that "our budget process is more secretive" than other institutions. Though there is a university fact book which contains information about the schools, there is no budget book for public consumption, no open meetings, and faculty do not serve on the budget committee. As one former Greenway administrator remembers:

> We used to joke at Greenway that we're a highly decentralized university except for the budget. We did maintain a great deal of central control over the budget, which allowed us to be fairly fleet of foot in reallocating, in changing cultures to do things differently, if we wanted to go into a restructuring effort of some sort it was much more easily orchestrated centrally. It gives capacity to minimize redundancy of function; we could decide what functions were best pushed down to the school level, what functions were most effectively maintained centrally, and so on. I just feel it gives you more flexibility.

The centralization does not, however, extend to the line-item level within schools. Once resources are allocated, the central administration does not rigidly monitor expenditures in the schools and departments, though some effort is made to make sure that schools live within their means. For the most part, schools spend money as they wish. One administrator sums up the allocation process: "Greenway is relatively centralized compared to many other institutions in terms of the allocations process, however, I consider us decentralized once the moneys have been allocated." According to one central business officer:

> We basically make sure they stay within their allocation money. When we make the allocations to a school, and they send us back their detailed departmental budgets and we just check the bottom line that they're working in that total. There are a lot of degrees of freedom on how they can move those resources around. They exercise that, and some of them do a real good job of moving resources around, and others never make changes. It just depends on the nature of the Dean.

The University has an integrated budgeting and accounting general ledger system that produces monthly reports which are delivered to individual managers in a department or center. Although the University's financial system could theoretically be used to block expenditures that create an overdraft in a certain line item, the system will allow a school to exceed a budgeted line item. One administrator states the rationale for this policy:

> So the system doesn't lock people out completely. We debated that when we first put the system in as to how tight we wanted to control people. I think this method has worked all right. We haven't really ever had to put [a hold] anybody . . . Although it is nice to have the option to say, 'Well if you really have been a bad actor and you just can't seem to get it together, we'll just slam the brakes and we can lock you out and nothing can get processed once you hit your budget limit.'

A major reason they decided against more direct control is that in many cases, direct control would mean that someone would not be paid. Once the moneys are allocated, the central budget committee has a bi-monthly budget meeting to examine where each unit stands relative to its budget. One administrator explains that if "problems are indicated, the Provost or other central administrator will sit down with the Dean to discuss the action and devise an appropriate plan." By the end of the year, the department or school must resolve any budget overdrafts. An administrator states that "The onus is on the school-level administrators and the academic side for all of their units to make sure that they are within bounds."

As this discussion may suggest, the planning and budget process is fairly structured and predictable. The process has been in place long enough that the deans are aware of the routine, whether or not they feel they receive the resources they need. A central administrator states:

> I think they understand the process, and people have incorporated the fundamentals of the process into their own planning cycles, and I think because it's been predictable and well managed for the most part, I think they feel like it's not like you don't get your opportunities. Everyone is

conditioned now to know what the drill is, so you know what you have to do in order to get your case made. That's important in these processes; people need to know that the processes are consistent and predictable and on time, and that you may not like the outcome but you can't say, 'Gee, speech got treated differently than music.'

GOODMAN'S LEADERSHIP

The previous section outlined the principle features of Greenery's resource allocation system. It is difficult, however, to separate the system from its champion and leader for most of the late decade, Jack Goodman. As one administrator summarizes, "You have to understand, Goodman was such a personal focus of this whole [process]." Unlike his predecessor, who "ran the university in a sort of wide open style in which the faculty were invited to participate fully in the budgetary process," Goodman centralized budget *authority* and made it clear that he—not the deans, and not the faculty—was in charge. At the outset, according to one administrator, Goodman promised to take swift action: "I'm going to grab a hold of this situation, I'm going to be in these meetings, and I'm going to make it clear that people understand!"

And he did. Goodman made it is his personal business to master the details of the University *and* the University budget. He wanted to understand how resources were being expended. Faculty and staff descriptions of Goodman's leadership style are remarkably consistent. They characterize Goodman as "a very strong personality," "an omnipresent person," "a tough guy," and someone who "made decisions [and] expected them to be carried out." He ran "a tight ship," he wasn't afraid to ask difficult questions or state his views categorically, and he "said no to a lot of people and irritated a lot of people." A trustee states that Goodman was "centrist in terms of his orientation." When asked to describe Greenway's resource allocation system, one dean bluntly states: "It's heavily centralized. With Goodman it was highly centralized in one person." One chair states, "He wanted to know the details of everything. You know, 'You don't need two economists that do international banking. One is enough.'" One dean recalls:

> [Goodman] wanted to know everything, and the more you told him, the happier he was. Of course, the tendency was to try to tell him as little as you could, because you didn't want to be micro-managed all the time. So in terms of financial matters, the previous management did really well... And he'd ask you questions, and sometimes you would say, 'Leave me alone, Jack. If you want to be the Dean, you be the Dean.' But basically it was just a close watching of everything.

Although the Provost is officially the chair of the university budget committee, Goodman is said to have been "very much involved with most budget decisions, major ones" during his tenure as President. One central administrator states:

> even if he didn't chair [the budget meetings], he was the Chair of them. He was his own best Provost. I think he would tell you . . . that the Provost was the Chair of the committee. I think no one believed that as a real practical matter, but I think in the last half of President Goodman's tenure there were many budget allocation meetings principally on the academic side that he did delegate to the Provost. Only appeals were really brought to his attention, or if he knew of a particular issue that he wanted to be involved in from the beginning . . .

Faculty were not very involved in the budget allocation process. According to one department chair:

> My impression is that whenever the faculty asked questions about how the resources were being allocated and why a decision was made or how a decision was going to be made, Goodman had his homework done. I mean, he was a man who was in command of the facts and figures.

Deans who "disobeyed" and who ran a deficit would be invited to the President's chambers for a personal conference. Administrators' accounts of this event are remarkably similar:

> President Goodman had a lot of what I would call stratagems. One of them was a private interview with the head of any unit that ran an operating deficit. This was an interview that you never wanted to have. It's not good. It's like taking a shower with a wire brush. He wants to know very specifically why the expenses are out of control, and he had a penchant for detail. He could run by the details, and the dean or the department head wouldn't be able to stay with him.

> Usually you would hear that in any one budget cycle, there would be two or three people who would get taken to the woodshed in their budget planning session, just for the sake of show . . . In some cases, they deserved it, and in some cases, they didn't, and it would come out of the blue, and you just wouldn't know. . . But it was the performance effect of saying, 'I'm going to make you sweat here for an hour and a half,' and by God, you got the message. 'This is what's going to happen.'

> And the sanction for negative performance is that negative things get brought to the President's attention. You didn't spend within his budget.

Then typically, there is a conversation between the President and the Dean if that has happened.

One of Goodman's other classic "stratagems" was something called the "constructive bribe" When approached by a dean for resources, he would normally agree to fund no more than one third the proposal. One third was to come from the school's current resources, and the remaining third was to be raised by the dean:

> And then he would believe that you would really then be tested; do you really believe in this program or don't you? He never gave a hundred percent of anything, and he never gave anything to the administrative side. He just never, never, never believed that administration needed anything.

Goodman's personal involvement in the resource allocation process was especially apparent during the first four or five budget cycles of his administration when he was trying to "get all of the behaviors in line with what he thought they should be." Subsequently, according to the same administrator, he wasn't quite as involved. Instead, one administrator states that he "just focused on the people who needed a little more help and understanding. It probably is just his personality. That's what he loved. He would cast it as academic priority setting."

Some faculty were critical of Goodman's style and believed that "decisions within the University were made as though the University were a business rather than an institution which ought to be interested in humanities and things that didn't have bottom-line significance." Indeed, Goodman's perspective is said to have been "very much a bottom-line oriented, unit-specific accounting procedure. " Even his critics commend Goodman for straightening out the university's finances. He is universally described as "a good fiscal manager" who turned around university finances and brought much needed discipline to the resource allocation process. His most ardent supporters describe him as "one of the really spectacular university managers in the business." They point to the institution's financial stability under Goodman's leadership:

> We've had very good discipline among the schools and units in not overrunning budgets, so there's a sanctity to the budget, and the expectation that once the budget is set, a unit cannot run over that budget and if they do they're liable for it. That was a change in the last ten years.

The other quality that distinguished Goodman's leadership was his firm belief in planning. In contrast to his predecessor, who did not believe in long-term planning, Goodman required a business plan before undertaking any new venture. One central administrator states:

I have never known him to go forward with any new undertaking for which there was not a business plan and a pro forma forecast of revenues and expenditures associated with the opportunity. He simply insisted on it. Academic as well as administrative. And sometimes those investments would not yield a return, and that was okay, but he wanted to know how much it was going to cost him, not just in the instant financial period, but over the long haul.

Equally important, Goodman institutionalized a University-wide program review and planning process that will be described in detail in the next section of this chapter.

PROGRAM REVIEW PROCESS

From the beginning, one of the main functions of the program review process has been to gather facts and figures "because [the previous president's] administration had not generated a very big data base, a very complete comprehensive data base on the structure of the University." According to one central administrator, program review is "intended to look at each of the major academic and programmatic areas of the university in a very systematic way—a very hard-nosed way." The program review office is coordinated by the central planning office and is a major responsibility of the Vice President for Planning. Though conducted once every seven years, a central administrator emphasizes that program review is "a continuous conversation; it's not an episodic one-time event."

For purposes of the review, the university is divided into 105 units. Units include administrative units as well as schools, departments, and organized research units. Every unit is on a seven or eight year cycle, after which a new cycle begins. Typically, three members of each department take responsibility for the self-analysis, a process which normally extends over a six month period. Afterward, an internal committee of faculty and staff will examine the departments' reports, and come up with their own findings and recommendation. Then, the University invites visitors from outside who have parallel experience in other academic institutions. The external team reviews the self-study and the internal committee's work, and conducts its own study. The sum of these three products is evaluated and integrated by a program review oversight committee into a final product that is given to the subject unit. At this stage, the unit under review is obligated to develop an action plan which responds to the program review and puts in place a series of commitments describing how the department will address the weaknesses identified in the program review. A final report is made to the president.

The program review process is universally praised by faculty and administrators, both central and school, as the following comments illustrate:

Greenway University 139

Department chair:

My view of it is that it has been good for the University, that it has helped us to understand where resources can be more efficiently used and that it. . . really has affected the way in which resources have been allocated within the university. You know, the Goodman administration had the view that the way you improve a place like Greenway, which basically came from mediocrity in the '50s up to pretty good stature by the early '80s and just continued to elevate. The way you improve is by devoting the resources to the better areas largely and making them stellar and then just prune out to the extent you can the operations you really don't need.

Central business officer:

Over time, and I've read a number of these program reviews and have been struck by the candidness with which they really do talk about the issues associated with either the problems or the opportunities or the general state of the departments that are being reviewed.

Department chair:

I think it's terribly critical. I think that our best institutions boldly challenge themselves to see how good they are, and if you take the time to develop and really put effort into the program review process, you engage the faculty to participate, you identify world-class external reviewers . . . [then], if you're told that you're dog meat, well, then you're dog meat. Accept it. If, however, you hear that in fact you're doing well, then that's good too. I think that if it's done properly, a good administration knows what to do with this information . . .

Planning officer:

We go area by area and look at the quality—the strengths and weaknesses—of each of our units, and what the needs are, and laying out an agenda for change unit by unit, which we obviously think is critical, because in a university, things happen in these departments and research centers, and if you don't get to the decision making at that level, then you're really . . . that's where the action happens. By having this process of program review, it creates an information base among all the major actors in terms of what our strengths, weaknesses, needs, and directions are and/or should be.

Former central administrator:

Program review is extraordinarily important for departments getting to understand themselves, for administrators getting to know the departments, for having faculty from other departments getting to know and feel invested in departments they never paid attention to before. It's a very important quality control mechanism.

> [Program review] has credibility with the entire community.

Program review is now in its second seven-year cycle. After reviewing every department in the University, the central planning office engaged in a one-year review of the planning process itself.

What is the impact of program review? According to administrators, after a program review has been completed, the central administration either recommends that the department continue in the same direction, perhaps taking advantage of some special opportunity, or the administration requires major changes. In some cases, for example, a review may suggest targeted investments which may bring a department to a new level of excellence. According to one department chair:

> My sense is that they [the central administration] are not using it as a way to go to the lowest common denominator or to even necessarily take the lowest units and bring them up to the best. You can't, at any university. You can't have every department the best. So they use it for selective enhancement.

This chair's department, in fact, received over four million dollars within months of an external review which the chairman states made "some very positive statements about what direction our department is going."

At the other end of the spectrum, the results of a program review may call for a major improvement program or restructuring. For example, administrators tell the story of one professional school that had fallen on hard times.

> About five years ago, [one of the professional schools] was in deep trouble. Its enrollments were falling, its costs were rising, it was experiencing deficits in the four-five million dollar range. So we basically went in and restructured the program. We cut the size of the program in half over a three-year program, so the total enrollment went down by half, the faculty went down by half, and we restructured the departments—they had something like eight or nine different departments and they now have three; and we financed a major breakthrough . . . The feeling was if we didn't do that, we would not be able to attract and retain the highest caliber professors in the country. I think it's going to be very successful, but we took a very big risk, so not only did we reduce the size and restructured and re-engineered the school, but we've made a major investment in

Greenway University

its future, and I think that will be very successful—lit looks as though it's going to be very successful but . . . it'll take us three or four years to figure that out.

In rare relatively rare circumstances, the recommendations from a program review have resulted in the elimination of a department or program. For example, when program review suggested that ecology and evolutionary biology suggested that the program was not viable due to its small size, and its Ph.D. program was not very successful, the department was phased out. One of the health sciences schools was also eliminated a few years ago when the University central administration decided after a review that "That thing will never support itself."

The program review process was the linchpin of the planning process under Goodman. Though other aspects of the academic planning process were relatively centralized, the program review system had its roots in the academic departments and faculty. A former senior central academic administrator feels that program review:

> . . . brings the faculty into the process in an interesting way. It was probably the single greatest strength of the Greenway system, where when a set of recommendations finally comes about, it can be as dire as suggesting closure. You don't have to go back and touch base with the faculty. They controlled the process that generated the recommendation, so when it hits your desk, you're ready to move immediately to an action plan.

Program review signaled the central administration's commitment to quality. In reflecting on the process, one administrator had the following comments:

> I think [the President] was trying to set a tone and indicate a future direction. . . . I think that he was instrumental in his tenure in really improving the quality of the place, and it was a general statement to that effect, but it wasn't an operational plan. It was not a multi-year operational, financial and programmatic and academic plan, per se, because it didn't have the resource potential that would otherwise have needed to have if he was really going to do that. And such things are dangerous, if you really do that in a highly explicit way. So it was more of an implicit document, a tacit document, than it was an explicit document. There are good reasons for that. There aren't many universities, if any, who have what I'm referring to as a more explicit resource-related five year future strategic plan. And the reason for that is because in order to do that, you have to make choices. And if you make choices, some will not be among the chosen, and those who will not be among the chosen will find it unacceptable; so you will have crafted, potentially, a political embarrassment.

... So we did have a framework for excellence, we did have a clear direction, and we had a way of informing ourselves under the Goodman regime—and still do. We retained this way of determining of whether or not we were in fact achieving quality. It's called program review.

Some administrators seem to consider the incremental, iterative nature of the program review process as a weakness in the absence of more global strategic planning. One central administrator states that

> It's a program review for this department, recommendations for that department. We don't see any overriding set of priorities. Up to now, we have always been left to guess as to what their priorities are. I would think the strongest system would have more exchanging of information so they would tell us periodically what their priorities were and we could tell them what our priorities are, and where there's a mismatch then there has to be some compromise. It would seem at our level we should have a better perception of the university priorities than we do.

The other weakness cited is the lack of explicit connection between resources and program review. One administrator states: "It does not simultaneously examine the resource issues or economic issues or constraints that are brought to bear on a given unit. That is one of the fundamental weaknesses in the process." Another administrator concurs with this view:

> It [program review] is not connected to the resource allocation process system. It is used as a tool, a piece of data—a very important data, highly credible in certain respects and it's used as the piece of information to say, 'Joan, your review didn't turn out that well, and you are coming in with this budget request when the review said you shouldn't be doing that.'

Others, however, believe that the connection between program review and resource allocation, though subtle and indirect, is clearly apparent. A business officer reports there is

> a very heavy spin-off into the resource allocation process, because all of the people who sit and advise the President in an informal budget review ... are knowledgeable about program review and its results, so the feedback from program review in the resource allocation process is very strong. And you could, if you were a mouse in the corner and you had your tape recorder with you, you could see the impact of program review on resource allocation. It's never been chronicled, but it's a true fact.

It may be that program review doesn't have much of an impact in those cases where a department or unit is not identified as falling at either end of the spectrum—that is, close to extinction or ripe for investment.

Nevertheless, this same business officer emphatically states that program review is not a panacea. In his experience:

> I have never seen program review actually be the seminal affair that leads to that leap that takes you from very good to distinguished. I've been involved in bringing departments to distinction, and when I look at the ones we did, it never was because of program review. It was because of other events that may have occurred, [such as] targets of opportunity.
>
> You have to be careful not to become a program review fundamentalist. When you let it substitute for the more entrepreneurial and innovative ways of now moving a department forward, you're really taking that leap . . . I think you sort of doom yourself to a linear growth.

It should be noted that the program review process also encompasses reviews of central administrative units. The effectiveness of the administrative reviews is unclear. It may be more difficult to conduct reviews of administrative operations. One administrator speculates that

> the reason it works better on the academic unit is because when we invite people to come and examine how well the academic units are doing, they already know before they get here, because they review the refereed journals. They know the quality of the faculty, because that's a much more public fact. It's a public fact because a lot of it is hooked to refereed journal publication. The quality of scholarship is more widely known, but the internal operations of the administrative units are not widely known.

FUTURE SYSTEM

At the time this case study was under development, Jack Goodman had just left the Presidency, and a new President and Provost had been named. Goodman will remain—as Chancellor of Greenway—but he will be much less involved in the day-to-day affairs of the University. " Though one administrator notes that "There is a whole series of agenda items we have to go through," and adds that the new president "has yet to lay down an agenda, " interviews with current administrators suggest several new directions for Greenway.

First, there will likely be less emphasis on incremental resource allocation as the following comments suggest:

Central administrator:

> We've come to the conclusion that we're too geared toward very margin-

al incremental budgeting, and we're going to try to refocus the process to making more strategic investments and preserving the incremental resources. Outside the necessity of addressing the annual faculty and staff salary increases, we're going to try to focus our marginal incremental resources on strategic plans and strategic productions, so we're trying to shift our annual allocation process to supporting things that are multi-year and are associated with moving towards some kind of a strategic goal.

Central administrator:

We've been changing that this year to try to get less of this sort of looking only at the margin of what their requests are and looking at the broader base, and asking them more fundamentally about what it is they're trying to achieve at their school, and how that relates to the budget.

School administrator:

The new President has made it clear that he wants to focus on some really big institutional initiatives for excellence. We just got new instructions for this year's resource allocation, where they're trying to unbundle that process and say, 'All right, let's take a look; five years—what do you think you will need in your area . . . what would be your strategic plan and objectives?'

Central administrator:

We look at what their special requests are, and then talk pretty generally about what they're doing. We've been changing that this year to try to get less of this sort of looking only at the margin of what their requests are and looking at the broader base, and asking them more fundamentally about what it is they're trying to achieve at their school, and how that relates to the budget.

Central administrator:

So we're going to talk about priorities and plans for the next five to ten years.

Central administrator:

The President . . . was actually hired by the trustees to sort of take Greenway to the next level of quality, and in order to do that, we really have to map out the strategic areas we're going to invest in over the next five to ten years. It will require a great deal of discipline to make sure we use our incremental resources to support those strategic initiatives. We're right now in the middle of a planning process that will help define what those strategic initiatives will be, and then that will be used to guide the budget allocation process.

The enhanced focus on longer-range priorities may be translated into several programmatic areas. While the University's professional schools are for the most part highly ranked, the University still needs to improve its core programs in the Arts and Sciences, many of which were not highly ranked in the recent ratings of the National Research Council. Under Goodman's leadership, several Greenway departments, in particular, Chemistry, Economics, and Sociology, made major strides in the national rankings. But many departments are still ranked less than 20th in the nation. "You'd like to see a lot more of them in the top ten," one administrator frankly admits. On a related issue, there is some feeling that graduate education needs attention. One central administrator states that

> Our graduate program needs a revolution, because it's very departmentally based and it's too large and it's not very good in major pockets. Our graduate students aren't particularly good. So what we have to do is take those resources back and redeploy them, and one of the ways that we think we need to redeploy them is to have more integrated graduate programs rather than departmentally-based programs.

More strategic allocation of resources may require that the University make even more difficult choices in the future, including, as this same administrator notes, examining base missions.

> You have to start from, what is our fundamental mission and what are our priorities? We have been successful in these last ten years, but we have never gone back and questioned base missions. We kind of just assumed that everybody thinks it's okay, then we kind of let that percolate from the level of the Deans of the academic side, which is fine. Very rarely in this process have we, in my experience, been more close to this in the last ten to twelve years . . . [but] have we ever institutionally said, 'We don't perform well in this particular area and your resource allocation is tied to our own determination of how you are going to perform well.'

Certain changes in the resource allocation process are likely to occur. First, the system is likely to be less centralized in the future. A central administrator states:

> Prior to this year, it was more centralized than it will be in the future. They're changing the supplemental budget request process. They're starting to decentralize larger sums of money to the Deans or other adminis-

trative heads that make decisions, but we will continue to monitor very closely, and will structure allocations to meet certain targets. But where possible, let's pass the decision making to the unit.

The system is likely to somewhat less adversarial and more open as following comments, one from a central administrator, the other from a dean suggest:

Central administrator:

> The one piece of feedback that we got from the latest round of feedback from the users, and the Dean's office in particular, is that they feel like it's turned into a little bit too much kind of a 'we-they.' they feel like the budget guys kind of give them a little bit of 'gotcha' analysis when they get into the meetings—the meetings are meant to, in the spirit of President Goodman, bring down the rationale for the request; that it's a little bit too much confrontational and not as much supportive and going in with a joint product that the school and the budget staff have jointly come to a conclusion, as opposed to having them do an analysis and a presentation and having the budget folks critique it, and then in the process try to poke holes in it. I think that was the main sense of it.

Dean:

> I think there's a sense schools are played off against each other. You're led to believe there's a pot of money that's divvied up into so many piles, and so you are competing with other schools. The process for the central administration has been rather confrontational. Until this year, we have never been invited over to talk about, informally, of our plans and our priorities.
>
> This year for the first time, the main budget person came over to talk about a lot of priorities, and they were interested in listening. They weren't confronting us. This is a mammoth change in attitudes, and it was certainly a step in the right direction. So this was a friendly, useful meeting. In other words, most of the 'our telling them' and they not providing us with many clues (and I don't think they know) as to what's going to happen.

Additionally, there is likely to be more money for university-wide and school priorities. "The previous administration just squeezed us very hard, and the result was that we became very financially stable," one dean explains. But now that the University has restored its financial health and has improved its academic standing, it may be time for the University to move forward. One dean feels that this new attitude may be translated into greater central spending: "Certainly, our impression is that we have a

President who is willing to spend, who expects to go out and raise some money to support our appetite."

Finally, there is likely to be much less of the President—both the old and the new. Goodman has remained as Chancellor, but, as noted, is now much less involved in the University:

> He seems to be less obtrusive . . . less visible in the day-to-day kinds of things. But I have a feeling that he spends a great deal of time in his office trying to understand the University . . . He's around the university, but he's certainly not intrusive.

As for the new President, one administrator states that "I think the trustees had in mind that this person wouldn't be involved in the nuts and bolts everyday running of the university." Responsibilities formally carried out by the President will likely be delegated to the Provost, one administrator believes:

> I think under [the new President] we might move to a more formally structured budget committee with the Provost as the Chair. I think [the new President] would like to have the Provost take over and I think most everybody supports the model that the Provost as the chief academic officer should be the one to make the principle resource allocation to the recommendations to the President, even for administrative areas, because administration should be supportive of academic ends and means. And so therefore the Provost should be the one who's bringing all those priorities together.

Despite the many changes going on at Greenway, there are no plans to move to a more decentralized resource allocation approach. "I think [the new President] is comfortable with the more centralized approach and is not advocating any major change in the way we manage our resources, so we'll probably continue with that kind of approach." The bottom-line is that the central administration likes the system and values its strengths. The following quotation from a central administrator captures this sense:

> The beauty of this highly centralized system is that you can make these [allocation] decisions, and they're not made by formula, or you don't have to go argue with deans to pull out the resources, because you've got the leverage. The levers, they're all central, and when you make a decision, or when you decide to do something, you can make it stick. The Provost and the President basically don't have to go beg for resources from the deans. They can say, 'These are the reasons we're doing it, and we're going to implement it.'

7
Garfield University

OVERVIEW

Garfield is also one of the oldest and most prestigious universities in the nation. In contrast to Shelton, Garfield offers a much wider portfolio of graduate and professional programs. Like Westmont, the University is known for its broad undergraduate liberal education. Many of its arts and sciences and engineering departments are highly ranked in the National Research Council ratings, though the University does not possess the all-around strength of Westmont or Garfield.

Over the last several years, Garfield University has adopted a substantially more decentralized resource allocation system. Historically, the university had used a relatively centralized system, whereby essentially all revenues came into the center and were subsequently allocated in block grants to each school using formulas that had been developed over time. The formulas were largely based on historical allocations with marginal increments, rather than a base budgeting review. One financial officer states that the formulas were driven by enrollment projections, and "some kind of baseline assessments in existing personnel levels," adding that the formulas did not revisit "intrinsic needs."

The deans were required to develop plans for how they would allocate these resources, which the Provost would review, critique, and suggest revisions. After the dean and Provost agreed upon the objectives, deans had considerable autonomy over how their allocated funds would be used.

Over time, the University became dissatisfied with this arrange-ment because, according to one senior academic officer, the system had "reverse incentives." He cites the example of a unit which grew its indirect cost recoveries substantially and received no apparent incremental returns. In fact, a certain portion of the indirect cost recoveries were credited to the originating school, but the transaction was not proportional to the revenue. Another central officer concurs with this view, stating that the system "tended very clearly to reduce the incentives of schools to take command and responsibility of their own operations, because no matter what, they would find themselves sharing the benefits of whatever revenues they brought in." Another university central administrator laments that "[t]here was just money disappearing out of every pore. There was no sense of accountability; there were disincentives for revenue generation, disincentives on fundraising . . ."

The logic underlying the central allocation system was never clear to the deans. A faculty leader notes that "it was never clear how much money there was available for what. The budgeting was never clear." Because costs and revenues were completely obscured, "some schools had a very strong sense that they were paying more than their share." For example, the central administration had historically charged the school of engineering a tax which supposedly represented a fair share of its "balance of trade"—coursework taken by engineering students in the faculty of arts and sciences in core disciplines such as mathematics and the sciences. However, since 1986, balance of trade adjustments have essentially been frozen—even though engineering enrollments have declined considerably. As a result the engineering school was paying more than its fair share of revenues in the form of taxes to the center.

One dean summarizes the problems with the resource allocation system:

> The budgetary and financial systems that we've had operating here have not permitted adequate transparency. In fact, the sources and uses of funds have not been clear enough to deans. I actually think that there are deans around here who do not mind at all 'subsidizing,' let's say, Arts and Sciences. But they don't like the idea of doing that and they don't know where the money is going and how it is being used. If they also feel it's not being well managed, they are very much concerned about it. Beyond that, they all have their own set of unmet needs and pressures within their own schools, so the notion of spinning off revenues in excess of expenditures that are going to be taken from them are reallocated somewhere else, is not something they particularly enjoy. The stronger the dean, the more likely they are to feel that way. The deans are in very, very difficult positions at these universities. They are middlemen—or women. They are supposedly serving the central administration, but they're also serving their own faculty and school's interest, and it's very difficult for them in some ways to walk the middle road of seeing the whole broader institutional needs, and still being a very staunch advocate for their local unmet needs.

Not unexpectedly, as one central administrator states, the resource allocation system has created a culture marked by "an ongoing argument about who's subsidizing who. Of course, the deans in the professional schools are fully convinced they're subsidizing the college, [and] the Arts and Sciences

Garfield University

more generally. I don't know who's subsidizing who." A faculty leader notes that "there was no way for anyone to see exactly what the revenues were or exactly what the academic costs were in any one school. Presumably someone in the central administration knew it."

The sense of inequity extended to the annual budget negotiations between the central administration and deans. Even though formulas formed the basis for general resource allocation decisions, significant off-line adjustments routinely occurred. A central financial officer mentions that the system "lent itself to a lot of high-level negotiation between the center and the individual schools," adding that "over time there was just barely a sense that some schools had played the game better than others and were finding themselves with the collected benefits or penalties of having had either good players or bad players in that game." This administrator feels that this was a key factor contributing to institutional efforts to reevaluate the system:

> The difficulty with the system, I think the thing that led to its collapse really was that it allowed arrangements to be made year by year between the central administration and individual schools. They kind of layered one on another, and eventually kind of clogged the system and also deprived it of any rooted rationality, because there would be a deal, for example, that would be worked out at the school in order to get a certain degree of net revenue, and it would plan to increase its enrollment. Then, depending on how eloquent it was in stating its needs, it might get to keep a particular share of that tuition income that came from the enhanced enrollment, and the center might keep the rest of it, but those ratios were not necessarily consistent across the school, so that it tended to create frictions and suspicion about who was getting better deals.
>
> Moreover, it became very complicated to administer, because those deals were meant to continue going forward for the most part, so that you would wind up with different cohorts in the layering of enrollment in the individual school. The revenues for each of those components could only be understood by going back to the original deals that they had been involved and whatever expansion to that point had occurred. It just was tremendously cumbersome.

When the University began to experience chronic budget deficits in the early 1990s, a Task Force on Budget Targets was convened in 1993-94 to examine opportunities for improving the resource allocation process. The Task Force report identified the major problems in the system then in place and its disadvantages:

> The Task Force was struck by the extremely complicated and arcane manner in which budget allocations at Garfield University have been set in the past . . . It is, to say the very least, a process that is difficult to understand

and that is even more difficult to comprehend in policy terms. Because it is essentially a formula-driven system, with little concern for the setting of spending priorities or differentiation among schools, it leaves the University's leaders with little opportunity to change the strategic direction of the institution, in general, or of any schools, in particular. Only the most sophisticated budget analysts understand precisely how such allocations are derived, and what drives those allocations up or down. As a result, the entire process is obscure and incomprehensible to most of the University community.

Moreover, the Task Force noted the psychological impact which the budget system cast on the community, and its negative effects.

> In difficult times, such a process tends to increase unease and suspicion. The Task Force found significant evidence of tension and distrust between, among, and within schools, as a result of the general lack of knowledge or understanding of budget policies, priorities, and/or procedures and their general outcomes. The fact that they are hidden from general view has not helped and the Task Force plans to turn its attention next to the philosophical issue of more open budgets and budget processes.
>
> The Task Force is convinced that current practices and their opacity have contributed to some of the suspicion (real and imagined) among faculty, deans, and others that the budget process is fundamentally slanted in favor of others and that is very much in need of reform. Quite apart from this consideration, however, one of the system's most glaring shortcomings is its lack of flexibility in the setting and resetting of the most basic and most important of the University's priorities, priorities that must vary over time.

Over time, as one central administrator describes, the system "lost all credibility." As a result, the Task Force concluded that:

> There is near unanimity within the Garfield community that the present budget system is inadequate and in need of significant reform. The current system contains insufficient incentives in some respects and perverse incentives in other respects. It is inordinately complex, lacks transparency, provides insufficient incentives to control costs or to generate new income, and distributes resources in a formulaic manner that makes strategic decision-making difficult.

At the same time the drawbacks of the system were becoming more apparent to central decision makers and leaders in the schools, the university was also facing serious budget deficits projected to be over eight million dollars over the next three and a half years. In the context of what one administrator describes as the "really substantial cutting that had to be

Garfield University

done," there was "pressure to resimplify the way in which the budgeting system worked:

> So what developed . . . was a radical shift that was first in operation for the 1994-95 fiscal year, in which essentially all revenues were credited directly to the schools, and the schools instead had to, instead of supporting their share of central costs had to pay essentially a fixed amount which one could describe as a tax, but it wasn't derived by some application of a percent of the revenues—it was derived historically instead. That tax simply represented what in the previous year had been the net that the central administration hung onto after collecting the revenues and then putting out the block grants.

The old budget system, in place throughout the '80's, began to change in the early 1990s during this period of budget deficit. The next section of this chapter discusses the transition to the new system.

TRANSITION TO THE NEW SYSTEM

In fiscal year 1994–95, the central administration (excluding the medical center) began crediting all schools with the unrestricted revenue that they generated, and assessing each a tax for "common costs." According to a description in a university document,

> The fundamental principles underlying the proposed new system—the full attribution of revenues and costs to the various units within the University, simplicity, transparency, appropriate incentives at the local level, greater discretionary resources at the central level-enjoyed support that the concepts embodies in the new system were necessarily appropriate for Garfield, or that the proposal being considered was right for Garfield.

In addition, starting in 1995–96, schools were given budget planning parameters for more than just the upcoming fiscal years, and were required to submit a budget proposal for the next two fiscal years. A university document notes that this will allow "a better assessment of the long-term financial implications of actions that will begin in 1995–96, particularly those related to capital projects which require incremental debt service to be absorbed into school budgets." Finally, the presentation of the budgets beginning in 1995–96 provides more information than was possible in early years about expenditures made by each school, and in particular distinguishes fungible from non-fungible sources of funding. A senior financial officer explains that the purpose of these changes is twofold:

Clearly, where we're moving towards is, first, a system that can make explicit to all the participants what resources from the center they're using. Second, as part of that, we're anxious to have that system provide feedback to the schools at the margin, so that as they make decisions, they either increase or decrease their use of central services, they will then have the impact of that reflected in their budgets, so that externalities are not hidden from them.

The budget allocation process in the new system also emphasizes more sophisticated financial planning at the unit level. The budget proposal process has pushed some of this financial planning closer to the academic units. As one dean states:

Our budget process for the schools is really one where they're not so much asking for money as asking for ratification that they have a sound financial plan, because they really are now operating substantially on their own, so we're looking to see whether all the projections they're making are realistic; what are the economics of tuition proposals that they're making. . . we're fundamentally inviting the schools to tell us what they think is prudent for them, in the context of the market they're competing in and also what their needs are.

The budget reform process, as it is known on campus, is ongoing and incomplete. One important issue that needs to be resolved pertains to the "balance of trade." Currently, historical numbers are being used, but in the future, one administrator notes, he hopes to "unpack" and reconcile the number. Presently, there is no algorithm for allocating tuition revenue on a credit unit basis. The University is proceeding cautiously on this matter, however, fearing that such a change may create undesirable incentives. One dean notes that:

You have to be careful. No matter what you do, the set of questions you have to ask, whether all the incentives are in the direction you want them to be in. When you start to move to transfer payments, you can create some real perversities in the system. You can get faculty giving courses simply to get enrollments. You can have the engineering school deciding it would be cheaper if they gave the same course themselves, and possibly not doing it as well. Where are the controls going to be, if they decide they're going to teach writing themselves rather than having it taught in arts and sciences. No matter which one you go to, there are always going to be some distorted incentives, and you just have to be aware of what they are and how you're going to manage it, so there have to be terms and conditions on whatever mechanism you put in place.

Another example of this conservative approach is seen in the development of a central tax system. In particular, the University central administration is still refining the formulas by which the central taxes are determined and allocated.

> The change that was made for the 1994–95 fiscal year, was dramatic, but it was also incomplete. In other words, it left us collectively—the schools and the central administration, needing to justify or recalculate—something we're actually now involved in this year—that central tax, because it was sort of a black box and it needed to be unpacked. It simply represented. . . the net of all these historical adjustments that had been made over time. It might tend, in a kind of general way, to represent the school by school use of central services, but not through any explicit allocation of costs or cost allocation model. If it's close to that, it's by some serendipity, not through careful, exact planning.

A faculty leader notes that these tax rates have historically not been clear: "Only by transferring the system to individual schools does the difference in costs become clear, and only now are people beginning to look at these questions." A central academic officer explains that the University is now in a position to begin assessing new tax rates:

> For the time being, the net that had been kept by the central administration to pay for central costs was simply inherited by the new system as the starting point for what the new tax would then be. The . . . system that we're currently using is historically driven, so the tax rates . . . are not closely matched, necessarily, to the university's academic priorities. There are disparities between the taxes paid by different schools, and there is not an easy mechanism to adjust those tax rates. That takes a great deal of time to make those adjustments. That's another weakness. I think that there isn't adequate flexibility in the system as well.

Over time, however, it has to modified so that it will reflect programmatic changes with implications for the recovery of central costs. Thus,

> if schools then decide to make enrollment changes or improve their grant recipient status and have more ICR, all of those incremental revenues would be credited directly to the school and the center would have no entitlement to any of that increment. The center had to be satisfied with simply receiving this year's version of that central tax amount.

Initially, the allocations were based on historical calculations. At the time this case study was being researched, the University was refining these calculations, "essentially providing a recalculation of what their uses of central services would be based on an explicit allocation model which may or may not fully match the historical numbers that were inherited." This officer thinks it unlikely the numbers will be the same after a recalculation: "It will be fairly surprising if all those other changes which were derived from an entirely different process did exactly tie . . . "

The larger question concerns the implicit subsidy historically provided by the university central administration for central services. Currently, the total cost of central services is about $107 million. The central administration only bills out $100 million. The $7 million dollar difference is made up through central offsets from the proceeds on earnings on some central endowments and certain other pieces of revenue that collectively sum to $7 million. Thus, all schools receive an automatic offset to their taxes—in essence, a rebate. Implicitly, each school receives a subsidy in proportion to the percentage total of taxes it currently receives. For example, a unit that pays 25% of the total taxes is getting 25% percent of the benefit of the $7 million dollar total subsidy. However, as one senior financial officer notes, "We can hold back those central revenues and in effect, define a bill for each school and then consciously decide at the Presidential and Provost level" what each school should receive. Right now, however, the University does not retain "participation fees" that could redistributed to cover expenses of other schools that have difficulty breaking even, or could be used to fund high priorities.

The new system, according to one dean, provides "a sense of budget discipline and accountability" lacking in the past, noting that deans are now

> responsible for any deficits and any savings, they can roll over and accumulate cookie jars if they want, to give them discretionary funding. They have freedom within the funds that are allocated to move things over budget lines. Otherwise you're never going to get folks that have a sense of accountability. Whatever system you have just has to have built into it the appropriate mechanisms for internal vigilance. Now, I think in the current times, in many respects the more centralized model serves institutions better because with the harsh landscape out there and the continued exposures that we keep hitting, you've got to be able to be fleet of foot.

Though the system has only recently been implemented, it does appear to be having an effect on behavior. One dean states:

> Everybody knows that they are going to live or die by their budget submissions. There is nobody to bail them out, and they'll carry debt with them, it will affect their next year allocations. I hold quarterly budget review meetings with all the [divisional] deans. Revenue targets are considered meaningful. . . We've really cranked up the fundraising, and just cut lots of specific deals with folks that begin to give them the idea of a culture where they can do things, but they have to make it work.

It's already begun to have an effect on the departments; they didn't care who was chair—now they care, because there were instances they didn't get the hiring authorizations they wanted, and they would say, 'Well, why didn't we get it?' and I would say, 'Well, the case wasn't presented very effectively.' They said, 'Who presented the case?' and I said, 'Your chair did that.' So then they'd start to fight with each other, but I notice that a number of chairs now are saying they're not going to continue and the departments are beginning to see they need a different kind of person.

You also have to give them some responsibility, moving around various kinds of . . . I'm a strong believer in the concept of the revealed preference, that I don't believe anybody's priority for anything until I know what they're willing to pay for. . . So I just try to convince everyone that is a co-venture. Don't come ask me for something until you know what you are going to put on the table, so that you come to me and say, 'Look, I can pay 25% on this.' If you're not willing to pay any of it, don't bother to ask. So that always has a rationing effect. We've done lots of things that have a rationing effect.

Ultimately, a senior financial officer hopes the system will increase the clarity of cost allocations and motivate a conversation between the deans and central administration over central services:

They're looking forward, in fact, to getting into the sort of conversation that you have with central services when you know exactly what you're paying for, and there's an issue of accountability there which I think is going to be a healthy development for central services. It will start to raise more specifics, for example, the issue like building maintenance or something like that where schools feel like they can make better arrangements might they be allowed to step outside of the centrally provided services that they use. It's a real option. It's a way of forcing fair competitiveness on the department of central services.

PRIORITIES

Discussions with university administrators point to several priorities in the years ahead. A recent university document summarizes the University's current strengths and strategic position:

Garfield continues to be among the relatively few American Research universities that represent the very best of higher education this country and, indeed, the world. It is unquestionably, in many of its parts, as well as in its overall achievements, a university that continues to earn its distinguished reputation. Second, there have been dramatic improvements in quality in virtually all of Garfield's schools over the past decade.

Many Arts and Sciences have made major improvements in the quality of their faculties, their attractiveness to students as represented in the number of applications, the qualifications for admission, the attractiveness of programs to those admitted, and most significantly, the achievements of their degree recipients. . .

> Complacency about these trends, however, would not serve us well. With these gains acknowledged, let us also note that Garfield's relative standing has improved significantly in some areas, but not in others. Much of what has been gained can be lost if we fail to meet the many challenges ahead. To improve our relative position—and this is within our grasp—we will have to carefully assess Garfield's comparative academic advantages, determine our academic priorities for the next decade, and be willing to make difficult choices among multiple, legitimate claims on our limited resources. We cannot forget that our competitive 'targets' are not stationary. These universities are also assessing their comparative strengths; many are making progress in meeting their strategic goals. Competition for excellence will only increase in the years ahead.

Another document concludes with a statement about the University's future strategy:

> The central message is clear: Garfield's future success will be measured by its ability to identify and build upon its inherent strengths, to support excellence where it is currently found, to grow and strengthen its programs selectively in a manner that will produce preeminence; and to demonstrate its willingness to part with some activities no longer academically vital or central to the future of the University.

Specific priorities are outlined in discussions with university administrators and described in recent planning documents. They include:

1. Undergraduate Education

The University recently completed an extensive strategic planning process, the outcomes of which were summarized in a document: The University is also moving toward strengthening its undergraduate program. The document notes that

> the Commission concludes that a rebalancing of the University is required to recognize and reflect the centrality of the undergraduate programs, and of Garfield College in particular. Such a rebalancing may require eventually a carefully managed expansion of the undergraduate student body, combined with a reallocation of University resources to support under-

Garfield University

graduate education. This investment is a necessary first step in positioning the university to compete in coming decades.

2. International and Interdisciplinary Work

The University is also interested in increasing it work in international and interdisciplinary areas:

> the Commission concluded that two obvious avenues to be immediately explored involved our observation that Garfield's research and academic profile does not sufficiently reflect the international and interdisciplinary resources available to the University. Perhaps Garfield's greatest asset is its diverse faculty boasting intellectual leaders in dozens of fields, and yet little institutional effort is expended to actively encourage work crossing traditional disciplinary boundaries—and where we already possess extraordinary intellectual strength in different schools. Interdisciplinary activities have not been adequately supported, and there exist organizational, fiscal and cultural barriers to interdisciplinary activity that must be eliminated or mitigated if dynamic research in cutting-edge disciplines is to be sufficiently supported.

3. Strengthening the Social Sciences

The University has earmarked the social sciences for improvement, as one recently appointed dean states:

> I announced very early on that one of my high priorities was going to be the revitalization of the social sciences here. Every one of those departments have been extraordinarily distinguished at some point in its history, and with the exception of the Department of History, there had been serious erosion. It's an area where with relatively modest resource investments, given the history of Garfield and given our location, we can get them back among that most distinguished group in very short order . . . They had really gone hypothermic. They got below critical mass. I felt the case was sufficiently compelling at face value that I wouldn't have to spend a lot of time justifying it; I could do it before the program reviews would come in because I knew what they were going to say. They obviously would give it in much richer detail—they would be very helpful in that regard—but people accepted it.

According to a university document, the University has supported cross-disciplinary research through its Strategic Initiative Fund, "which applies a portion of the University's income from intellectual property to new research ventures, promotes cross-disciplinary research, and invests in faculty members and research groups in ways that will yield academic as well as financial returns."

A senior academic officer states that

> A lot of what we use for discretionary income here is, believe it or not, the return on patents and licenses as a source of revenues . . . That money is used for central investments in high priority academic concerns, particularly leveraging purposes for growth within the university.

The fund, has for example, supported a new center which joins research from several schools and departments, and institutions outside the university, to focus on the science of habitat management. The University provided $3 million in funds for the center.

An academic officer also mentions that the University is creating an Earth Institute, "which is going to build upon the strengths of the geological sciences, but try to look at the problems of the earth, conservation, preservation, social policy, science as one integrated system across the university."

In the longer term, however, the central administration believes that it must find other ways to fund central priorities. Right now, a central academic officer notes that income from intellectual property is an important source of funds:

> One is that those discretionary funds, at the moment, depend on hitting home runs in the world of patents and licenses. As long as we do, as long as we have an extraordinarily able office that is able to do this, we'll be in reasonably good shape

The lack of certainty in this revenue stream suggests the importance of diversifying revenue sources.

THE FUTURE

The central administration realizes that for the resource allocation system to be effective, it must be linked to the achievement of institutional priorities. Recently, the University has moved toward a more explicit revenue center model of resource allocation. The next step, however, will be to develop a central pool of resources, through explicit taxes and possibly a system of "participation and subvention" commonly associated with other revenue-center budgeting systems. One administrator describes this as "the main mechanism for the decisions at the margin about the allocation of resources among the schools on the main campus," adding that the system has yet to be full articulated. He states that "We are going to need to set out a set of objectives and goals that will, in effect, reward schools to the extent that they participate in reaching those goals and in effect reduce the

Garfield University

somewhat supplemental increment that would be given to schools that don't reshape their activities [in accordance with central goals]." Most importantly, he wants to avoid one of the most commonly cited pitfalls of this type of system.

> [the Provost] is not interested in finding himself trapped in the system, which in a way has no discretionary money at the center . . . That sort of leaves the leadership at the center without resources to push their vision of the university. I think within the context of the new fundraising campaign that we just kicked off a week ago, or an extension of the previous one which had a roughly three million dollar target and has now been renewed for essentially another three million over the next five years—and now one of his goals is to raise central funds that are in fact a sort of pool for initiatives, so that would be a further set of resources that got put on the table.

A faculty leader states the problem this way:

> Whether the next step should be taken and move from the clarity of costs and revenues to responsibility for costs and revenues or whether the university should be saying, as I think it will, to some degree, certain things within the university are priorities, are important to the university as a whole not really to any one faculty within it, and hence it's the responsibility of the central university administration to allocate resources and revenues and costs independent of where they are actually accruing . . . The central administration likely wants to have some leeway in the budget for initiatives, exchanges, interfaculty, the new environmental center is clearly one of those, and that's just fine. Then the question is, whose budget is it coming from? It is to a degree a zero-sum game, and there are questions that are not simply financial questions; they are real questions of educational institutional priorities that are reflected in the budget.

The resources might be used to support university wide priorities, as one administrator explains, and in turn motivate the behavior of schools toward attainment of these priorities:

> So, for example, if one were trying to foster interdisciplinary program development . . . schools that have initiated developments in that area would be more likely to receive a share of discretionary central revenues that would have been applied at the margin to push to overall community in the direction that the president wanted to go. If you wanted to make that goal explicit, you would then act on it to the extent the schools brought forward to you past actions and plans that were consistent with that goal.

The issue is complicated by the politics of institutional resource allocation and the struggle for scarce resources that occurs on any university campus. The question, and problem, will be to determine how the system of subsidies will operate across the schools—in effect, who will be the benefactors, and who will be the recipients in the system:

> Which schools need to be under pressure to either subsidize the other schools more or else get their management together more. That's going to be a highly interesting analytic exercise and its obviously going to be highly political and difficult to carry out. We think we have, in effect, then, a hybrid model, but we think we understand clearly the principles of that hybridization . . . It doesn't pretend that there's some sort of mechanical bottom line—it sets a standard and admits that life is not that simple, and that there's a qualitative issue that has to get applied there. We're just trying to make the terms and the framework for it as explicit as we can.

The problem of central subsidies is complicated by institutional economics. A senior academic officer notes that Garfield doesn't have "cash cows" from which to spin off revenues:

> In fact, many of the schools struggle to be competitive with richer institutions, so there is resistance to, if you will, institutional altruism, giving up their resources for other, even higher priorities.

CONCLUSION

In the last two fiscal years, 1995 and 1996, Garfield has achieved a balanced operating budgeting. Now that financial stability has been restored, the University is moving toward refining its new resource allocation system and understanding the relationship between resources and decisions. One central administrator believes there will now be

> less of a concern with getting the bottom line numbers correct and now reviewing with much greater care what we can do and what we cannot do in the future and how we want to shift resources around and what flexibility we have to do that. That will involve more academic planning and work among the deans and among the schools for one, to try to achieve the economies that can be obtained by greater cooperation among the schools. So I think certainly that will be part of our future. I think it will be much easier for Deans and their staffs to know precisely what the algorithms are that are being allocated in terms of cost allocations; there will be more discussions about those allocation mechanisms and taxation mechanisms, and I think that they'll probably have a better general understanding of the bases on which resources are distributed, and an articula-

tion of why the priorities have been set and how the money is being used, and hopefully whether or not it's done any good.

One central administrator is optimistic that this can be accomplished and predicts the following:

> I think that there will be more visibility, more transparency, more accountability in the way in which we allocate resources. I'm hoping we'll get to a point where will begin to get a base budgets more than growth at the margins. An awful lot of the analysis that has gone on over the last decade been examining everything at the margins—growth at the margins, decline at the margins—but not really peeling back the onion and seeing what is that the money is going for, and whether nor not there ought to be some systematic changes over time in the base allocations. I think more of that will go on.

Over time, the University central administration hopes that it will be able to develop a statement of the relative position of the schools in relation to one another, but thus far they yet not yet defined what types of internal benchmarks would be appropriate.

The move toward decentralization is likely to persist, though over time both central and school administrators will need to determine the proper balance between centralization and decentralization necessary to create appropriate unit incentives and achieve University-wide priorities. The following two quotations capture this point:

Dean:

> I think the eventual driving forces are going to push it towards increasing decentralization. In these things, where you stand depends on where you sit. It's to my advantage to have it become increasingly decentralized, but it's also to my advantage to have the institution work as effectively as possible. I frankly don't think we should [adopt] the fully decentralized model, even though I certainly could argue that as a self-interest case. I think the central administration has to maintain some resource allocation capability to meet broader institutional interests. We all tend to be very, very balkanized, and there are initiatives that should span many schools that we know historically just don't happen if there isn't somebody who stands over them who's going to provide the stimulating seed funds, who's going to negotiate all the contractual arrangements that are necessary to make it work effectively, who's going to smooth transfer of payment issues. If I just decentralized completely out to my departments, it would be destructive to the curriculum. They would all be pursuing
> their own self-interests. I've got to hold something back that I can take

away or give, to [motivate their] behavior. Otherwise I can't build in any rewards.

Central administrator:

The thing that concerns me most about strict decentralization and movement towards tubs is that I think it allows budget structures to dominate academic priorities, or it puts a very heavy emphasis on budgetary controls, budgetary accountability, and local needs rather than creating the united university. The universities under these highly decentralized systems tend to become holding companies rather than real universities, and I think that in fact, in the future we have to put the "uni" back in the university. Those [universities] that don't will have comparative disadvantages in the future.

8
Summary Case Analyses

The previous case chapters describe in detail the resource allocation process in the six universities selected for this study. This section presents a summary analysis of the resource allocation process and the current challenges facing each university, as revealed in the case studies.

BUCHANAN UNIVERSITY

Buchanan University gradually developed a decentralized resource allocation system during the 1970s and 1980s, as individual schools negotiated formula agreements with the university central administration. By the early 1990s, every Buchanan school was operating under such an agreement. Though apparently patterned after a traditional responsibility center system, certain features of the Buchanan system are inconsistent with the model. In particular, the Buchanan system fails to incorporate an explicit system of subvention and participation. Furthermore, the central administration does not fully recover expenses for central shared services typically billed to revenue centers in traditional responsibility center systems. The formulas used in calculating the annual resource allocation are not widely known within the university community.

The Buchanan formula system provides incentives for deans to wisely manage resources and engage in entrepreneurial, revenue-generating activities. This entrepreneurial culture enabled the University to recruit innovative deans willing to develop new schools or revamp existing programs. Although the University's academic standing has improved during the period in which the formula system was developed, the formula system has apparently also had negative consequences for the institution. Buchanan is described as a "confederation," rather than a unified entity. While it is difficult to know whether the institution would operate in a more integrated fashion under a more centralized resource allocation system, it appears that the formula system is at least partly responsible for the fragmented culture described in the interviews.

From the perspective of the central leadership, a main weakness of the system is its relative inflexibility. It is exceedingly difficult for the recently appointed central leadership to reallocate or distribute resources in support of university-wide priorities. Only modest sums of money are available to the Provost and President for allocations outside the individual formula agreements. The University recently completed a strategic planning exercise, which identified a number academic priorities that transcend school and department boundaries, including improving the quality of undergraduate life and building interdisciplinary research programs in selected areas. Recently, the executive leadership has been meeting with the deans to communicate university priorities and build the trust required for resource allocation reform that might address the lack of central resources. The central administration is also developing benchmarks by which to evaluate its academic programs as well as the quality of its administrative services.

Despite the central administration's frustrations over the lack of central funds, no dramatic changes are contemplated for the near future, though the central leadership remains optimistic that over time, through communication and persuasion, they can begin to address some of the perceived shortcomings of the current system and more effectively address university-wide academic priorities.

PIERCE UNIVERSITY

Pierce University has used full-responsibility center budgeting since the early 1980s. Prior to that time, Pierce operated under a very highly centralized system where the locus of budget authority was tightly controlled by the executive administration. Budget allocation at Pierce incorporates the classical features of RCB, including attribution of revenues and expenses to academic and administrative units, and central billing of each responsibility center's calculated share of central administrative expenses. The system also incorporates explicit taxes on certain unit revenues, which are returned to the central administration and which become available for redistribution. Explicit payments and rebates known as subvention and participation are also features of the system.

Though Pierce's resource allocation system is highly decentralized, the central administration nevertheless reserves considerable oversight over the system itself, through careful financial monitoring, communication with deans and administrative officers, and through a system of recovery for shared administrative expenses. Additionally, the Provost is responsible for determining whether an individual school is entitled to a rebate on its "participation," or whether it contributes a portion of its resources to the central administration (and, indirectly, the other units in the University). The President delegates much of the responsibility for resource allocation decisions to the Provost. Faculty participation in the system is relatively limited; they sometimes serve in advisory capacities to the dean within their respective schools or as members of specially appointed University committees. Faculty also serve on a University budget committee which is described primarily as an educational experience rather than as a policy-setting group.

In recent years, the University's Budget Advisory Committee studied the status of the responsibility budget system and its effects—both positive and negative—on the institution. On the positive side, the system encourages academic entrepreneurship, empowers deans, and holds them accountable for decisions and resources. The result is a business-like environment where deans can develop innovative programs. The system holds the central administration accountable for the quality and cost-effectiveness of central services. Because resource flows are open and visible to members of the community, suspicions and jealousies among the deans may be minimized. The rules of the games are identical for all units, regardless of size or status.

On the negative side, the system has contributed to what critics describe as "intellectual balkanization" and a lack of "university-wide" vision." And while the system is said to promote a businesslike environment, it is criticized for its overly commercial characteristics. Because schools vie for attributed tuition, there is greater pressure to offer courses on the basis of perceived popularity rather than educational value. There are disincentives for interdisciplinary programs and other cross-school initiatives are discouraged. Finally, RCB leads to duplication—of faculty, courses, research agendas, and administration.

Despite its deficiencies, the faculty, deans, and central administrators interviewed for this study believe the system works well and are comfortable with the trade-offs which this highly market-driven system demands.

A major concern expressed by the central administration is that the priorities of the University, articulated in a recent plan, transcend school and department boundaries. These include improving undergraduate education, and building interdisciplinary research and teaching programs in the health sciences. Funding these initiatives will demand a more strategic allocation of resources University-wide. The central administration is now expecting schools and departments to provide more compelling arguments for why they deserve subvention. In the longer term, the central administration would like to increase system-wide taxes so that a significantly greater proportion of revenues is available for reallocation according to central priorities. The Provost is trying to communicate to the deans the value of a more cooperative culture, through a mixture of market incentives and personal leadership. Through these measures, the university central administration hopes to ensure a more direct connection between resource allocation and the attainment of university priorities.

The central administration has also moved toward developing a system of feedback whereby every academic department in the University will be expected to evaluate its performance against the competition, and use the collected data as the basis for benchmarking improvement.

WESTMONT UNIVERSITY

Westmont University's resource allocation system is in a state of transition. The University has historically had a highly centralized resource allocation system which offered deans little flexibility. Budgets were centrally determined and rigorously monitored. Schools were in no way responsible for managing revenues, and except for ensuring that they did not overspend their budget, deans were not held accountable for their finances. The centralized resource allocation model allowed deans and faculty to focus on intellectual goals, such as outstanding scholarship and good teaching, qualities for which the university is reknown.

In the early 1990s, a combination of budget deficits and a change in the central leadership led the University to develop a new, more decentralized resource allocation model, one which gave deans considerably greater authority over resource allocation. The system created powerful economic incentives for deans to share in the responsibility of reducing the university budget deficit through cost-cutting and revenue generation. Although the system resembles responsibility center budgeting, it stops short of RCB in two important ways: participation and subvention are absent from the system, and the University has not tried to develop an explicit system of taxes to recover shared administrative expenses. Instead, the University has proceeded cautiously, preferring to manage those subsidies at the center rather create explicit taxes. The net result is that the University has maintained some of the centralization of the old system.

Deans responded to the new incentive structure by developing new professional and other terminal master's degree programs to raise the tuition revenues required to improve their school's net position—the difference between a unit's calculated revenue and expense. These changes have stimulated a more entrepreneurial culture which many faculty worry could compromise the University's academic character. Interestingly, the University's emphasis on revenue generation is entirely consistent with the economic model of non-profit organizations. Massy (1996) notes that tensions between the values of the academy and the realities of the marketplace are accentuated during periods of fiscal distress. At such times, the economic choices of a non-profit organization may begin to approach the profit-maximizing behavior of a for-profit firm. Because money is scarce, its marginal utility increases. The institutional response is to raise revenues, even if this means expanding programs with relatively lower marginal intrinsic value. In Westmont's case, the University central administration has created explicit incentives for the various schools to offer revenue-generating programs which would otherwise interest the faculty very little.

The central administration, especially the Provost, has communicated the necessity of these changes throughout the University community and has tried to reassure the faculty that the University's intrinsic values will not be compromised. In addition, the central administration is trying to be sensitive to concerns raised by faculty and deans.

In an effort to reduce administrative costs, the University recently completed an extensive study which resulted in recommendations for consolidating numerous administrative functions and streamlining certain processes.

The University's main priorities in this period of fiscal distress are to maintain its position as a leading research university and to strengthen its undergraduate programs. But there is no strategic plan that outlines specific academic priorities. A great deal of energy in the last few years has concentrated on closing the University's looming budget deficits and implementing the new resource allocation policies. Now that the University's financial difficulties appear to be turning around, the University can refocus its energies on shaping academic priorities.

SHELTON UNIVERSITY

Shelton University's resource allocation system is relatively centralized. All unrestricted revenues flow to the center, and are subsequently distributed to the academic units. Though Shelton has had a centralized resource allocation policy for many decades, the system in place since the 1970s represents a significant departure from the previous system. Prior to the 1970s, resource allocation was tightly controlled by the chief academic and executive officers, with little direct involvement from other members of the campus community, in particular, the faculty. When the university began to feel the effects of a more constrained resource environment in the late 1960s, the University central administration, with assistance from a major foundation, developed the resource allocation system it still uses today.

While the current system is still centralized, it encompasses much broader participation from a permanent University committee, known as the Priorities Committee. The Priorities Committee, composed of faculty and staff, is responsible for developing and endorsing the University's annual operating budget. The Priorities Committee meets intensively each fall, and, working with central business officers who serve as *ex officio* members of the Committee, reviews the previous year's annual budget and hears requests for incremental resources from academic officers. Little attention is given to the base budget. The final budget is submitted to the Board of Trustees for its approval.

The Priorities Committee's final recommendations are published annually in widely circulated public document that summarizes the University operating budget, and describes allocations and current priorities in key areas, including undergraduate tuition and fees; graduate student support; undergraduate financial aid; faculty and staff salaries; employee benefits; faculty staffing; computing and information technology; library; research support facilities; and administration and academic support services.

The process appears to serves several purposes. The first is the development of the annual operating budget—the fundamental task of the Priorities Committee. The second is educational. Each year, a subset of the University community becomes intimately acquainted with University financial affairs. The annual written report of the Priorities Committee offers an opportunity for other members of the community to understand institutional academic priorities and their resource consequences. Third, the process serves to reinforce the shared values of openness and participation consistent with the institution's central values.

The University also uses a formula system for allocating administrative budgets to the schools and departments. Recently, the formula was revised to more appropriately reflect the resource requirements of natural science and engineering departments. It is hoped that the revised formula will curtail the off-formula negotiations routinely associated with these departments. Deans and department chairs will still be free to negotiate directly with the university central administration for additional academic or administrative resources beyond those requested during the annual Priorities Committee deliberations or formula allocation process.

The system appears to work for a number of reasons, including the University's relatively small size, its narrow portfolio of teaching and research programs, and a dedicated and responsive senior central administration.

No major changes in resource allocation system are currently contemplated, however, the University has recently acknowledged the need or more long-range financial planning and priority-setting in the face of growing financial constraints.

GREENWAY UNIVERSITY

Greenway University's resource allocation system is relatively centralized. The central administration determines the annual operating budgets of the University's major academic units, however, schools are generally free to allocate funds as they wish after the central allocations have been made. A central budget board, consisting of the senior central administrative and academic officers, is responsible for annual allocations, which generally consist of a base-budget increment, and approved special budget requests. Though the committee is chaired by the Provost, until recently, Greenway's President exerted considerable authority in University resource allocation matters. No one discusses the resource allocation process at Greenway without also mentioning Goodman's leadership. Goodman balanced the

University's books and instilled a sense of fiscal discipline through direct involvement, and where necessary, personal intervention with the deans. Deans who overspend "Goodman's budget" can expect a personal visit from the President.

Though deans have an incentive to manage costs wisely—they can generally roll over surpluses without penalty—incentives for deans to raise revenues are apparently weaker, relative to more market-based budget allocation systems. "Entrepreneurship" was not mentioned as a University value by anyone interviewed for this case study.

One of the hallmarks of the University's planning system is a centrally-coordinated program review process. Every administrative and academic unit in the University is reviewed on a regular, published schedule. The system is universally praised by faculty and administrators, but the association between the program review process and resource allocation is less clear.

Greenway recently appointed a new president and provost. Academic priorities for the new administration are still being shaped. As for the resource allocation process, the University has no plans to drastically alter the current system, although discussions with administrators suggest that the University may look more strategically at marginal increments, using them to fund yet undefined institutional initiatives for excellence. The central administration is likely to be somewhat less confrontational with the deans than it has been in the past, and may decentralize larger amounts of money to the schools. Raising the number of highly ranked academic departments in the arts and sciences, and enhancing the quality of graduate programs are also mentioned as possible priorities.

GARFIELD UNIVERSITY

Garfield University's resource allocation process is presently in a state of transition. Historically, the University's resource allocation system was relatively centralized. All unrestricted revenues flowed to the center, and were subsequently allocated in blocks to the major academic units by means of formulas which had been developed over time. The system also operated with significant off-formula agreements which had been negotiated over time between the academic units and central administration. Academic units had few incentives to raise revenue, because the formulas did not necessarily reward such efforts with attributed income.

Over time, the resource allocation system lost credibility in the community. The basis for the formulas was unclear, and because the system obscured the locus of cross-subsidies, an on-going argument developed over "who was subsidizing whom." Suspicions intensified during the early 1990s when the University found itself facing a series of budget deficits. In the face of these pressures, the central administration undertook resource allocation reform in fiscal year 1994–1995. The new system incorporates typical features of responsibility center budgeting, including the full attribution of revenues and costs to various academic units, and a central tax. The new system gives deans stronger incentives to raise revenues, and, equally important from the central administration's standpoint, encourages deans to engage in more rigorous financial and general business planning. Resource allocation is a significantly more open process than it had been in the past.

Although the University has achieved a clarity of costs and revenues absent from the old system, resource allocation reform is incomplete and on-going. The University central administration continues to refine the formula by which the central tax is determined. Over time, the administration hopes the tax will more appropriately reflect each unit's fair share of central services. Additionally, the central administration may develop a system of participation and subvention that would allow central administrators to adjust unit bottom lines to the extent that unit behavior is in accordance with central objectives. At present, however, subsidies are still determined at the center. Like Westmont, there is a strong sense that too much change too quickly may have undesirable consequences.

Such adjustments will become more crucial as the University moves ahead with ambitious plans to promote more cross-disciplinary research, promote more global research, and improve undergraduate education.

As the previous case studies may suggest, the six institutions in this study face a variety of unique challenges. Each university's resource allocation approach is shaped by myriad factors, including institutional history, mission, leadership, and economic conditions. These unique factors were highlighted in the individual case studies and summary case analyses.

9
Cross-Case Analysis and the Future Directions

In reviewing the cases collectively, a number of other insights emerged which suggest broader conclusions about resource allocation in the six university sample, conclusions which might possibly apply to other research universities as well. These insights are discussed below:

1. Difficult financial conditions may lead an institution to redevelop its resource allocation approach. The transition to a new resource allocation model is also influenced by the views of the executive leadership and the community's readiness for change.

Three of the six institutions—Westmont, Greenway, and Garfield—implemented a new resource allocation approach following a fiscal crisis marked by chronic budget deficits. In all three cases, the new approach was seen as an antidote to the budget crisis. Interestingly, two of the institutions, Westmont and Garfield, responded by developing relatively decentralized resource allocation systems, while the third, Greenway, essentially became more centralized in the sense that the President became much more active in directing resource allocation process and policies. Regardless of strategy, the net result was the same: fiscal stability and collective relief that university finances were finally under control.

The choice of system appears to be as much a function of institutional leadership as of financial conditions. At Westmont, Greenway, and Garfield, the conversion to a new system followed a transition in senior leadership. The attitudes of the new leadership appears to be the major determinant in whether an institution selected a more decentralized or centralized resource allocation philosophy following a period of fiscal instability.

Pierce also developed a decentralized resource allocation system following a transition in leadership, though fiscal constraint does not appear to be the major impetus for change. Buchanan's recent measures to reform its resource allocation system also occurred following a change in executive leadership. Perhaps these leaders felt they could achieve greater management flexibility by adopting a new resource allocations system. Their apparent objective was to instill financial accountability of academic units as well as generate surpluses to fund central or university-wide priorities.

In addition to leadership, the receptivity of the community to change appears to be a key explanatory variable in the type of system ultimately developed. Neither Westmont nor Garfield introduced full responsibility budgeting, though both implemented one key element of RCB—the attribution of revenues and expenses to major academic units—while avoiding the more controversial allocation of (explicit) subvention and participation. Neither institution is averse to the idea of introducing explicit subsidies—indeed administrators at Garfield raise it as a distinct possibility—but leaders at both institutions seem cautious about introducing too much change at once. The leadership at Buchanan—a university already on a formula system based on the attribution of revenue and expense—is anxious to reform the resource allocation system, but cautious about introducing dramatic change. In all three cases—Westmont, Garfield, and Buchanan—there is the sense that change must occur incrementally. At all three institutions, the central leadership, and especially the Provost, is spending a great deal of time trying to convince the community that resource allocation reform is necessary, explaining the benefits for the university as a whole and for local academic units.

In contrast to the more incremental approaches adopted at Westmont, Garfield, and Buchanan, Pierce adopted full responsibility center budgeting at the outset. Total RCB was built from the ground up. Why were administrators at Pierce so successful in making a complete transformation? Several members of the recently recruited central leadership had arrived from an institution which had spearheaded decentralized incentive budgeting. Their sense of confidence dovetailed with a community anxious for a more equitable, visible, and entreneurial resource allocation system. Although change also occurred at Greenway, the mandate for a more tightly centralized resource allocation system came from the governing board and the rather aggressive (and sometimes confrontational) style of the newly appointed President.

Central administrators undoubtedly gain flexibility when they appoint deans who are sympathetic to their resource allocation and willing to play by the new rules. The "new deans" at Westmont, Pierce, Buchanan, and Garfield, appear to have been screened at least partly for their willingness to function within the new resource allocation model. A key job requirement is willingness to serve as ambassador for a school and as citizen of the university. While this job description was probably always implicit in a dean's appointment, there appears to be greater emphasis on the importance of the latter role.

Shelton adopted its present resource allocation in the late sixties. A more constrained resource environment was one of the primary reasons the university shifted from a budget allocation approach controlled by a few central administrators, to one which embraced broader participation by other members of the academic community. The system is still centralized in the sense that the senior central administration still manages the process (and to some degree the outcomes), but the system is far more participatory than in the past. It is interesting to note that while Shelton was facing financial constraint when it adopted its new resource allocation process, its financial condition at the time still placed it near the top of American research universities.

It is interesting to observe that the two institutions transitioning from one resource allocation system to another both moved toward more-market driven systems with explicit attribution of revenues and expense. Neither institution had taken the next step and incorporated the explicit taxes, participation, and subventions typical in responsibility-center systems. Both institutions, however, appear to be benefiting from greater transparency of institution-wide financial information, as well as sharpened focus on unit financial planning.

2. The free flow of reliable information is a key ingredient in a successful resource allocation system.

Information is the cornerstone of any successful resource allocation system. In decentralized, incentive-based systems, reliable information is required to accurately attribute revenues, expenses, and central administrative overhead. The reliability of such information is crucial to the credibility and integrity of the system. Furthermore, although RCB decentralizes resource allocation management to the unit level, the central administration still provides necessary oversight. At Pierce, for example, the central financial administration systematically reviews the projected bottom-line of every responsibility center on a monthly basis, in order to ensure that no unit finishes the year with a budget deficit.

Information is also essential for achieving improved financial and academic planning. One of the reasons that Garfield and Westmont adopted decentralized systems was to encourage better planning at the local level where academic decisions are typically made. In order for such planning to occur, units need accurate and timely information about their financial condition. Such information is necessary for making trade-offs about various academic and administrative investments.

One institution, Greenway, has developed an unusually comprehensive academic information system. Under the leadership of a vice president for planning, the planning office collects a variety of data about the financial and academic performance of the University's schools and academic departments. No other institution in this sample had developed a database as comprehensive. In fact, the academic feedback loop in these institutions seems to be an informal collection of indirect measures (such as National Research Council rankings), the results of occasional department reviews, and the direct knowledge of the dean or provost of each department's subjective quality.

Institution leaders endorse the value of building more systematic performance measurement systems, but recognize the difficulty developing such systems for the academic enterprise. Nevertheless, Pierce and Buchanan are both attempting to develop comprehensive performance benchmarks. When this occurs, will these institutions explicitly link the attainment of specific outcomes to the allocation of resources? That remains to be seen.

Interestingly, demands for central information appear to increase when a university adopts a more highly decentralized resource allocation system. The central administration must process more data in order to ensure that units are living within their financial means and contributing to the overall academic mission of the university. Evidence from the cases suggests that central administrators are better equipped to handle complex financial planning, though the better deans will make investments in administrative personnel over time.

3. Institutional leaders express a growing need to raise central resources for university-wide academic priorities.

Evidence from this study suggests that academic priorities are increasingly no longer confined to a single academic unit, but transcend school and disciplinary boundaries. In a world of limited resources and either stable or diminishing revenues, institutional leaders are searching for the biggest "bang for their buck." They have adopted this strategy because it is the only financially feasible way to improve their institution's academic reputation and to achieve distinctiveness within the increasingly competitive higher education market. Historically, institutions have tried to improve programs across-the-board. It is debatable whether this strategy ever really "worked." In any event, institutional leaders seem to be reaching the conclusion that strategic investments are the wisest use of limited resources.

The leaders of three institutions—Pierce, Garfield, Buchanan—have proposed ambitious cross-disciplinary research and teaching programs. Such programs build on existing institutional resources. These programs may enable each institution to become "better" and distinctive in the higher education market. But in all three cases, the institutions are struggling with the problem of building a pot of central resources to fund these university-wide priorities. In the decentralized environment, very little money is left at the center unless the central administration is able to

Cross-Case Analysis and the Future Directions 177

wrest money from the deans through direct or indirect taxation. Central leaders at Pierce are trying very hard to raise the additional required funds by increasing taxes and by trying to communicate the value of these university-wide initiatives to the deans. At Buchanan, central leaders are grappling with the same issues, and, like leaders at Pierce, are meeting with deans to discuss University priorities. Garfield is still transitioning to a new decentralized system, but central administrators there have made it clear that the system that ultimately emerges must include central resources for university-wide priorities. In all likelihood, the deans at Buchanan and Garfield will resist subsidizing the center, but ultimately may have no choice if central leaders adopt a firm stand (as they have at Pierce).

4. Resource allocation systems vary in the incentives they create for academic unit heads to act in accordance with central goals. The incentives are a function of the assumptions underlying the resource allocation system and its intended outcomes.

The impact of incentives on unit behavior is a major theme in this research. In formula-based systems, deans apparently have the strongest incentives to raise revenues through attributed tuition and external fund-raising. At Pierce, such incentives were especially pronounced; deans are likened to corporate entrepreneurs managing a business enterprise. A key job requirement is readiness to thrive in an entrepreneurial, academic environment. Such pressures to generate income may further reflect the institution's relatively small per-capita endowment, very modest reserves, and historically large portfolio of academic programs. Similar incentives for deans to raise revenues were also evidenced in the formula-based systems used at Buchanan and Westmont. There was little evidence of an entrepreneurial culture at Garfield, despite its recent transition to a system based on general responsibility center principles. The absence of entrepreneurship may be due to the fact that the units have not yet found a way to introduce additional revenue-generating programs.

At Pierce, incentives for fund-raising included external as well as internal fund-raising. Over time, in the RCB environment, where subvention and participation are at stake, perceptive deans cultivate their relationship with the Provost and try to demonstrate the success of their academic unit, justifying why it deserves a subsidy. Perhaps this reflects the fact that the deans in the RCB system can see precisely how much subsidy each unit in the University is receiving from the central administration. The dean is likely under pressure from his or her faculty to ensure that this subsidy is a high as possible. In a real sense, the subsidy serves as a performance measure for a dean. In other systems were the subsidy is hidden, there is apparently less pressure on the deans. At Buchanan, for example, deans are more likely to regard central subsidies as an entitlement rather than as something to be earned.

At Shelton and Greenway, deans seem to have fewer incentives to raise revenues or to engage in entrepreneurial endeavors. At Greenway, the central administration calculates the gross margins of major academic units and works with units with negative margins to improve their bottom line. But the impetus originates in the central administration, not in the dean's office. One Greenway professional school which has consistently had a negative gross margin has been encouraged by the central administration to enroll a larger entering class. But since the additional tuition is funneled back to the central administration, the dean may or not benefit from enrolling larger class. At Shelton, deans are more inclined to raise revenues by direct negotiation with the central administration, rather than by enrolling larger numbers of students. This process may reflect the university's unusual abundance of resources and lack of financial pressures.

5. Once a resource allocation is in place, it is difficult to change the "rules of the game"—in a minor or major ways that impact university-wide resource allocation.

Changing the "rules" of a resource allocation process is a politically sensitive and usually very difficult exercise. This observation was highlighted in numerous interviews and across several institutions. The senior central administrators at Buchanan are in agreement that the institutional resource allocation process should be realigned to achieve current and future objectives, however, they realize that tweaking the system will take time and leadership—and that any changes are likely to ruffle feathers. Senior administrators at Pierce are also finding resistance as they attempt to alter the distribution of institutional resources to support current university objectives.

In the case of Westmont, which made a dramatic change from a highly centralized to a highly decentralized process, resistance was mitigated, to some extent, by the central leadership's personal influence, support, and guidance during the transitional period. And while the changes made were significant, the leadership avoided deeper changes, such as introducing explicit taxes. Garfield's leadership has also proceeded cautiously during the transition from a highly centralized to a highly decentralized system, and has avoided introducing explicit taxes.

The one exception appears to be Greenway. Resource allocation reform occurred rather swiftly under Goodman's leadership.

6. Value-outcomes principles are attractive to university central executives. Their full implementation is more difficult.

Two of the institutions in this sample are apparently gravitating toward value-outcomes principles in their resource allocation process. Buchanan and Pierce currently use formula allocation systems with price-regulation features (though it might be said that Pierce has exploited price-regulation more effectively then Buchanan). Both universities, however, seem to be moving toward the value-outcomes model in their stated goal of using explicit performance measures to link university priorities with resource allocation. Greenway, through it's elaborate strategic planning process and other central planning mechanisms, uses certain VO principles in determining academic priorities.

It should be noted, however, that no university in this sample has really embraced the elaborate budget allocation model and performance measurement system indicative of value-outcome systems. The difficulty in developing performance measures may be one reason why this system is not more fully utilized. The politics of withholding and dispensing funds may make such a system controversial for the Provost charged with its administration. And perhaps the one-year budget time-frame is too narrow to link budgets with outcomes. Finally, the incremental funds available to university provosts for distribution on annual basis appear to be relatively small as many of the costs of the university budget are fixed. A large percentage of the annual operating budget—tenure-line faculty—is fixed and not open to redistribution.

Still, there is evidence that university provosts and presidents are increasingly demanding outcomes for their investments. These outcomes may not be discernible in one year or two years. But in the intermediate term, these senior central administrators expect to see the results—the value—of their investments during their tenure.

RESOURCE ALLOCATION AND AGENCY

At the outset of this study, I demonstrated how concepts from principal-agent theory illuminate the resource allocation process in academic organizations. Central administrators, acting as principals, allocate resources to faculty and non-faculty agents in schools, departments, and administrative units. Throughout the cases, there is ample evidence that university central administrators seek to influence "agent" behavior through direct and indirect control. In the Massy model, the standard approaches of university principals map into three resource allocation systems: 1) Direct Control; 2) Price Regulation; and 3) Value-Outcomes.

While this research did not seek to confirm the validity of this model for private research universities, evidence from the cases does shed light on its appropriateness for understanding the resource allocation process in this class of higher education organizations.

A major observation is that the complexity of the resource allocation process can rarely be reduced to a single category or system. University resource allocation models are dynamic, fluid, and evolving systems. Garfield and Westmont, for example, were in the process of transitioning from one resource allocation system to another. The details of their respective systems were still under development at the time these case studies were researched. Even established systems exhibit multiple resource allocation approaches. Greenway, for example, allocates resources in major blocks and uses a rigorous strategic planning process to determine how well units are meeting their negotiated goals. Though the process has characteristics associated with value-outcomes systems, Greenway's president also exerted tremendous *direct* control over the resource allocation process policies. He often closely monitored the expenditures of academic units. Shelton's resource allocation system, a process characterized by the university Priorities Committee, does not fit very well into *any* of the three postulated models. Collectively, this evidence does not invalidate the Massy typology, but does suggest that the model might be expanded to incorporate the complexities suggested in this research. A fourth model, "Communal control" might be added to incorporate cases like Shelton.

Evidence from the cases does, however, validate the general agency problem facing university central administrators. Central administrators do attempt to influence the economic behavior of deans—through economic incentives, direct and indirect taxes, and direct control over expenditures. But the cases also suggest that university central administrators also use non-economic measures, including appeals to citizenship and the greater good of the university, to motivate the actions of deans. Central administrators are not always successful in these appeals, but it is clear that deans can and do respond out of a sense of civic duty. On some level, however, their actions are motivated by self-interest. Simply stated, a dean serves at the pleasure of the Provost.

The data from this study do not offer a magic bullet for resolving the agency problem facing central administrators. Tensions between central administrators and their agents (primarily deans) persisted across resource allocation systems. The data do suggest that institutional leaders must determine, for their universities, the right mix of incentives and monitoring devices for managing the agency problem. The proper blend will vary from institution to institution depending on values, goals, history, and financial resources. The data also imply that successful resource allocation systems combine market incentives with executive communication and leadership. Leaders in these universities communicate the economic as well as subjective value of their incentive systems. In other words, they embed the incentive system within the larger values of their university and in the context of its strategic direction.

PREDICTIONS

What will university resource allocation look like in the future? Based on a close reading and analysis of the data collected in this study, the author makes the following predictions:

1. Market-based resource allocation systems will be restructured to achieve a better balance between university-wide and unit goals. Restructuring will occur through a combination of standards economic incentives and central leadership interventions. Institutions will seek ways to improve the feedback loop between academic units and central administration in order to instill accountability and measure results. In essence, these institutions will move toward values-outcomes principles.

2. In the face of growing competition and stable or declining resources, successful institutions will seek the greatest "bang for their buck" by tapping synergies among traditional academic departments. Resource allocation strategies will support these cross-department initiatives.

3. Resource allocation processes will continue to reflect the values and objectives of institutions and their leaders. Since none of these variables remains static, resource allocation systems will, over time, undergo change and transformation. On balance, the changes will legitimize the prerogative of the central administration to develop resource allocation policy that supports the objectives of the overall university and the accountability of decentralized units.

4. Central administrators will continue their quest to generate resources for university-wide priorities through reallocation of existing funds. Realizing that the funds available for reallocation will never meet total institutional needs, they will supplement these efforts to achieve growth-by-substitution through aggressive funding-raising and other revenue-generating strategies.

5. Deans in market-based resource allocation systems will increasingly seek revenue-generating opportunities as a means of improving their unit bottom-line. When confronted with the politically and personally difficult challenge of downsizing or eliminating academic programs, deans will opt to raise new funds.

6. Emphasis on values-outcomes will force institutional leaders to articulate more forcefully "what really matters"—i.e. the university central priorities—in their respective universities.

7. The refinement of resource allocation processes will occur in parallel to the development of enhanced information systems for sophisticated and timely tracking of financial data.

Sample Interview Protocals

ACADEMIC DEAN

1. Describe how the resource allocation process works at (name of institution). Who are the people you deal with and how does the process work? What is your role in the overall resource allocation process? How do you influence resource allocation decisions of the central administration?

Probes

a) Would you describe the system as centralized (i.e. significant direct control over how resources are used by academic units), or relatively decentralized (i.e. funding is assigned to academic units in blocks with general expectations or understandings about how it is to be used?) How does the administration monitor the way resources are used by your School? What kinds of data or documentation are required about use of funds? Does the central administration attempt to monitor the "productivity" of your school?

b) What kinds of incentives and/or sanctions are built into the system for your school to use funds in accordance with central goals? How do they work? How well would you say they work? Do they have any influence on the way your school uses funds?

2. In your mind, what are the top frustrations of the resource allocation system used as (name of institution)? How would the academic deans critique the system and process?

3. How has the changing fiscal and market environment for higher education affected your institution's resource allocation polices?

4. As dean of (name of school) what specific goals are you trying to accomplish? If your goals are not in agreement with central mandates, how much leeway do you have to spend funds as you see fit?

5. In what ways does the resource allocation system used in your institution support your ability to accomplish the goals you mentioned? What do you see as primary weaknesses in the system? How would you modify the resource allocation system at (name of institution) to more closely achieve your goals?

6. What features would an ideal resource allocation system possess?

CHAIR OF BUDGET/FINANCE COMMITTEE OF FACULTY SENATE

1. How does the resource allocation process work at (name of institution)?

Probes

a) What is your committee's role in the process? What is your committee's role in designating how much money is allocated to schools? Do faculty have enough voice in the process? Who else participates in policy development and/or implementation, including allocation decisions?

b) Would you describe the system as centralized (i.e. significant direct control over how resources are used by academic units), or relatively decentralized (i.e. funding is assigned to academic units in blocks with general expectations or understanding about how it is to be used)? How does the administration monitor the way resources are sued by academic units?

c) What kinds of incentives and/or sanctions are built into the system for schools to use funds in accordance with central goals? How do they work? How well would you say they work?

d) In your mind, what are the top frustrations of the resource allocation system used at (name of institution)? How would you modify the system?

2. How has the recent fiscal and market environment for higher education affected your institution's resource allocation policies?

3. What features would an ideal resource allocation system possess?

ACADEMIC DEPARTMENT CHAIR

1. How does the resource allocation process work in your school? What is your role in the process? What types of unrestricted funds are allocated to your department by the dean's office?

Sample Interview Protocals

2. Does the dean's office monitor the way you spend unrestricted funds? How much leeway do you have to spend unrestricted funds as you wish? What kind of information do you provide to the dean on use of funds?

3. Are you required to provide information to the dean on your department's performance? Productivity?

CFO/CHIEF BUDGET OFFICER

1. Would you describe in detail the resource allocation process used at (name of institution)?
Probes:
a) What is your role in the overall resource allocation process? What is your role in designating how much money is allocated to schools? Who else participates in policy development and/or implementation, including allocation decisions?

b) Would you describe the system as centralized (i.e. significant direct control over how resources are used by academic units), or relatively decentralized (i.e. funding is assigned to academic units in blocks with general expectations or understandings about how it is to be sued)? How does the administration monitor the way resources are used by academic units? What kinds of data are collected?

c) What kinds of incentives and/or sanctions are built into the system for schools to use funds in accordance with central goals? How do they work? How well would you say they work? What do the academic deans think of these policies?

d) In the central administration's allocation of unrestricted funds to academic units, are you trying to influence the ways schools should use their restricted funds? Do you use consolidated budgeting in your institution? Do you use revenue-constrained budgeting your institution?

e) In your mind, what are the top frustrations of the resource allocation system used at (name of institution)?

2. How has the recent fiscal and market environment for higher education affected your institution's resource allocation policies?

3. Can you describe to me a recent period in institutional history when having an effective resource allocation process really mattered—such a period of downsizing, budget shortfall, or projected deficit? How well did your resource allocation system work?

4. What are the specific institutional goals the President and Provost are trying to accomplish at (name of institution)? In what ways does your resource allocation system enable them to accomplish these goals? What do you see as primary weaknesses or gaps in the system? How would you modify the resource allocation system (at (name of institution) to more closely achieve institutional objectives?

5. What features would an ideal resource allocation system possess?

Notes

Chapter 1

1. Garvin (1980) points out that economists have paid little attention in general to the nonprofit sector, and most of the research that has been done has tended to focus on return on investment in higher education rather than institutional behavior. James (1990) adds that economists have devoted little attention to what happens inside organizations.

2. See also the work of James (1990) and Garvin (1980).

3. The operating budget is actually a subset of the total institutional budget. Other important budget subsets include capital budgets, auxiliary enterprise budgets, hospital operations budgets, service center budgets, and restricted budgets separated from the operating budget (Meisinger, 1984).

4. This section is based heavily on Dressel and Simon (1976) and Dickmeyer (1994).

5. In a line-item budget, each expenditure category is denoted as an independent item. Line-item budgets are typically prepared for each independent operating unit (for example, a school, department, or free-standing administrative unit). In an incremental system, a unit budget is usually the same as the previous year (with an adjustment for inflation), unless the unit head can convince the provost or dean to provide an additional allocation for some specified new line of expenditure (see Meisinger, 1984; Caruthers and Orwig, 1979; Massy, 1994; Dickmeyer, 1994).

6. This emphasis is illustrated by the Carnegie Commission's 1966 monograph, *Planning for Effective Resource allocation in Universities*. The Carnegie document discusses concepts for resource planning that attempt to link budgeting and academic planning with no hint that financial stringency might soon dictate such efforts.

7. In most public universities, the university budget begins with a core budget for continuing, recurring expenses, and a categorical component is designated for new programs or special projects (Smartt, 1984).

8. Examples of models developed at this time include CAMPUS (Computerized Analytical Methods in Planning University Systems) at the University of Toronto;

RRPM (the Resource Requirements Prediction Model); and SEARCH, developed by Peat, Marwick, Mitchell and Company (see Schroeder, 1973; Weathersby and Weinstein, 1970).

9. A technical review of these models is beyond the scope of this paper. For a comprehensive review and structural comparison of these models, see Weathersby and Weinstein (1970). Hopkins and Massy (1981) also discuss the technical features of several of these models.

10. Although certain cost accounting methods have been devised to estimate and assign resources to individual outcomes (Wallhaus, 1980).

11. Stanford allocates unrestricted funds to the University's Graduate School of Business and the School of Medicine using a formula tied chiefly to enrollment, tuition, and indirect cost recovery on sponsored research (Stanford University Operating Budget Guidelines, 1993-94).

12. These are taken directly from Banta and Fisher (1984, p.30-31):1) the percentage of programs eligible for accreditation that are accredited; 2) the percentage of programs that have undergone peer review, administered a comprehensive exam to majors, or both within a five year period; 3) the value added by the general component education curriculum as measured by the American College Test College Outcome Measures Project (COMP) exam and by comparisons with the performance of seniors at comparable institutions; 4) demonstrations that generalizations about program quality are supported by surveys of enrolled students, alumni, community members, and employers; 5) implementation of a campus-wide plan for instructional improvement based upon information gathered from the outlined procedures and other sources.

13. For examples and evidence, see the collection of essays in Part II of Hubbard's (1993) *Continuous Quality Improvement: Making the Transition to Education*.

14. However, the system is presently being modified to better meet the dual objectives of accountability and improvement.

15. Responsibility Center Budgeting is sometimes known as Revenue Center Management.

16 Dunwork and Cook present similar arguments for a decentralized resource allocation in their 1976 article.

17. Pfeffer and Moore also found that departments with more highly developed paradigms tend to be more successful both in attracting grant and contract income and in the allocation of budget and faculty positions.

18. One may legitimately question whether the principal has the "right" to dictate agent behavior. I am inclined to accept the argument posited by Hopkins and Massy write (1981, p.103): "There may be an issue as to whether the central administration has any right to manipulate the allocation decisions of deans in the first place. We would argue that such a right exists unless it has been given up explicitly—for instance, by the institution's constitution or equivalent, or by a specific agreement with a dean or faculty."

19. Rodenhouse, 1996.

Notes

20. Critical studies of resource allocation under conditions of retrenchment support this claim. See, for example, Slaughter (1993) and Gumport (1993).

Chapter 3

1. RCM, responsibility center management, is used synomously with RCB.

Chapter 4

1. Individual faculty do not participate in the resource allocation process centrally.

Bibliography

Altschul, Arthur G. et al. "Higher Education Must Change." *AGB Reports*, Vol. 34, No. 3:7–9 (1992).

Albright, Brenda N. "Quality Incentives in the Budget," in D.J. Berg and Gerald M. Skogley (editors). *Making the Budget Process Work*. New Directions for Higher Education, no. 52, San Francisco: Jossey-Bass, December 1985.

Arns, Robert G. and William Poland. "The Role of Program Review and Evaluation to Academic Planning and Budgeting," in Micek, Sidney (editor), *Integrating Academic Planning and Budgeting in a Rapidly Changing Environment: Process and Technical Issues*. Boulder, CO: National Center of Higher Education Management Systems, 1980.

Arrow, Kenneth J. "The Economics of Agency," in Pratt, John W. and Richard J. Zeckhauser (editors), *Principals and Agents: The Structure of Business*. Boston: Harvard Business School Press, 1985.

Ashar, Hanna and Jonathan Z. Shapiro. "Are Retrenchment Decisions Rational? The Role of Information in Times of Budgetary Stress," *Journal of Higher Education*, Vol. 61, No. 2:121–141 (1990).

Attiyeh, Richard. "Survey of the Issue," in Lumsden, Keith G. *Efficiency in Universities: The La Paz Papers*. New York: Elsevier Scientific Publicizing Company, 1974.

Baldridge, J. Victor, David V. Curtis, George P. Ecker, and Gary L. Riley. "Alternative Models of Governance in Higher Education," in Baldridge, J. Victor and Gary L. Riley (editors), in *Governing Academic Organizations: New Problems, New Perspectives*. McCutchan Publishing Corporation: Berkeley, CA, 1977.

Banta, Trudy W. and Homer S. Fisher, "Performance Funding: Tennessee's Experiment," in J. Folger (editor), *Financial Incentives for Academic Quality*. New Directions for Higher Education, No. 48. San Francisco: Jossey-Bass, December 1984.

Becher, Tony, *Academic Tribes and Territories: Intellectual Enquiry and the Culture of Disciplines*. Bristol, PA: Open University Press, 1989.

Birnbaum, Robert. *How Colleges Work: The Cybernetics of Academicc Organization and Leadership*. San Francisco, CA: Josses-Bass Inc., Publishers, 1988.

Borchert, F.R. Jr. and V.C. Mickelson. "Creating a Financial Management System," in *Strategies for Budgeting*. New Directions for Higher Education, Vol. 1, No.2:5–18 (Summers, 1973).

Bowen, William G. *The Economics of Major Private Universities*. Berkeley, California: Carnegie Commission on the Future of Higher Education, 1968.

Breneman, David W. "Strategies for the 1980s," in Mingle, James R. (editor), *Challenges of Retrenchment*. San Francisco: Jossey-Bass, 1981.

Bruegman, Donald C. "Management Ingenuity: Reallocation of Resources in the Nineties," *NACUBO Business Officer*, Vol. 27, No. 10: 28–31 (April, 1994).

Carnegie Commission on Higher Education. *The More Effective Use of Resources: An Imperative for Higher Education*. Berkeley, California: Carnegie Commission on Higher Education, 1972.

Caruthers, J. Kent and Melvin Orwig. *Budgeting in Higher Education*. AAHE–ERIC/Higher Education Research Report No. 3. Washington: American Association for Higher Education, 1979.

Chaffee, Ellen Earle. *Decision Models in University Budgeting*. Ph.D. Dissertation, Stanford University, 1980.

Cheit, Earl F. *The New Depression in Higher Education: A Study of Financial Conditions at 41 Colleges and Universities*. Carnegie Foundation for the Advancement of Teaching, 1971.

Clark, Burton R. *The Higher Education System: Academic Organization in Cross-National* Perspective. University of California Press: Berkeley, CA, 1983.

Clotfelter, Charles. *Buying the Best: Cost Escalation in Elite Higher Education*. Princeton, New Jersey: Princeton University Press, 1996.

Cohen, Michael D. and James G. March. *Leadership in Ambiguity*. New York: McGraw-Hill, 1974.

Craven, Eugene. "Evaluating Program Performance," in Jedamus, Paul and Marvin W. Peterson (editors), *Improving Academic Management: A Handbook of Planning and Institutional Research*. San Francisco: Jossey-Bass Inc. Publishers, 1980.

Cunliff, Ed, Sharon Martin, and Joyce Mounce. "A Study in Change: The Integration of Planning and Budget at Central Oklahoma," *NACUBO Business Officer*, Vol. 26, No. 8: 32–36 (1993).

Cyert, Richard M. and James G. March. *Behavioral Theory of the Firm*. Englewood Cliffs, New Jersey, 1963.

Dickmeyer, Nathan and K. Scott Hughes. "Financial Self-Assessment," in C. Frances (editor). *Successful Responses to Financial Difficulty*. New Directions for Higher Education, No. 38. San Francisco: Jossey-Bass, June 1982.

Dickmeyer, Nathan. "Budgeting," in Green, Deirdre McDonald (editor), *College and University Business Administration*. Washington, D.C.: National Association of College and University Business Officers, 1994.

Dressel, Paul L. and Lou Anna Kimsey Simon. "Approaches to Resource Allocation in Departments," in *Allocating Resources Among Departments*, New Directions for Institutional Research, Vol. 3, No. 3:7–25 (1976).

Dunworth, John and Rupert Cook. "Budgetary Devolution as an Aid to University Efficiency. *Higher Education*, Vol. 5, 1976.

El-Khawas, Elaine and William F. Massy. *"Britain's Assessment-Based Systems* in Massy, William F. editor, (forthcoming).

Furman, James. The Integration of Fiscal and Academic Planning," in Leslie, Larry L. and Otto L. Health (editors). *Financing and Budgeting Postsecondary Education in the 1980s*. Tucson, Arizona: Center for the Study of Higher Education, 1980.

Furubotn, Eirik G. and Svetozar Pejovich, "Introduction," in Furubotn, Eirik G. and Svetozar Pejovich. *The Economics of Property Rights*. Cambridge, MA:Ballinger Publishing Company, 1974.

Garvin, David A. *The Economics of University Behavior*. New York: Academic Press, Inc., 1980.

Geffrion, A.M. *et al.* "Academic Department Management: An Application of an Interactive Multicriterion Optimization Approach." Berkeley, CA: Ford Foundation Program for Research in University Administration, 1971.

Green, John L. Jr. and David G. Monical. "Resource Allocation in a Decentralized Environment," in D.J. Berg and Gerald M. Skogley (editors). *Making the Budget Process Work. New Directions for Higher Education*, no. 52. San Francisco: Jossey-Bass, December, 1985.

Gumport, Patricia. "The Contested Terrain of Academic Program Reduction." *Journal of Higher Education* (1993).

Hackman, Judith Dozier. "Power and Centrality in the Allocation of Resources in Colleges and Universities," *Administrative Science Quarterly*, Vol. 30:61–77 (1985).

Heath, Robert. "Responsibility Center Budgeting: A Review and Commentary on the Concept and the Process." *Journal of Communication Administration*, No. 1:1–10 (1993).

Heveron, Eileen D. "Boosting Academic Reputations: A Study of University Departments," *The Review of Higher Education*, Vol. 11, No. 2: 177–197.

Heydinger, Richard B. "Planning Academic Programs," in Jedamus, Paul and Marvin W. Peterson (editors), *Improvement Academic Management: A Handbook of Planning and Institutional Research*. San Francisco: Jossey-Bass Inc. Publishers, 1980.

Hills, Frederick S. Hills and Thomas A. Mahoney. "University Budgets and Organizational Decision Making," *Administrative Science Quarterly*, Vol. 23: 454–465 (1978).

Hoenack, Stephen A. "Direct and Incentive Planning with a University," *Socio-Economic Planning Science*, Vol. 11:205–212 (1977).

Hoenack, Stephen A. "Recent Research on Incentives in Institutions of Higher Education," in Wilson, Robert A. (editor), *Administering and Managing the Finances of Colleges and Universities*. Topical Paper No. 23. Selected Proceedings of the Annual Conference on Higher Education. Tucson, Arizona: Center for the Study of Higher Education, 1984.

Hoenack, Stephen A. *Economic Behavior within Organizations*. New York: Cambridge University Press, 1983.

Hoenack, Stephen A. "Economics, Organizations, and Learning: Research Directions for the Economics of Education," *Economics of Education Review*, Vol. 113, No. 2: 147–162 (1994).

Hoenack, Stephen A. and David J. Berg. "The Role of Incentives in Academic Planning," in *Academic Planning for the 1980s*, New Directions for Institutional Research, Vol. VII, No. 4:73–96 (1980).

Hopkins, David S.P. and William F. Massy. *Planning Models for Colleges and Universities*. Stanford, California: Stanford University Press, 1981.

Hubbard, Dean (editor). *Continuous Quality Improvement: Making the Transition to Education*. Maryville, MO: Prescott Publishing Company, 1993.

Hyatt, James A., Carol Herrstadt Shulman, and Aurora A. Santiago. *Reallocation: Strategies for Effective Resource Management*. USA: National Association of College and University Business Officers, 1984.

James, Estate. "Decision Processes and Priorities in Higher Education," in Hoenack, Stephen A. and Eileen L. Collins. *The Economics of American Universities: Management, Operations, and Fiscal Environment*. Albany, New York: State University of New York Press, Albany, 1990.

Jencks, C. and Riesman, David. The *Academic Revolution*. Garden City, N.Y.: Doubleday, 1969.

Kaludis, George. "Emerging Principles for Budgeting," in *Strategies for Budgeting*. New Directions for Higher Education, Vol. 1, No. 1. 2:97–102 (Summer, 1973).

Kerr, Clark. *The Uses of the University*. Cambridge, Massachusetts: Harvard University Press, 1982.

Jones, Dennis. "Budgeting for Academic Quality: Structures and Strategies," in J. Folger (editor), *Financial Incentives for Academic Quality*. New Directions for Higher Education, no. 48. San Francisco: Jossey-Bass, December, 1984 (43–56).

Jones, L. R. *University Budgeting for Critical Mass and Competition*. New York: Praeger Publishers, 1985.

Keller, George. "Free at Last? Breaking the Chains that Bind Education Research," *The Review of Higher Education*, Vol. 10, No. 2:129–134 (1987).

Levin, Henry. "Raising Productivity in Higher Education," *Higher Education Extension Service Review*, Volume 4, No. 3 (1993).

Long, Durward. "Linking Academic Planning and Budgeting," in Micek, Sidney (editor) *Integrating Academic Planning And Budgeting in a Rapidly Changing Environment: Process and Technical Issues*. Boulder, CO: National Center for Higher Education Management Systems, 1980.

Bibliography

Massy, William F. "Balancing Values and Market Forces: Perspectives on Resource Allocation." Discussion Paper. Stanford Institute for Higher Education Research, April 1994.

Massy, Williams F. "Budget Decentralization at Stanford University," *Planning for Higher Education*, Vol. 18, No. 2:39–55 (1989–90).

Massy, William F. "A Paradigm for Research on Higher Education," in Smart, John C. (editor), *Higher Education: Handbook of Theory and Research*, Volume VI. New York: Agathon Press, 1990.

Massy, Williams F. *Resource Allocation Reform in Higher Education*. Washington, D.C.: National Association of College and University Business Officers, 1994.

Massy, Williams F. and David S.P. Hopkins, "The Case for Planning Models," in Wyatt, Joe B. (editor), *Financial Planning Models: Concepts and Case Studies in Colleges and Universities: Proceedings of a Workshop*. Princeton, New Jersey: EDUCOM, 1979.

Massy, William F. and Michael C. Hulfactor, "Optimizing Allocation Strategy," in Altbach, Philip G. and D. Bruce Johnstone (editors). *The Funding of Higher Education: International Perspectives*. New York: Garland Publishing, Inc., 1993.

Meisinger, Richard J. Jr., and Leroy W. Bubeck. *College and University Budgeting: An Introduction for Faculty and Academic Administrators*. Washington, D.C.: National Association of College and University Business Administrators, 1984.

Meisinger, Richard J. Jr. "Introduction to Special Issue on the Relationship Between Planning and Budgeting," *Planning for Higher Education*, Vol. 18, No. 2: 1–7 (1989–90).

Micek, Sidney S. *Integrating Academic Planning and Budgeting in a Rapidly Changing Environment: Process and Technical Issues*. Boulder, Colorado: National Center for Higher Education Management Systems, 1980.

Millard, Richard M. "Power of State Coordinating Agencies," in Jedamus, Paul and Marvin W. Peterson (editors), *Improving Academicc Management: A Handbook of Planning and Institutional Research*. San Francisco: Jossey-Bass Inc. Publishers, 1980.

Millard, Richard. "Quality Promotion in the Steady State," in Leslie, Larry L. and Otto L. Health. *Financing and Budgeting Postsecondary Education in the 1980s*. Tucson, Arizona: Center for the Study of Higher Education, 1980.

Millett, John D. *The Academic Community: An Essay on Organization*. New York: McGraw-Hill, 1962.

Millett, John D. *Resource Allocation in Research Universities*. Washington, D.C.: Academy for Educational Development, Inc. June, 1973.

Mortimer, Kenneth P. and Michael L. Tierney. "The Three 'R's" of the Eighties: Reduction, Reallocation and Retrenchment," AAHE–ERIC/Higher Education Research Report, No. 4. Washington: American Association for Higher Education, 1979.

Morgan, Anthony W. "Resource Allocation Reforms: Marginal Utility Analysis and Zero-Based Budgeting in Higher Education," *Higher Education Review*, Vol. I, No. 3:1–17 (Spring, 1978).

Olsen, Jeffrey E. "Values Implicit in the Resource Allocations of University," Ph.D. Dissertation, Stanford University, 1989.

Orwig, Melvin. "Financial Responses for the 1980s," in Leslie, Larry L. and Otto, L. Health (editors). *Financing and Budgeting Postsecondary Education in the 1980s.* Tucson, Arizona: Center for the Study of Higher Education, 1980.

Orwig, Melvin D. and J. Kent Caruthers, "Selecting Budget Strategies and Priorities," in Jedamus, Paul, and Marvin W. Peterson and Associates. *Improving Academic Management.* San Francisco: Jossey-Bass Publishers, 1980.

Pew Higher Education Research Program. "Double Trouble." in *Policy Perspectives*, Vol. 1, No. 3 (1989).

Pew Higher Education Program. "The Lattice and the Ratchet." in *Policy Perspectives*, Vol. 2, No. 4 (1990).

Pew Higher Education Program. "Learning Slope." in *Policy Perspectives*, Vol. 4, No. 1, Section A. (1991).

Pew Higher Education Research Program. "Testimony From the Belly of the Whale." in *Policy Perspectives*, Vol. 4, No. 3 (1992).

Pfeffer, Jeffrey and William L. Moore. "Power in University Budgeting: A Replication and Extension," *Administrative Science Quarterly*, Vol. 25:637–63 (1980).

Pickens, Williams H. "Performance Funding in Higher Education: Panacea or Peril?" Paper Presented at a Conference on Survival in the 1980s: Quality, Mission and Financing Options. Tucson, AZ, December, 1982.

Pondy, Louis R. "Toward a Theory of Resource Allocation," in *Power in Organizations.* Nashville: Vanderbilt University Press, 1970.

Pratt, John W. and Richard J. Zeckhauser. "Principals and Agents: An Overview," in Pratt, John W. and Richard J. Zeckhauser (editors), *Principals and Agents: The Structure of Business.* Boston: 1985.

Pyhrr, Peter A. Zero-Base Budgeting. New York: John Wiley and Sons, 1973.

Schmidtlein, Frank A. "Why Linking Budgets to Plans has Proven Difficult in Higher Education," *Planning for Higher Education*, Vol. 18, No. 2: 9–23 (1989–1990).

Schroeder, Roger G. "A Survey of Management Science in University Operations," *Management Science*, Vol. 19, No. 8: 895–906 (1973).

Scott, W.R. *Organizations: Rational, Natural and Open Systems.* Englewood Cliffs, J.J.: Prentice Hall, 1981.

Shirley, Robert C. and J. Fredericks Volkswein. "Established Academic Programs Priorities," in Micek, Sidney (editor), *Integrating Academic Planning and Budgeting a Rapidly Changing Environment: Process and Technical Issues.* Boulder, CO: National Center for Higher Education Systems, 1980.

Simon, Herbert. "A Behavior Model of Rational Choice," *The Quarterly Journal of Economics*, Vol. 69, No. 1:99–118 (1955).

Skolnik, "If the Cut is so Deep, Where is the Blood? Problems in Research on the Effects of Financial Restraint," *The Review of Higher Education*, Vol. 9, No. 4:435–455.

Slaughter, Shiela. "The Political Economy of Restructuring Postsecondary Education," *Journal of Higher Education* (1993).

Smartt, Steven. "Linking Program Reviews to the Budget," J. Folger (editor), *Financial Incentives for Academic Quality*. New Directions for Higher Education, no. 48. San Francisco: Jossey-Bass, December, 1984 (43–56).

Spremann, Klaus, "Agency Theory and Risk Sharing," in Bamber, Gunter and Klaus Spremann (editors), *Agency Theory, Information, and Incentives*. New York: Springer-Verlag, 1987.

Stanford University Operating Budget Guidelines, 1993–94. Submit for action to the Board of Trustees, Stanford University, 1993.

Stonich, Paul J. *Zero-Base Planning and Budgeting: Improved Cost Control and Resources Allocation*. Homewood, Illinois: Dow Jones-Irwin, 1977.

Strauss, Jon, John Curry, and Edward Whalen. "Responsibility Center Budgeting," in Massy, William F. (editor) (forthcoming).

Stroup, Herbert. *Bureaucracy in Higher education*. New York, 1966.

Temple, Charles M. and Robert O. Riggs. "The Declining Suitability of the Formulas Approach to Funding Public Higher Education: Rationale and Alternative," *Peabody Journal of Education*, Vol. 55, NO. 4:351–357 (July, 1978).

Thelin, John R. "The Search for Good Research: Looking for" Science" in All the Wrong Places," *The Review of Higher Education*, Vol. 10, No. 2:151–158 (Winter, 1986)

Tonn, Joan C. "Political Behavior in Higher Education Budgeting," *Journal of Higher Education*, Vol. 49, No. 6:575–587 (1978).

Tuckerman, Howard P. and Cyril F. Chang. "Participants Goals, Institutional Goals, and University Resource Allocation Decisions," in Hoenack, Stephen A. and Eileen L. Collins. *The Economics of American Universities: Management, Operations, and Fiscal Environment*. Albany, New York: State University of New York Press, Albany, 1990.

Van Vijt, Alfons P., and Jack E. Levine. "The Pros and Cons of Existing Formula Financing Systems and a Suggested New Approach," Paper Presented at the College of Applied Arts and Technology Design Workshop, Ottawa. New York: Ford Foundation, 1969.

Walthaus, Robert A. "Analyzing Academic Program Resource Requirements," Jedamus, Paul and Marvin W. Peterson (editors), *Improving Academic Management: A Handbook of Planning and Institutional Research*. San Francisco: Jossey-Bass Inc. Publishes, 1980.

Weathersby, George B. and Weinstein, Milton C. "A Structural Comparison of Analytical Models for University Planing," Berkeley, CA: Ford Foundation Program for Research in University Administration, 1970.

Weick, Karl E. "Educational Organizations as Loosely Coupled Systems," *Administrative Science Quarterly*. Vol. 21, No. 1:1–19 (March, 1976).

Whalen, Edward L. *Responsibility Center Budgeting: An Approach to Decentralized Management for Institutions of Higher Education*. Bloomington, Indiana: India University Press, 1991.

White, William D. "Information and the Control of Agents," in *Journal of Economic Behavior and Organization*, Vol. 18:111–117 (1992).
Wildavsky, Aaron. *The Politics of the Budgetary Process*. 1964.
Williams, Harry. *Planning for Effective Resource Allocation in Universities*. Washington, DC: American Council on Education, 1966.
Wilson, Robert A. (editor), *Administering and Managing the Finances for Colleges and Universities*. Topical Paper No. 23. Selected Proceedings of the Annual Conference on Higher Education. Tucson, Arizona: Center of the Study of Higher Education, 1984.
Wyatt, Joe B. editor. *Financing Planning Models: Concepts and Case Studies in Colleagues and Universities*. Proceedings of a Workshop (Indianapolis, IN, August 27–29, 1978). Princeton, New Jersey: EDUCOM, 1979.

Index

agency theory, 20–26

Block-Incremental Budgeting, 15–16
Buchanan University, 31–49,
  165–166
  formula system, 31–32, 33–40
  priorities, 41–43
  strategic direction, 47–48

direct control system, 22, 24

Garfield University, 171–172
  resource allocation history,
    149–153
  resource allocation reform,
    153–157
  priorities, 157–160
Greenway University, 127–147,
  170–171
  presidential leadeship,
    135–138
  program review, 138–143
  resource allocation history,
    127–128
  resource allocation processes,
    128–135
  summary views of resource
    allocation systems, 143–147

Pierce University, 51–73, 166–168
  institutional priorities, 61–64
  responsibility center budget-
    ing, 64–72
  responsibility center princi-
    ples, 57–61
planning and resource allocation,
  6–17
  formula budgeting, 10–11
  history, 6–7
  incremental line-item budget-
    ing, 8–9
  performance budgeting, 13–14
  planning, programming, and
    budgeting systems (PPBS),
    11–12
  quantitative modeling, 9–10
  zero-based budgeting, 12–13
price regulation systems, 22–24
property rights theory, 24–25

rational choice theory, 17–18
responsibilty center budgeting, 4,
  14–15

Shelton University, 103–126,
  169–170

199

institutional priorities,
119–121
priorities committee, 105–115
resource allocation history,
103–106
resource allocation system
strengths, 121–124

value-outcome systems, 23–24

Westmont University, 75–101,
    168–169
    decentralized resource allocation model, 80–86
    entrepreneurship and revenue generation, 87–91
    institutional priorities, 95–99
    resource allocation history,
    75–79
    summary views of new allocation system, 91–95